PEANUTS
ALL-STARS

Charles M. Schu[...]

Ballantine Books
New York

Published in the United States by Ballantine Books,
an imprint of The Random House Publishing Group,
a division of Random House, Inc., New York.

BALLANTINE and colophon are registered trademarks of Random House, Inc.

The comic strips in this book were originally published in newspapers worldwide.

ISBN 0-345-47982-3

Printed in the United States of America

www.ballantinebooks.com

2 4 6 8 9 7 5 3 1

Design by Diane Hobbing of Snap-Haus Graphics

PEANUTS ALL-STARS

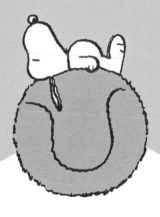

Basketball

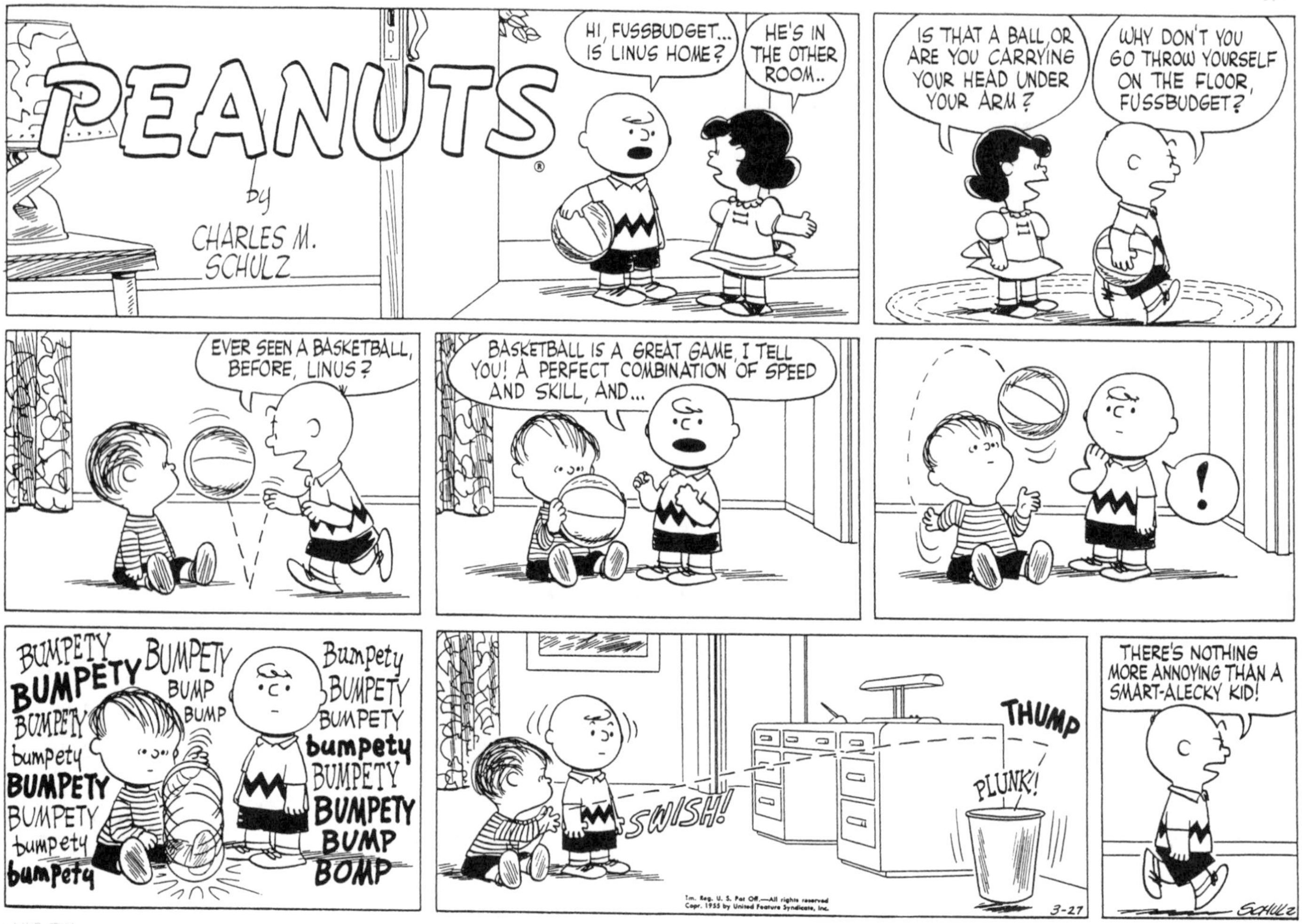
PEANUTS
by CHARLES M. SCHULZ
HI, FUSSBUDGET... IS LINUS HOME?
HE'S IN THE OTHER ROOM..
IS THAT A BALL, OR ARE YOU CARRYING YOUR HEAD UNDER YOUR ARM?
WHY DON'T YOU GO THROW YOURSELF ON THE FLOOR, FUSSBUDGET?
EVER SEEN A BASKETBALL, BEFORE, LINUS?
BASKETBALL IS A GREAT GAME, I TELL YOU! A PERFECT COMBINATION OF SPEED AND SKILL, AND...
!
BUMPETY BUMPETY BUMPETY bumpety BUMPETY BUMPETY bumpety bumpety
BUMPETY BUMP BUMP
Bumpety BUMPETY BUMPETY bumpety BUMPETY BUMPETY BUMP BOMP
SWISH!
THUMP
PLUNK!
Tm. Reg. U. S. Pat Off.—All rights reserved
Copr. 1955 by United Feature Syndicate, Inc.
3-27
THERE'S NOTHING MORE ANNOYING THAN A SMART-ALECKY KID!
SCHULZ

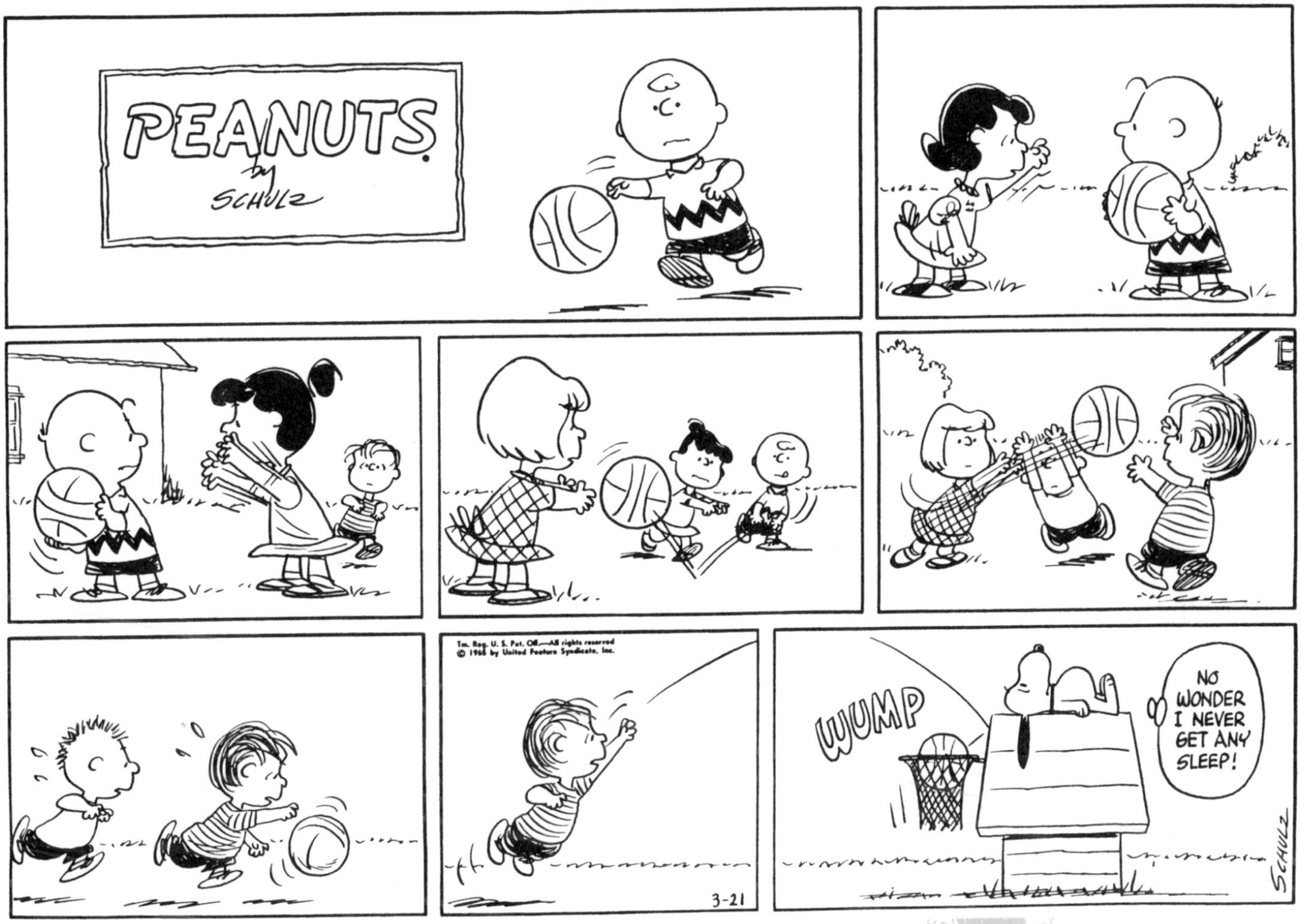
PEANUTS
by SCHULZ
Tm. Reg. U. S. Pat. Off.—All rights reserved
© 1965 by United Feature Syndicate, Inc.
3-21
WUMP
NO WONDER I NEVER GET ANY SLEEP!
SCHULZ

PEANUTS
Tm. Reg. U. S. Pat. Off —-All rights reserved
© 1973 by United Feature Syndicate, Inc.
9-21
SCHULZ

PEANUTS
!
Tm. Reg. U. S. Pat. Off.—All rights reserved
© 1973 by United Feature Syndicate, Inc.
9-22
SSSSSS!!
SCHULZ

PEANUTS
MY DAD USED TO PLAY ON A BASKETBALL TEAM IN HIGH SCHOOL...
HE SAID HE CAN'T REMEMBER EVER LOSING A GAME....
Tm. Reg. U.S. Pat. Off.—All rights reserved
©1974 by United Feature Syndicate, Inc.
THEY MUST HAVE HAD A GREAT TEAM..
1-4
NO, HE HAS A TERRIBLE MEMORY!
SCHULZ

THAT'S A NEAT LOOKING BASKET-BALL, CHUCK

THE ONE THEY GAVE US GIRLS TO PLAY WITH ISN'T HALF THAT GOOD

9-26

YOU'RE NOT AGAINST WOMEN'S SPORTS ARE YOU, CHUCK?

⚹ SIGH ⚹

© 1979 United Feature Syndicate, Inc.

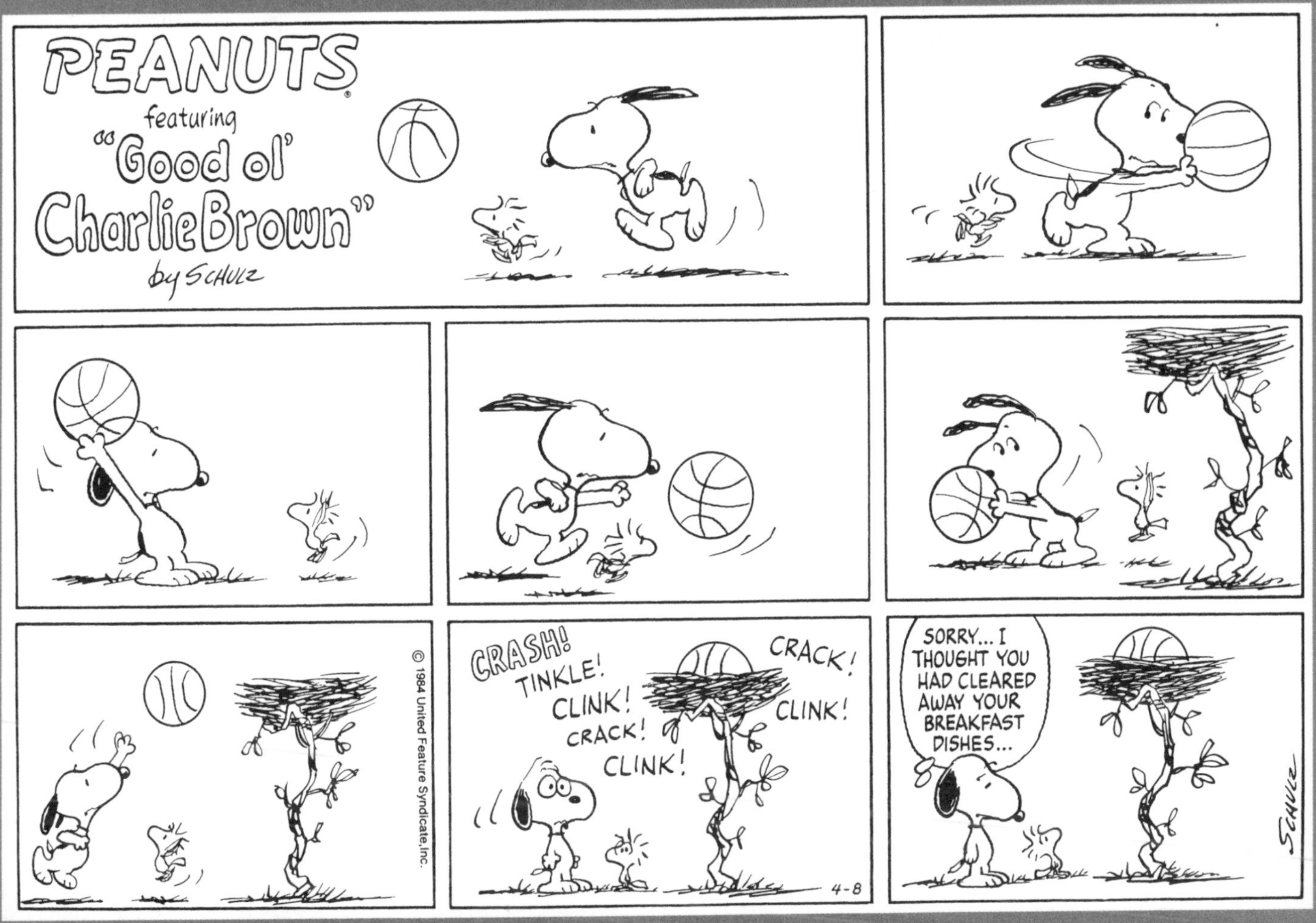
PEANUTS
featuring
"Good ol' Charlie Brown"
by SCHULZ
© 1984 United Feature Syndicate, Inc.
CRASH!
TINKLE!
CLINK!
CRACK!
CLINK!
CRACK!
CLINK!
4-8
SORRY... I THOUGHT YOU HAD CLEARED AWAY YOUR BREAKFAST DISHES...
SCHULZ

| FIRST WE'LL SHOOT A FEW BASKETS.. | 10-4 | THEN WE'LL PLAY A LITTLE ONE-ON-ONE.. | OR MAYBE ONE-ON-ONE-FOURTH... |

© 1984 United Feature Syndicate, Inc.

SCHULZ

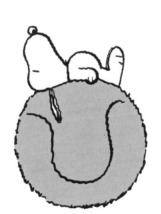

PEANUTS featuring "Good ol' CharlieBrown" by SCHULZ

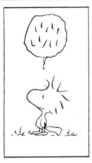

© 1985 United Feature Syndicate, Inc.

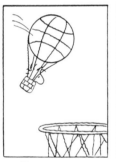

B-25

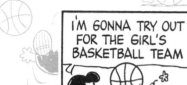

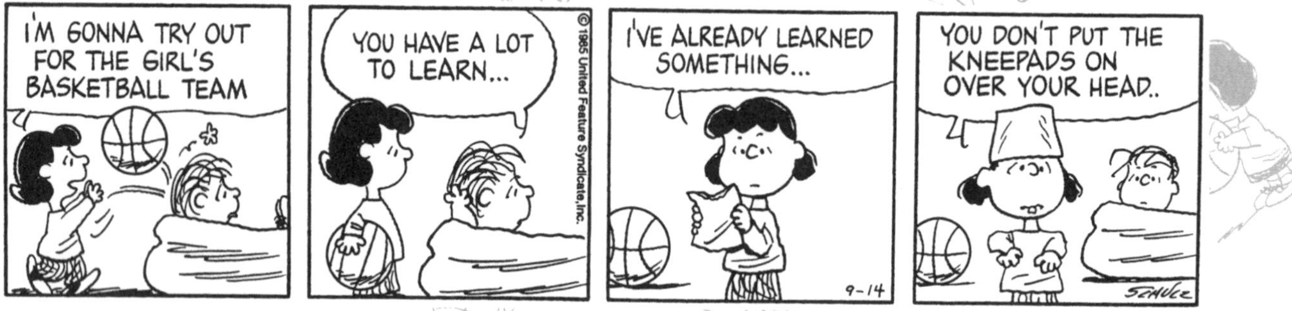
I'M GONNA TRY OUT FOR THE GIRL'S BASKETBALL TEAM
YOU HAVE A LOT TO LEARN...
© 1985 United Feature Syndicate, Inc.
I'VE ALREADY LEARNED SOMETHING...
9-14
YOU DON'T PUT THE KNEEPADS ON OVER YOUR HEAD..
SCHULZ

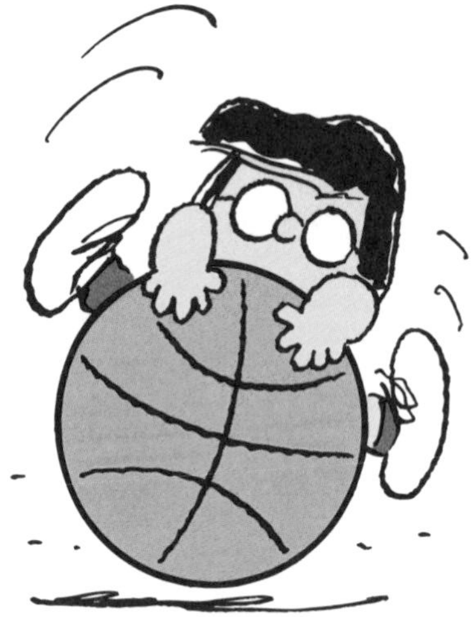

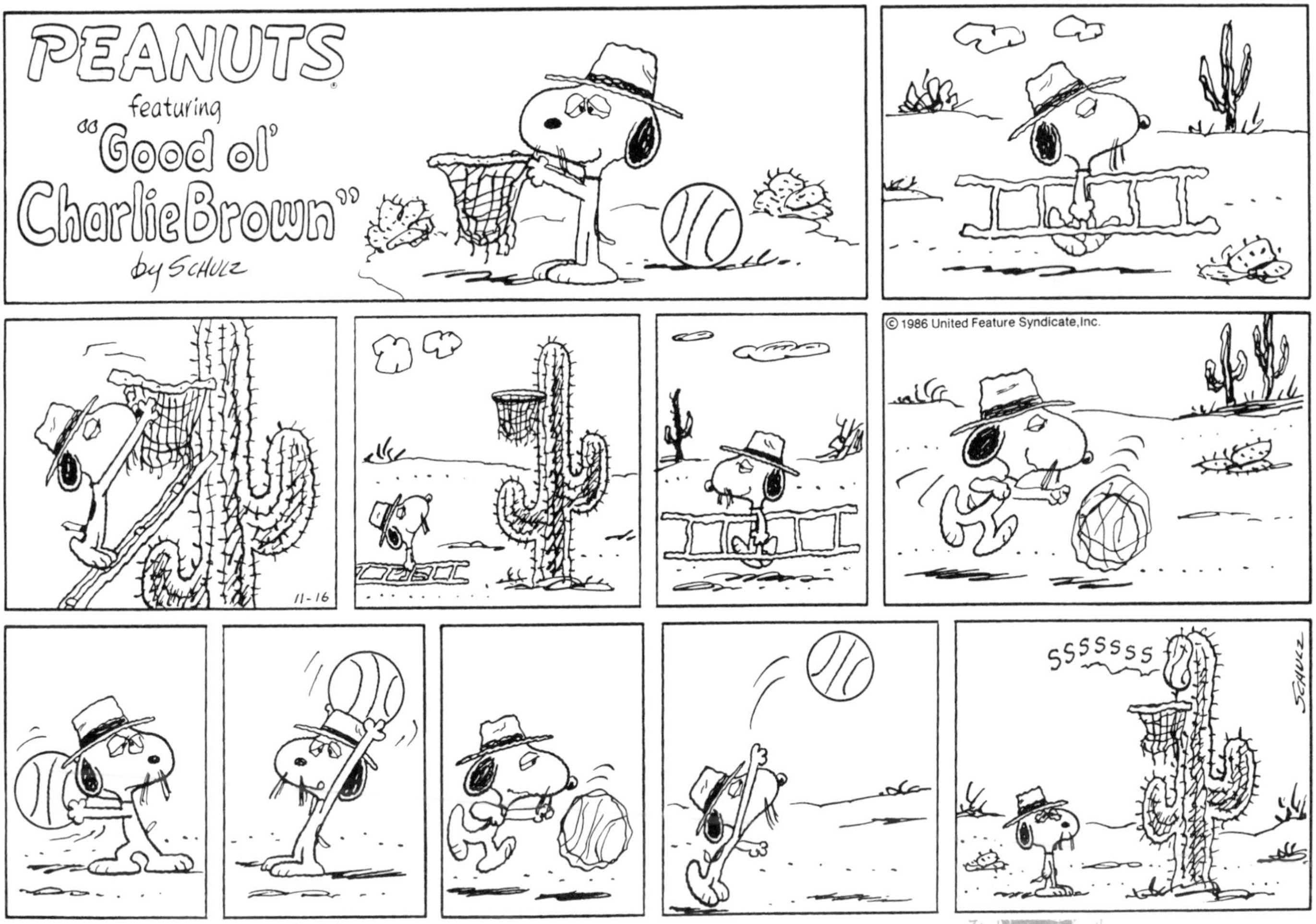
PEANUTS
featuring "Good ol' Charlie Brown"
by SCHULZ
11-16
© 1986 United Feature Syndicate, Inc.
SSSSSSS
SCHULZ

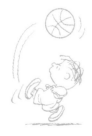

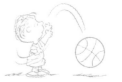

5-14
THERE'S NO HURRY, I GUESS, BUT LET ME KNOW WHEN I CAN HAVE YOUR SUPPER DISH...
© 1990 United Feature Syndicate, Inc.

RATS!
© 1993 United Feature Syndicate, Inc.
NO MATTER HOW HARD YOU TRY, YOU CAN'T DRIBBLE A TUMBLEWEED!
SCHULZ
3-6

OKAY, SHOOT!
7-29
© 1993 United Feature Syndicate, Inc.
YOU DIDN'T SAY, "NICE TRY"
SCHULZ

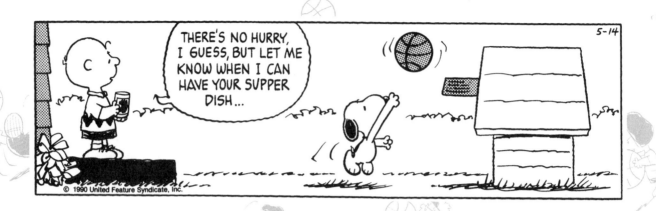

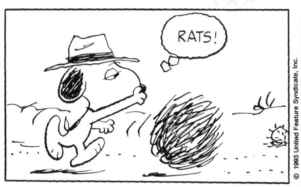

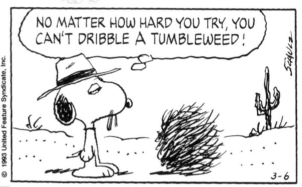

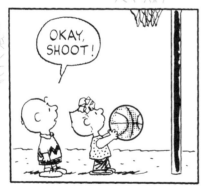

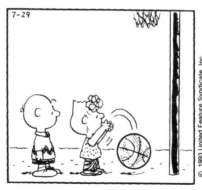

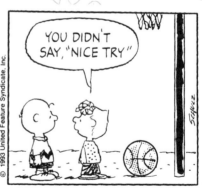

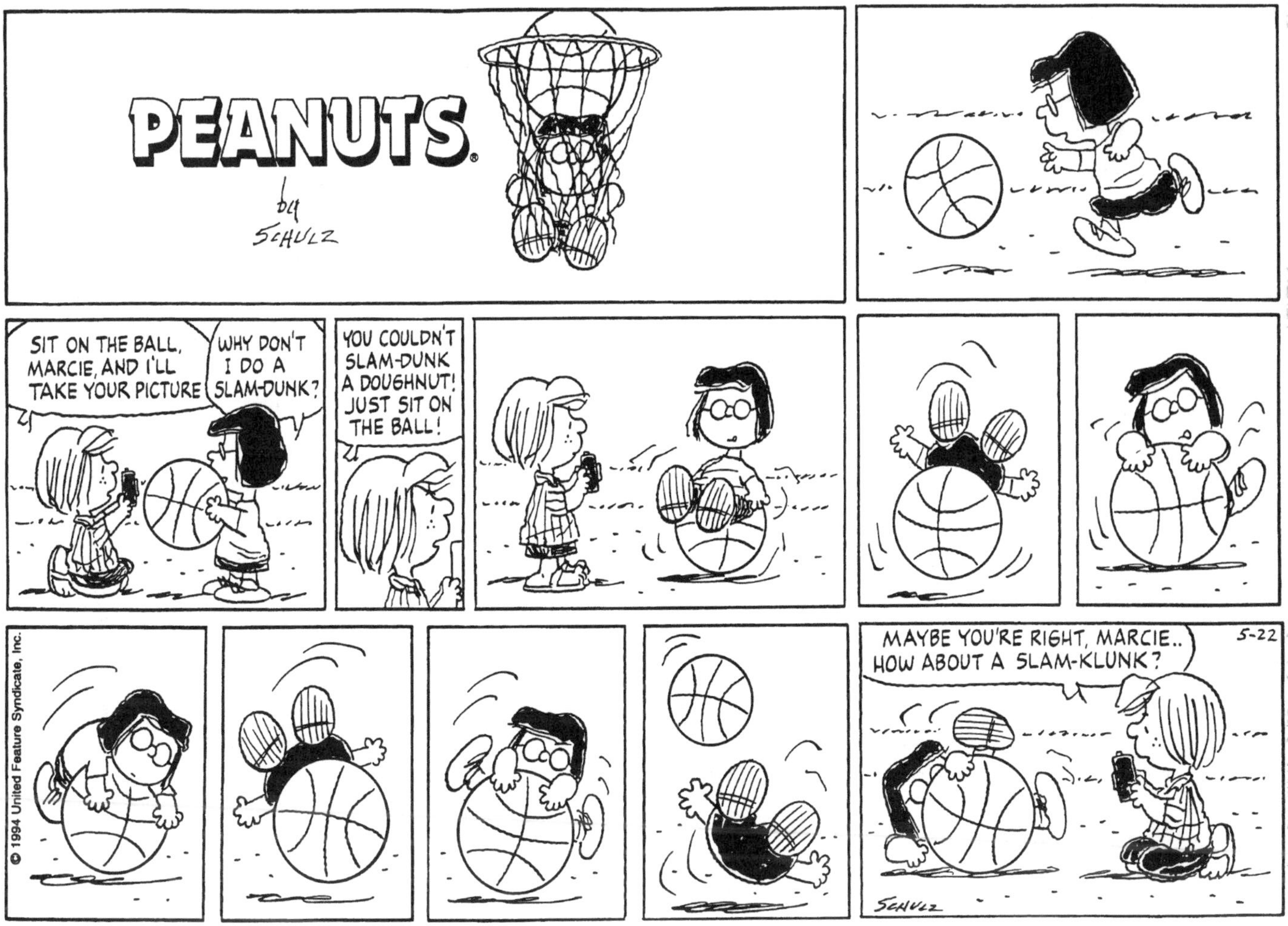
PEANUTS
by SCHULZ
SIT ON THE BALL, MARCIE, AND I'LL TAKE YOUR PICTURE
WHY DON'T I DO A SLAM-DUNK?
YOU COULDN'T SLAM-DUNK A DOUGHNUT! JUST SIT ON THE BALL!
© 1994 United Feature Syndicate, Inc.
MAYBE YOU'RE RIGHT, MARCIE.. HOW ABOUT A SLAM-KLUNK?
5-22
SCHULZ

THIS IS HOW WE SHOOT BASKETS, RERUN
SEE, WE BOUNCE THE BALL A COUPLE OF TIMES TO GET OUR RHYTHM..
THEN WE FLIP IT THROUGH THE BASKET!
© 1994 United Feature Syndicate, Inc.
7-28
WHY?
SCHULZ

© 1994 United Feature Syndicate, Inc.
8-16
SCHULZ

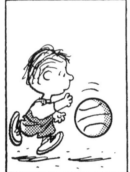

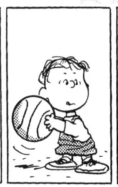

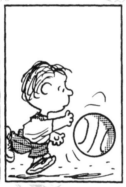

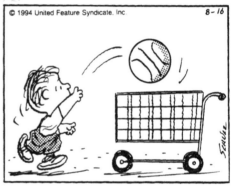

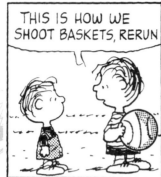

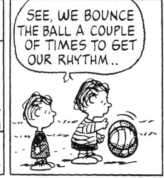

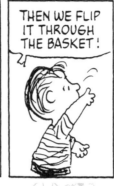

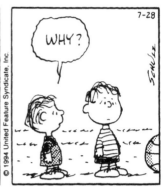

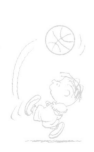

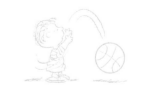

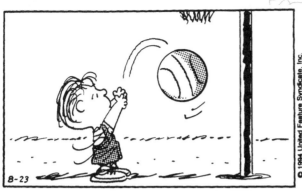

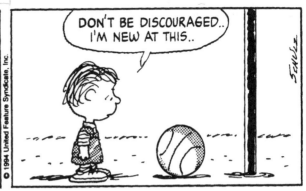

8-23
© 1994 United Feature Syndicate, Inc.
DON'T BE DISCOURAGED.. I'M NEW AT THIS..
SCHULZ

8-30
© 1994 United Feature Syndicate, Inc.
WE DON'T HAVE TO DO THIS, YOU KNOW..

9-1
© 1994 United Feature Syndicate, Inc.
WELL, I'LL SAY THIS FOR YOU.. YOU'RE VERY PATIENT..
SCHULZ

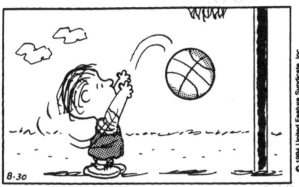

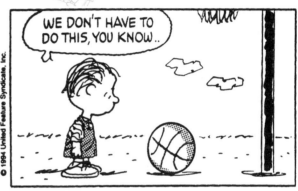

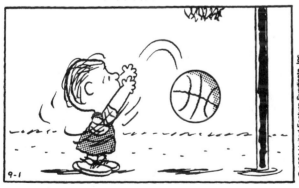

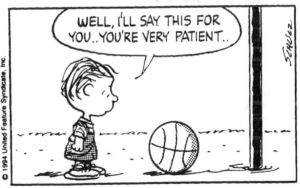

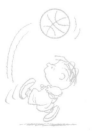

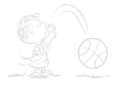

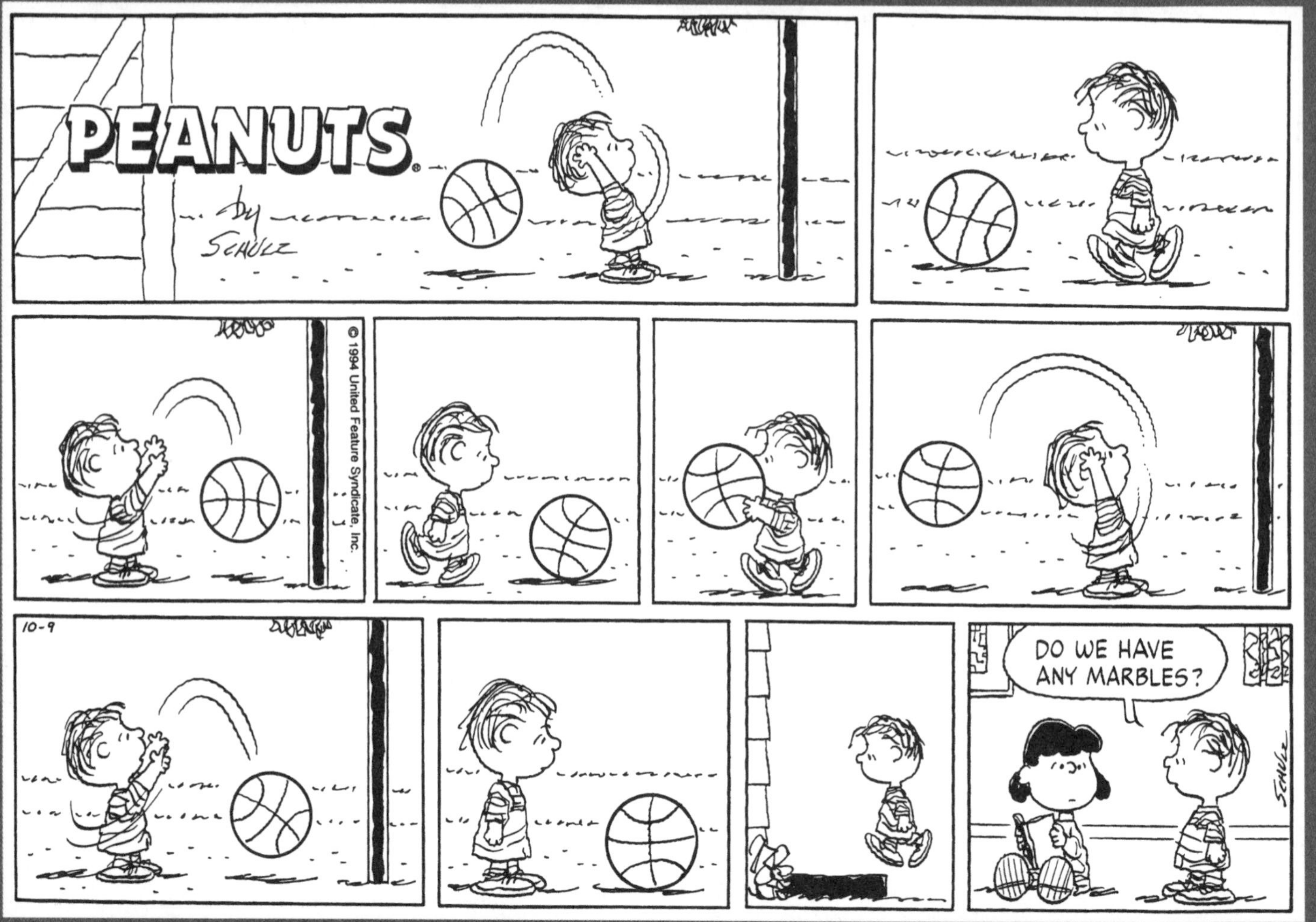
PEANUTS
by SCHULZ
© 1994 United Feature Syndicate, Inc.
10-9
DO WE HAVE ANY MARBLES?
SCHULZ

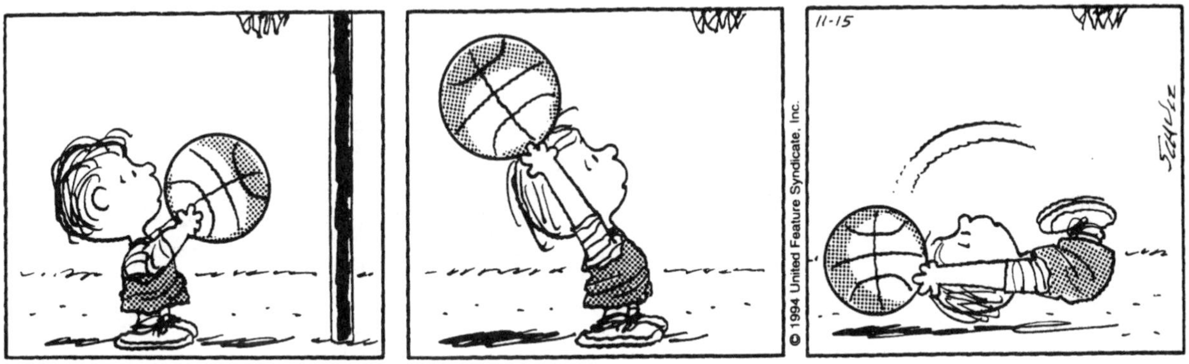
© 1994 United Feature Syndicate, Inc.
11-15
SCHULZ

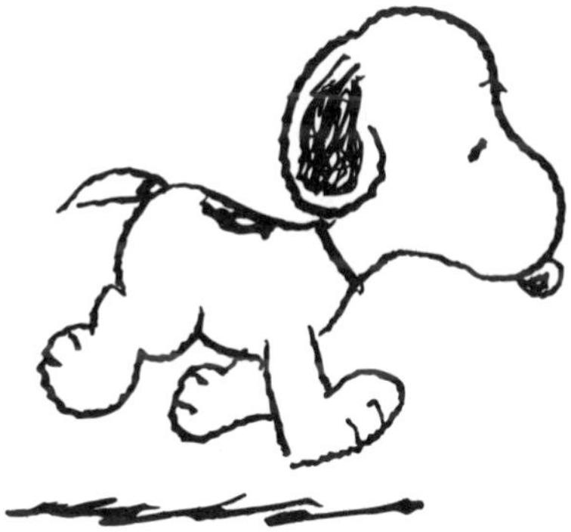

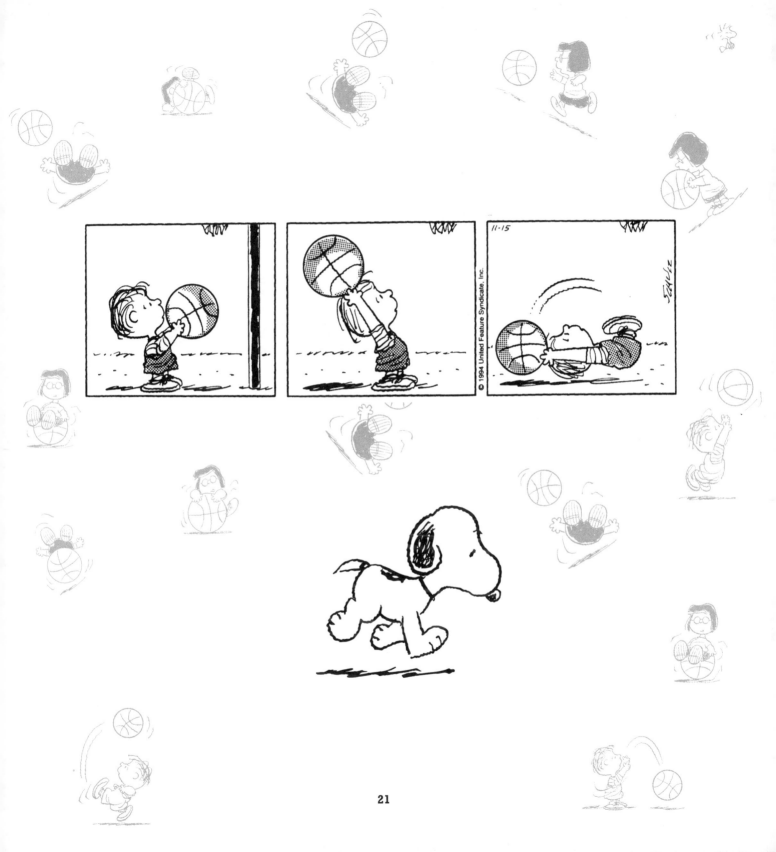

4-25 © 1995 United Feature Syndicate, Inc.
WHAT WAS THAT ?
THAT WAS MY FAMOUS JUMP SHOT..
SCHULZ

DON'T WAIT UP FOR ME.. I'M GOING OUT TO PLAY A LITTLE MIDNIGHT BASKETBALL..
© 1995 United Feature Syndicate, Inc.
WELL, MAYBE A LITTLE NOON BASKETBALL..
4-26
SCHULZ

© 1995 United Feature Syndicate, Inc.
6-6
SCHULZ

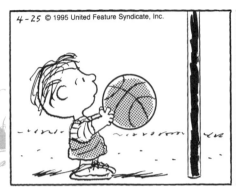

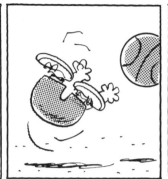

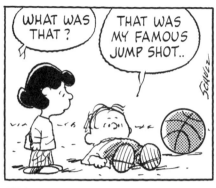

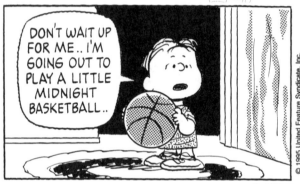

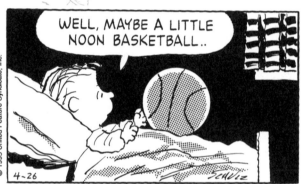

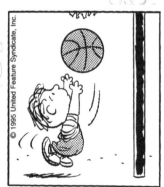

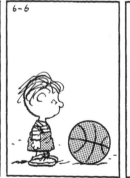

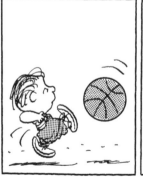

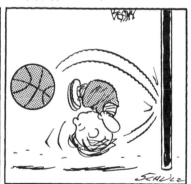

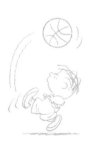

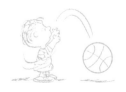

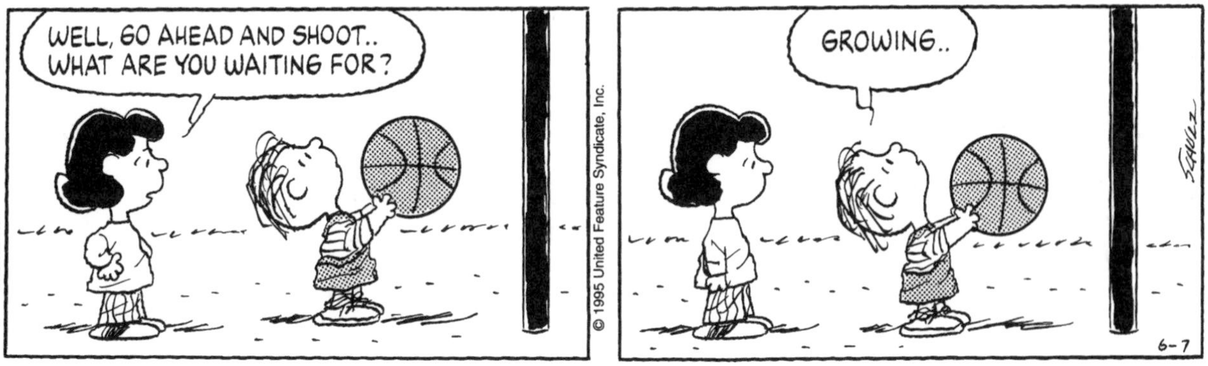
WELL, GO AHEAD AND SHOOT..
WHAT ARE YOU WAITING FOR?
© 1995 United Feature Syndicate, Inc.
GROWING..
SCHULZ
6-7

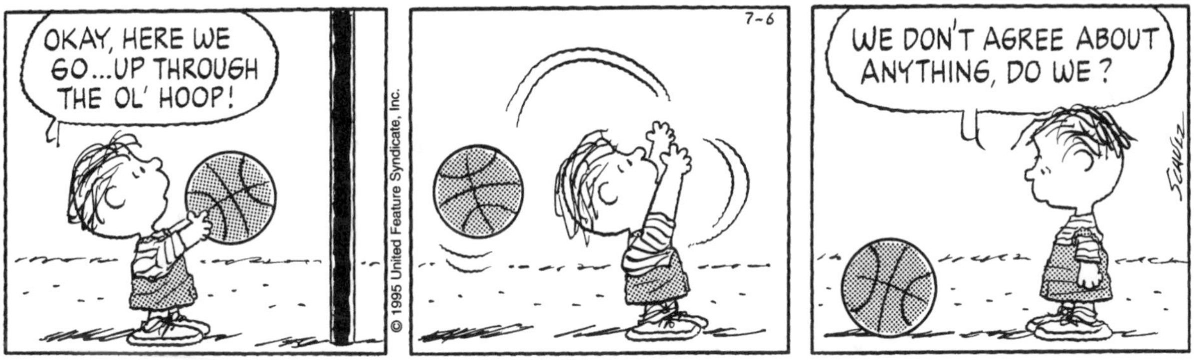
OKAY, HERE WE GO...UP THROUGH THE OL' HOOP!
© 1995 United Feature Syndicate, Inc.
7-6
WE DON'T AGREE ABOUT ANYTHING, DO WE?
SCHULZ

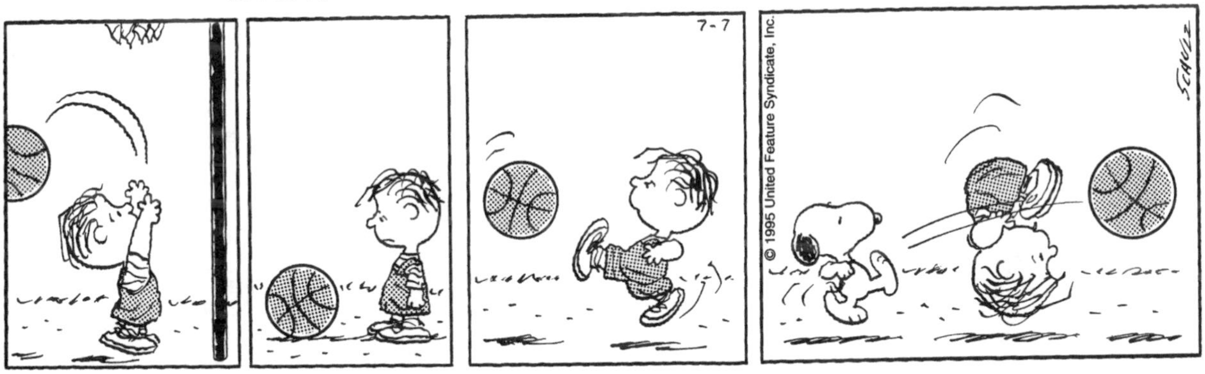
7-7
© 1995 United Feature Syndicate, Inc.
SCHULZ

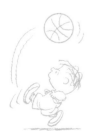

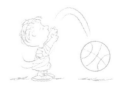

HERE WE GO! SLAM DUNK!
LOTS OF SLAM, BUT NO DUNK..
© 1995 United Feature Syndicate, Inc.
9-18

I CAN DO IT! I'VE MASTERED THE TECHNIQUE!
11-4
NOTHING CAN STOP ME FROM PUTTING THIS BALL THROUGH THE HOOP!
NOTHING!
© 1995 United Feature Syndicate, Inc.

ALL RIGHT, HERE'S THE WAY IT'S GONNA WORK..
I TOSS THE BALL INTO THE AIR, AND IT GOES THROUGH THE HOOP..
11-20
© 1995 United Feature Syndicate, Inc.
I WAS TALKING TO **YOU**!

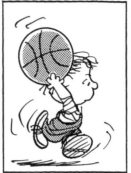

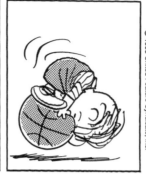

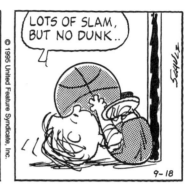

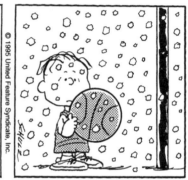

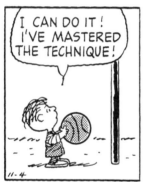

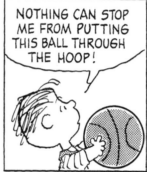

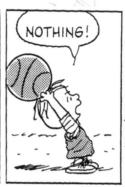

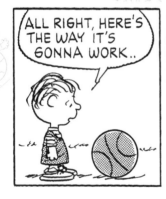

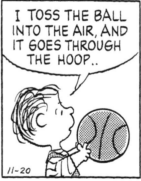

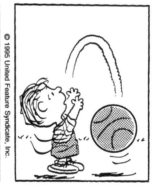

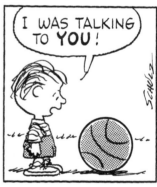

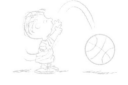

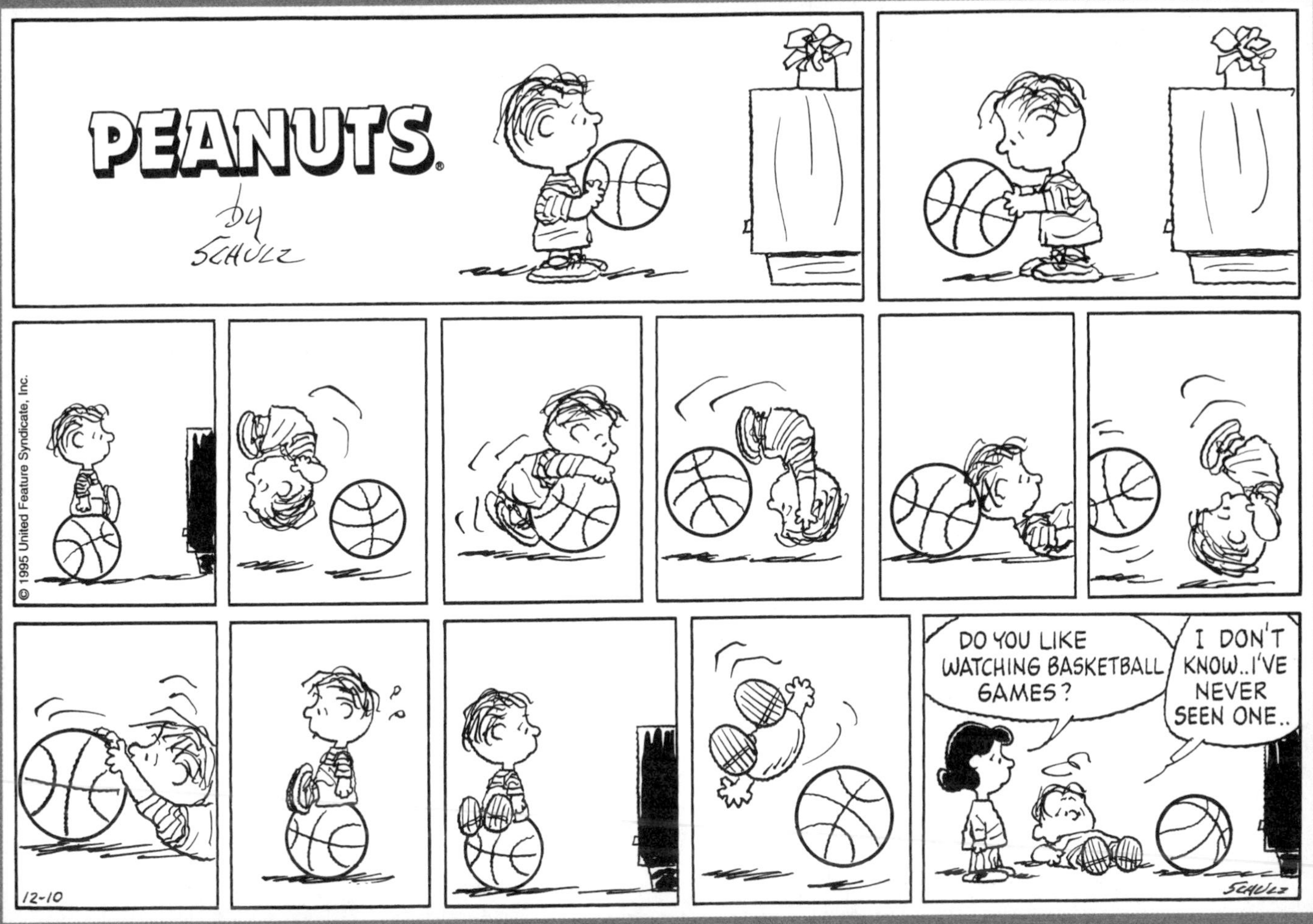
PEANUTS
by SCHULZ
© 1995 United Feature Syndicate, Inc.
12-10
DO YOU LIKE WATCHING BASKETBALL GAMES?
I DON'T KNOW..I'VE NEVER SEEN ONE..
SCHULZ

THE SCORE IS TIED! THREE SECONDS TO PLAY!
HE TURNS! HE SHOOTS!
© 1996 United Feature Syndicate, Inc.
1-22
SORT OF.. MORE OR LESS..
SCHULZ

YOU SHOOT, AND I'LL GO UP FOR THE REBOUND..
1-24
BONK!
© 1996 United Feature Syndicate, Inc.
THAT WAS THE REBOUND..
SCHULZ

© 1996 United Feature Syndicate, Inc.
8-9
SCHULZ

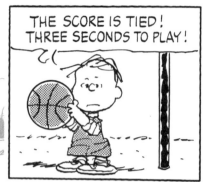

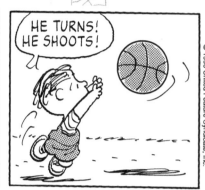

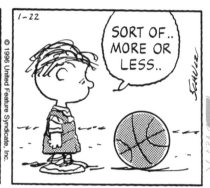

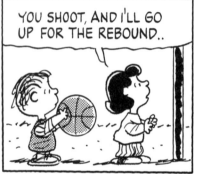

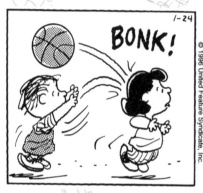

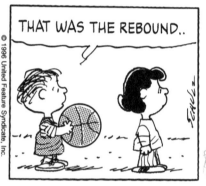

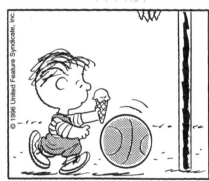

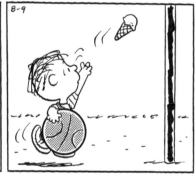

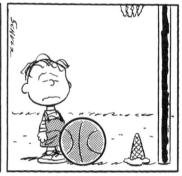

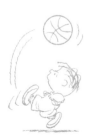

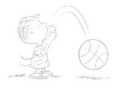

8-22
www.unitedmedia.com
© 1996 United Feature Syndicate, Inc.
WHAT DID YOU STOP FOR?!
SCHULZ

UP YOU GO! SLAM DUNK! THROUGH THE HOOP! GO! GO! GO!
8-23
www.unitedmedia.com
YOU TALK TO IT! IT NEVER LISTENS TO ME!
© 1996 United Feature Syndicate, Inc.
WOOF!
SCHULZ

www.unitedmedia.com
© 1996 United Feature Syndicate, Inc.
BANG!
SCHULZ
9-25

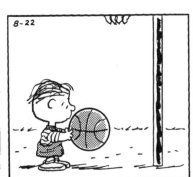

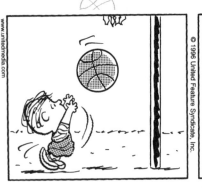

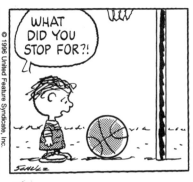

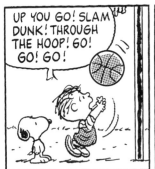

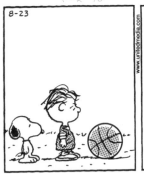

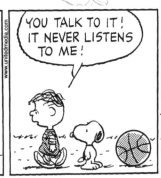

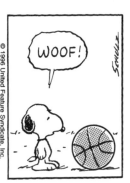

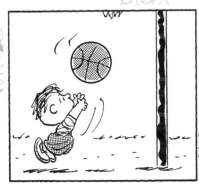

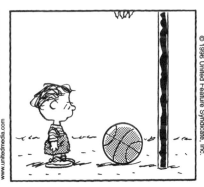

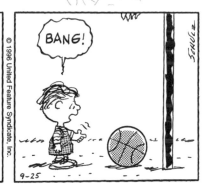

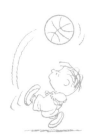

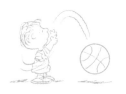

1-6-97
© 1996 United Feature Syndicate, Inc.
HERE'S A LIST OF THE ATHLETES' NAMES..ALL YOU HAVE TO DO IS FORGE THEIR SIGNATURES..YOU CAN START WITH THE BASKETBALLS..
SCHULZ

WHAT'S THIS? THIS ISN'T A BASKETBALL PLAYER'S AUTOGRAPH!
I DON'T DO FAKE AUTOGRAPHS..THAT'S MY DAD'S NAME... HE'S A BARBER..
www.unitedmedia.com
A FAMOUS BARBER?
© 1996 United Feature Syndicate, Inc.
TELL HIM TO AUTOGRAPH A BARBER POLE! WE COULD SELL IT!
SCHULZ
1-7-97

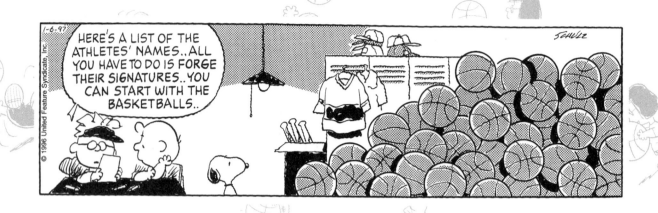

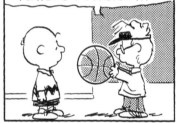

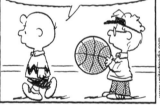

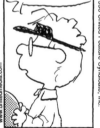

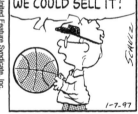

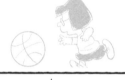

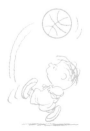

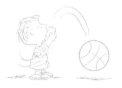

1-11-97
www.unitedmedia.com
© 1996 United Feature Syndicate, Inc.
YOU JUST DON'T UNDERSTAND, DO YOU?
SCHULZ

www.unitedmedia.com
3-15
© 1997 United Feature Syndicate, Inc.
SCHULZ

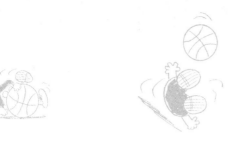

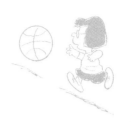

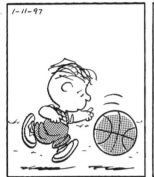

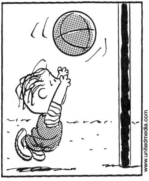

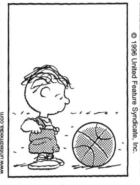

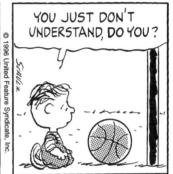

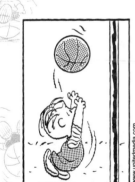

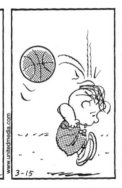

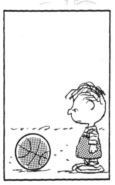

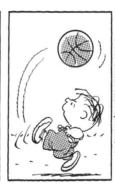

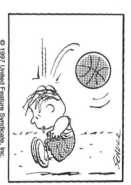

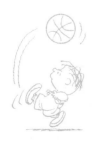

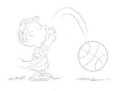

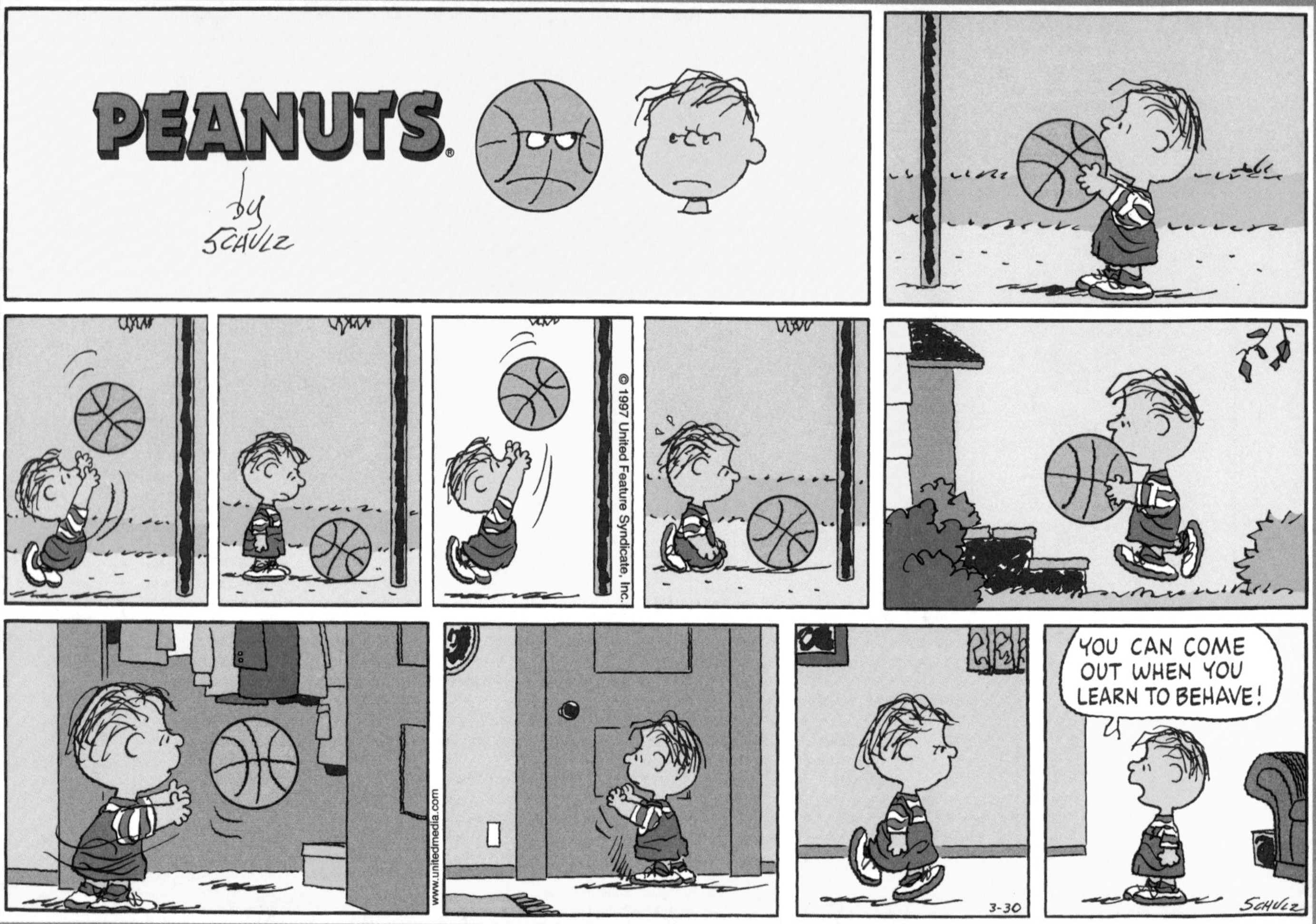
PEANUTS
by SCHULZ
© 1997 United Feature Syndicate, Inc.
www.unitedmedia.com
3-30
YOU CAN COME OUT WHEN YOU LEARN TO BEHAVE!
SCHULZ

4-3
AAUGH!!
WHAT'D YOU DO THAT FOR?!
I DIDN'T MEAN TO.. IT WAS A DOG THING..
SCHULZ
© 1997 United Feature Syndicate, Inc.
www.unitedmedia.com

BONK!
I HIT YOU ON THE HEAD SO I THINK THAT MEANS YOU GET A FREE SHOT...
7-4
BONK!
SCHULZ
© 1997 United Feature Syndicate, Inc.
www.unitedmedia.com

THE GOVERNMENT'S "MIDNIGHT BASKETBALL" PROGRAM HAS STILL TO REACH SOME OUTLYING AREAS..
7-9
SCHULZ
© 1997 United Feature Syndicate, Inc.

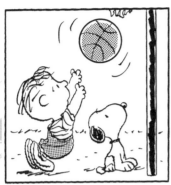

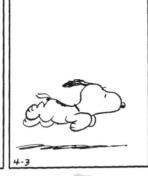

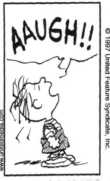

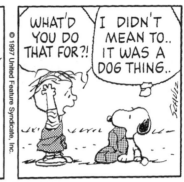

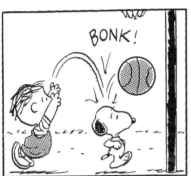

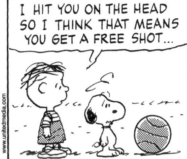

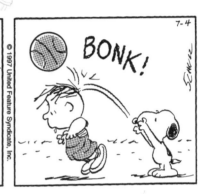

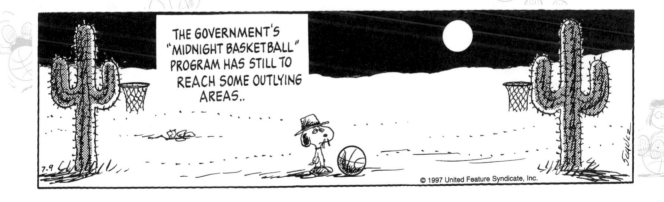

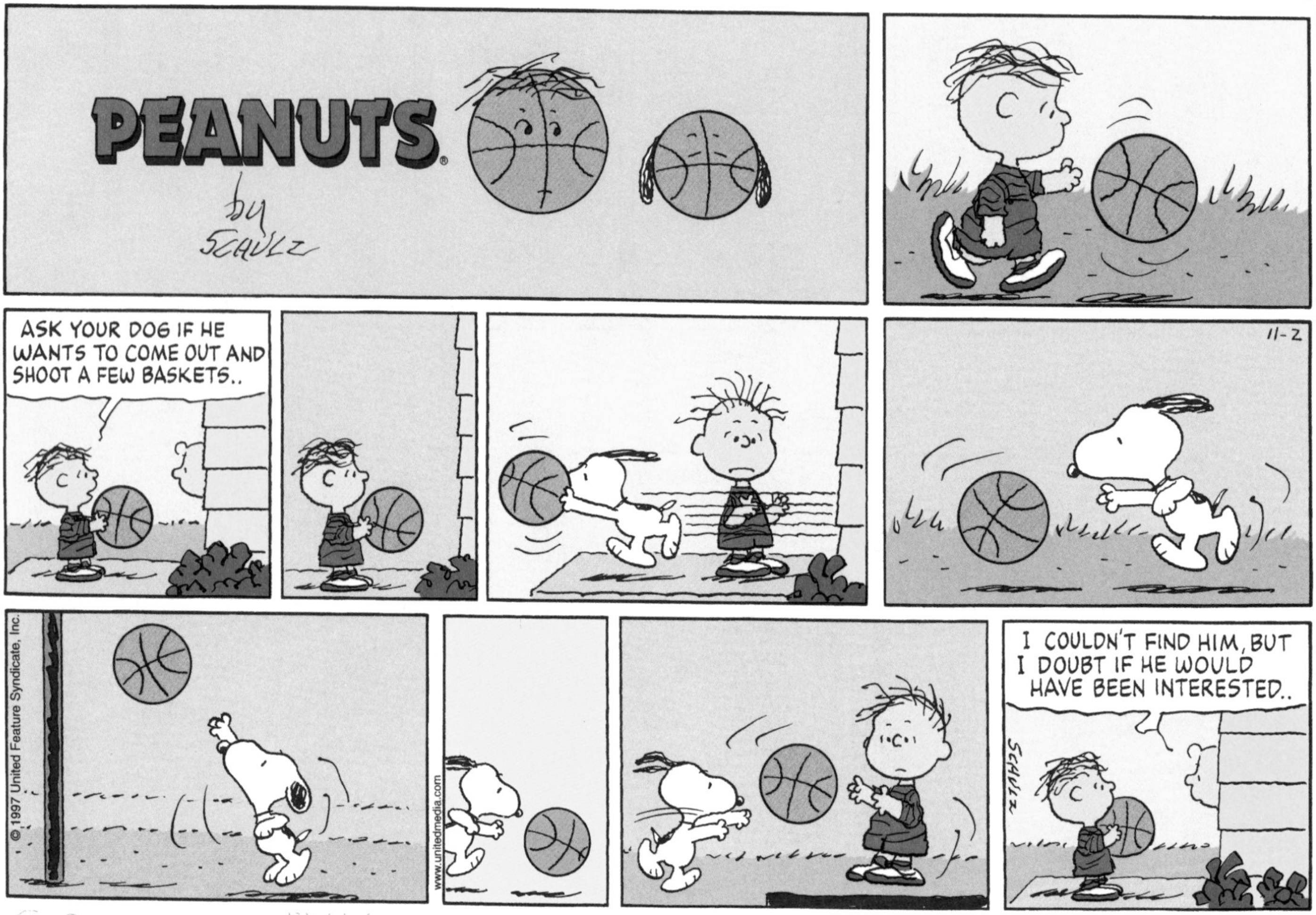
PEANUTS
by SCHULZ
ASK YOUR DOG IF HE WANTS TO COME OUT AND SHOOT A FEW BASKETS..
11-2
© 1997 United Feature Syndicate, Inc.
www.unitedmedia.com
I COULDN'T FIND HIM, BUT I DOUBT IF HE WOULD HAVE BEEN INTERESTED..
SCHULZ

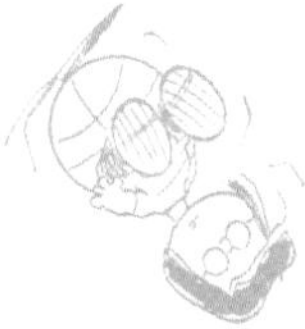

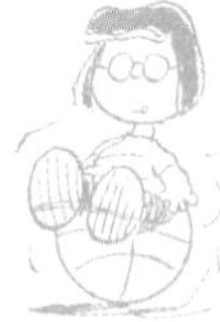

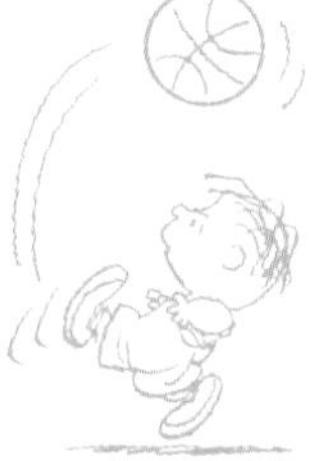

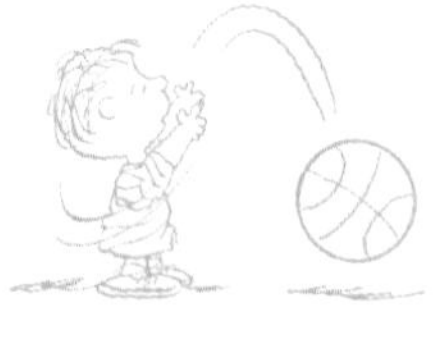

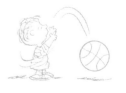

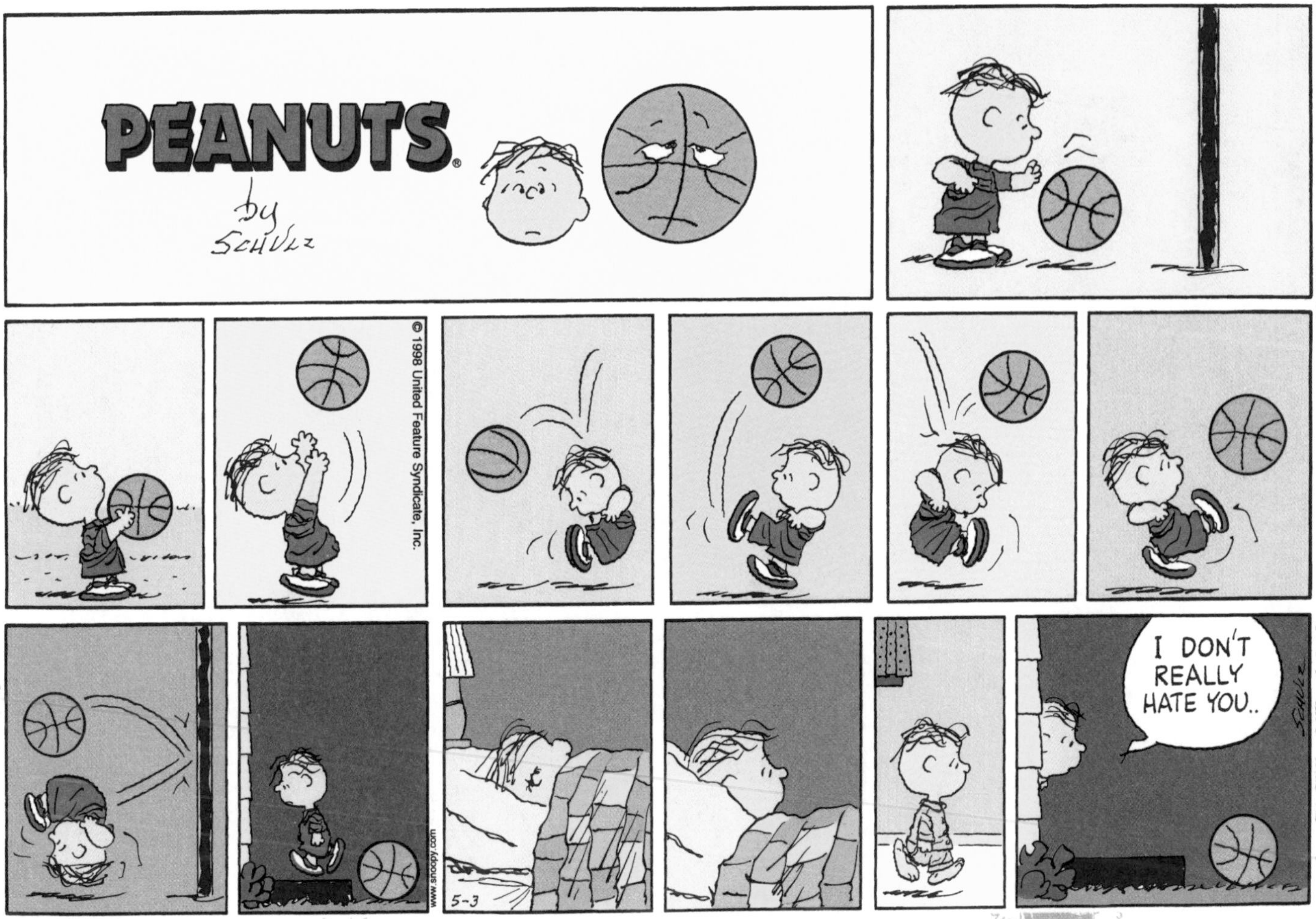
PEANUTS
by SCHULZ
© 1998 United Feature Syndicate, Inc.
www.snoopy.com
5-3
I DON'T REALLY HATE YOU..
SCHULZ

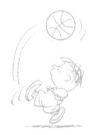

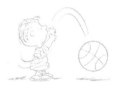

PEANUTS
TEN SECONDS ON THE GAME CLOCK.. RERUN COMES OFF THE BENCH..
I BLOCK THE PASS! THE BALL IS MINE!
I WHIRL..
I DRIBBLE DOWN THE SIDE! WE'RE ONE POINT BEHIND..
I FAKE A PASS, AND WHIRL AGAIN..
© 1999 United Feature Syndicate, Inc.
THREE SECONDS ON THE GAME CLOCK..
2-28
www.snoopy.com
I SHOOT..
IT'S IN!!
THEY LET ME HAVE THE GAME BALL..

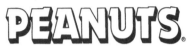

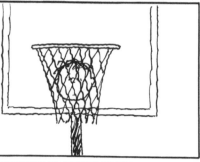

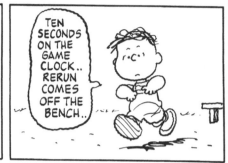

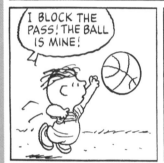

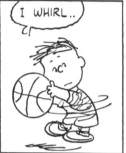

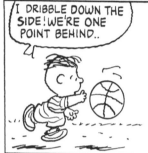

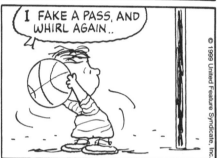

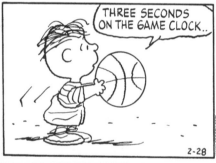

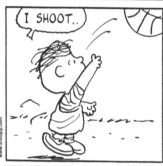

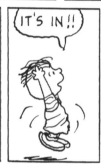

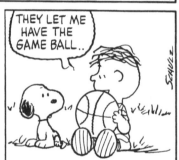

6-17
LET ME ASK YOU SOMETHING...
DO YOU KNOW WHY WE'RE OUT HERE?
www.snoopy.com
© 1999 United Feature Syndicate, Inc.
SCHULZ

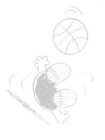

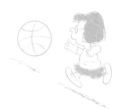

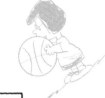

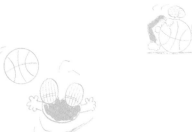

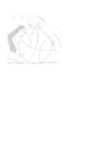

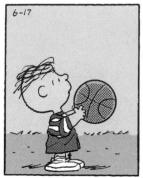

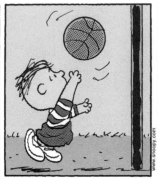

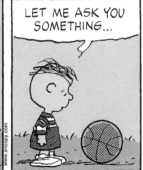

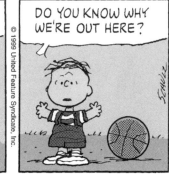

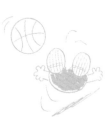

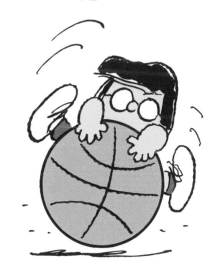

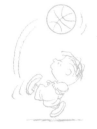

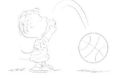

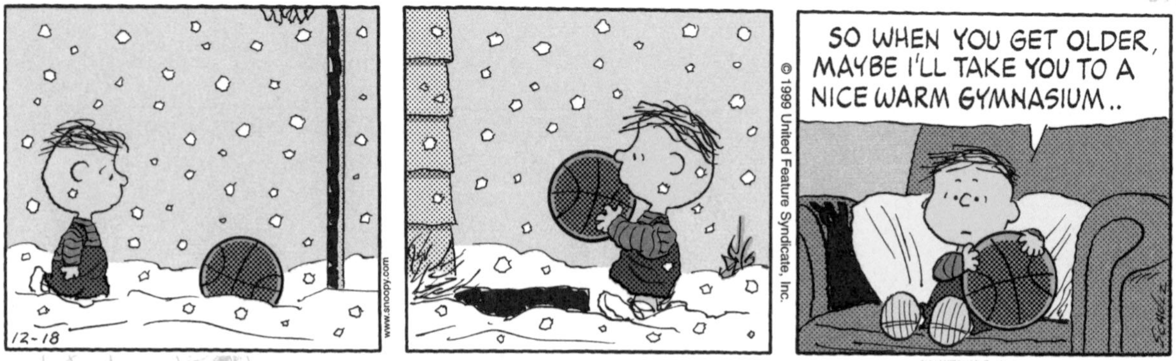
12-18
www.snoopy.com
© 1999 United Feature Syndicate, Inc.
SO WHEN YOU GET OLDER, MAYBE I'LL TAKE YOU TO A NICE WARM GYMNASIUM..

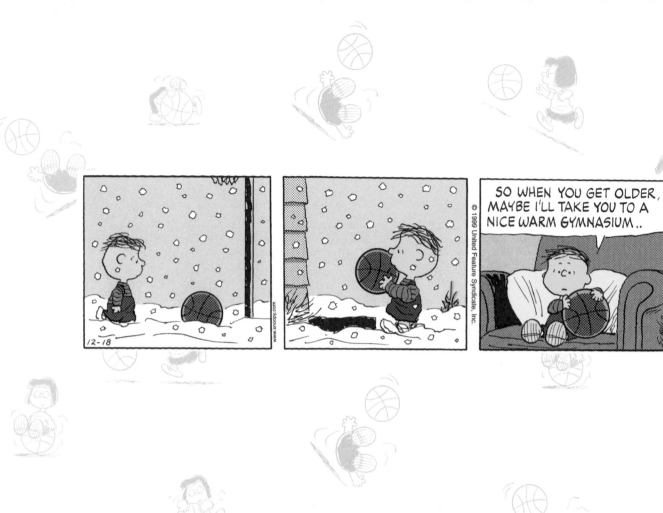

Football

"PEANUTS"

SIGNALS! ONE! SIX! THREE! TWO! FIVE! HIKE!

TIME OUT!

SAY, CHARLIE BROWN... ABOUT THE WAY YOU CALL THOSE SIGNALS..

I THINK YOU SHOULD TRY MIXING UP THE NUMBERS INSTEAD OF SAYING THEM IN THEIR RIGHT ORDER!

"PEANUTS"

"PEANUTS"

RATS!

IT'S NO USE... I GIVE UP!

WELL, DON'T FEEL SO BADLY ABOUT IT, CHARLIE BROWN.... AFTER ALL..

..MOST COLLEGE PLAYERS ARE BIGGER THAN US!

"PEANUTS"

AND THERE GOES CHARLIE BROWN THRU RIGHT GUARD!

HE SHAKES OFF ONE TACKLER.. AND ANOTHER.. TEARING.. TWISTING.. TURNING..

AND NOW HE'S IN THE CLEAR! HE'S..HE'S... HE'S....

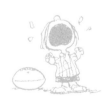

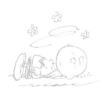

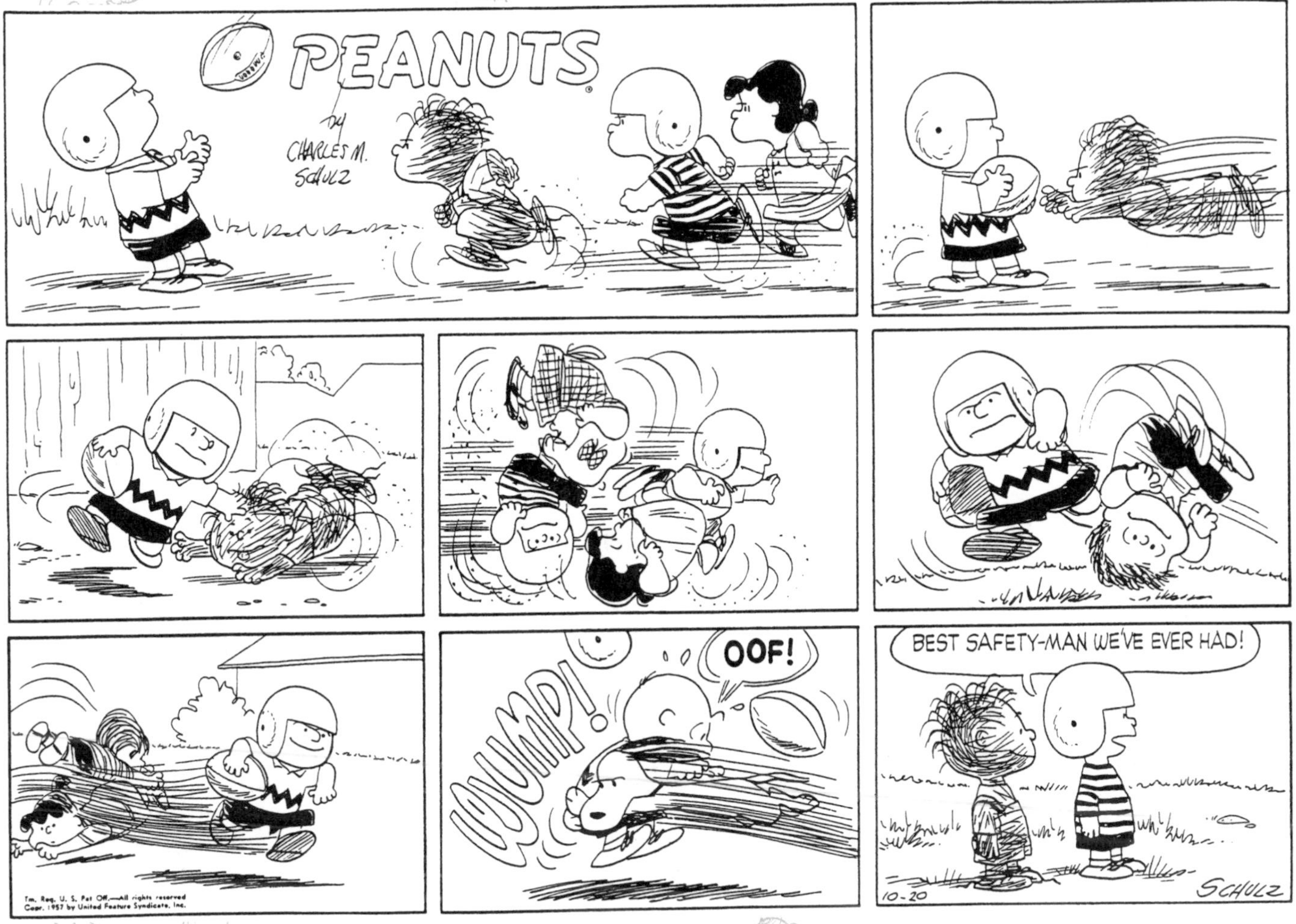
PEANUTS
BY CHARLES M. SCHULZ
Tm. Reg. U. S. Pat. Off.—All rights reserved
Copr. 1957 by United Feature Syndicate, Inc.
WUMP!
OOF!
BEST SAFETY-MAN WE'VE EVER HAD!
10-20
SCHULZ

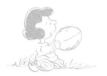

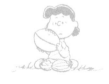

PEANUTS by CHARLES M. SCHULZ

NOW'S THE TIME FOR A GOOD PASS PLAY!

ALL RIGHT, MEN, LET'S GET IN THERE THIS TIME, AND SMEAR 'EM!

NOW, LISTEN CAREFULLY

SCHROEDER HIKES THE BALL TO YOU, LINUS, AND YOU FADE BACK, AND THROW ME A LONG PASS..

NOW, ARE YOU SURE YOU UNDERSTAND?

OF COURSE, I UNDERSTAND!

WELL, I HOPE SO..

SIGNALS! THIRTY-THREE! EIGHTEEN! FORTY-NINE!

HIKE!

PASS IT!

SCHULZ

10-27

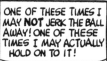

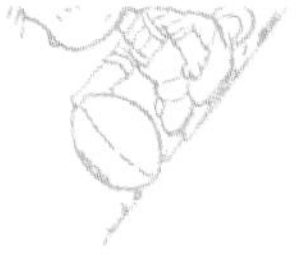

PEANUTS

YOU SAY YOU LEFT YOUR FOOTBALL IN THE BACKYARD LAST NIGHT?

UH HUH... AND THEN, ABOUT TEN O'CLOCK, I WOKE UP, AND I COULD HEAR SOMEONE PUNTING IT ALL OVER THE YARD

BUT WHO IN THE WORLD WOULD BE PUNTING A FOOTBALL AROUND AT TEN O'CLOCK AT NIGHT?

I CAN'T IMAGINE! 12/20

PEANUTS 12-21

PUNT

HAVE YOU SEEN MY FOOTBALL, CHARLIE BROWN? IT SEEMS TO HAVE DISAPPEARED

YOURS, TOO?

THE "MAD PUNTER" HAS STRUCK AGAIN!

IS THERE NO STOPPING THIS FIEND? WILL HE NEVER BE CAUGHT?

51

52

54

PEANUTS

10-22

WHOP!

I LOVE TOUCH FOOTBALL!

SCHULZ

AAUGH!

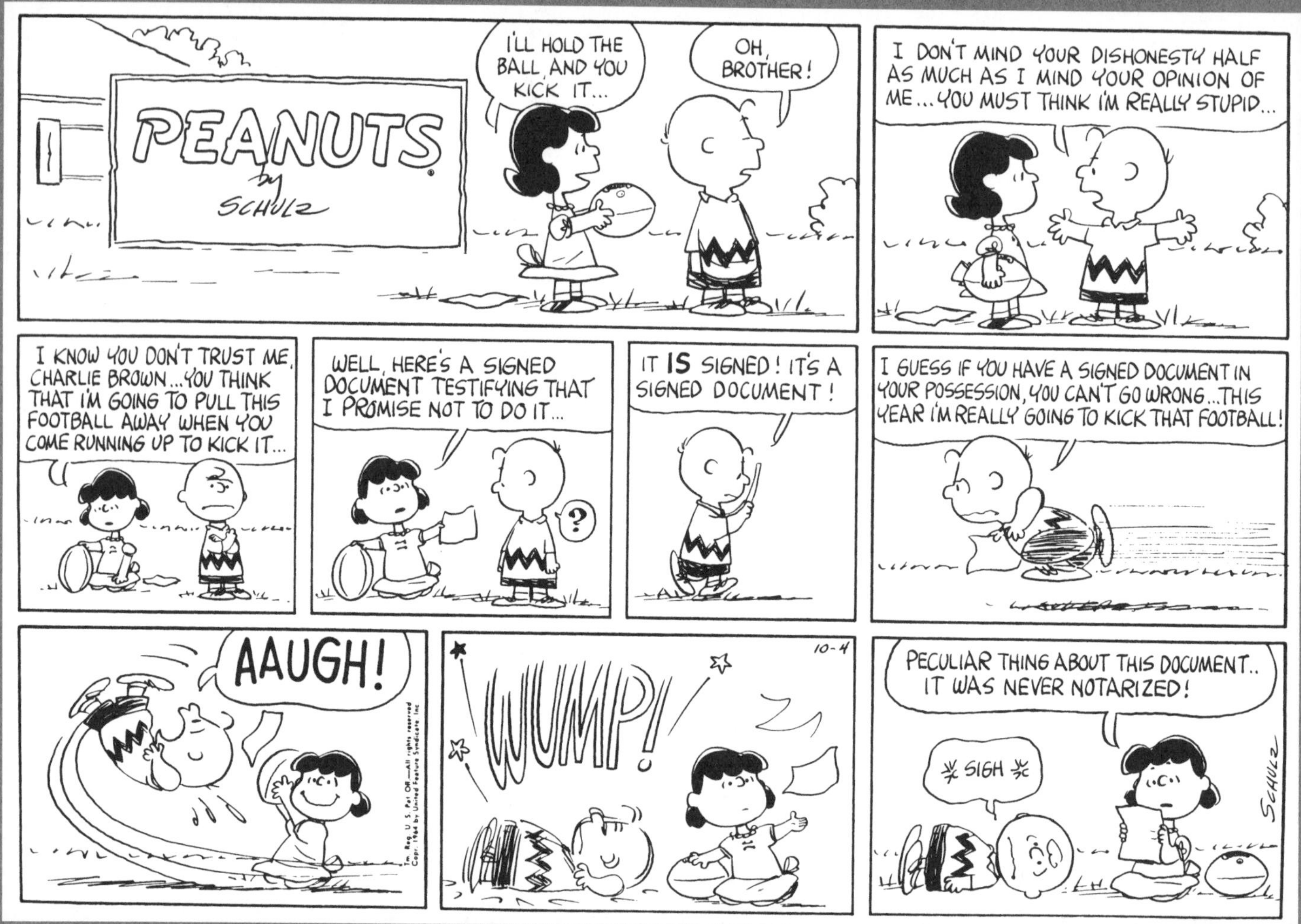
PEANUTS
by SCHULZ
I'LL HOLD THE BALL, AND YOU KICK IT...
OH, BROTHER!
I DON'T MIND YOUR DISHONESTY HALF AS MUCH AS I MIND YOUR OPINION OF ME... YOU MUST THINK I'M REALLY STUPID...
I KNOW YOU DON'T TRUST ME, CHARLIE BROWN... YOU THINK THAT I'M GOING TO PULL THIS FOOTBALL AWAY WHEN YOU COME RUNNING UP TO KICK IT...
WELL, HERE'S A SIGNED DOCUMENT TESTIFYING THAT I PROMISE NOT TO DO IT...
?
IT IS SIGNED! IT'S A SIGNED DOCUMENT!
I GUESS IF YOU HAVE A SIGNED DOCUMENT IN YOUR POSSESSION, YOU CAN'T GO WRONG... THIS YEAR I'M REALLY GOING TO KICK THAT FOOTBALL!
AAUGH!
10-4
WUMP!
PECULIAR THING ABOUT THIS DOCUMENT.. IT WAS NEVER NOTARIZED!
SIGH
SCHULZ

PEANUTS by SCHULZ

OH, BROTHER!

WELL?

HOW ABOUT IT, CHARLIE BROWN? I'LL HOLD THE BALL, AND YOU COME RUNNING UP AND KICK IT...

BOY, IT REALLY AGGRAVATES ME THE WAY YOU THINK I'M SO STUPID!

I GUARANTEE THAT THE ONLY THING THAT WILL MAKE ME PULL THE BALL AWAY THIS YEAR WILL BE AN INVOLUNTARY MUSCLE SPASM!

NOW, YOU CERTAINLY WILL AGREE THAT THE ODDS MUST BE ASTRONOMICAL AGAINST SUCH AN INVOLUNTARY MUSCLE SPASM OCCURRING AT THE VERY MOMENT YOU TRY TO KICK THE BALL...

SHE'S RIGHT! THIS YEAR HAS TO BE THE YEAR I KICK THAT OL' BALL!

SO HERE I GO!

AAUGH!

WUMP!

I'VE LOOKED IT UP, CHARLIE BROWN... THE ACTUAL ODDS AGAINST SUCH AN INVOLUNTARY MUSCLE SPASM OCCURRING AT THAT PRECISE MOMENT WERE TEN BILLION TO ONE!

SCHULZ

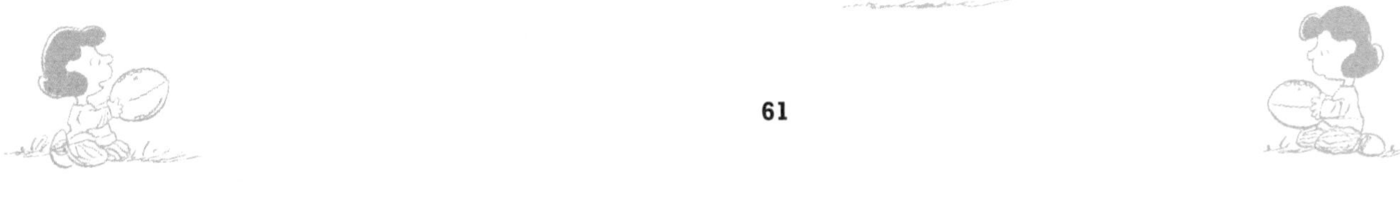

9-25

PEANUTS
Tm. Reg. U. S. Pat. Off.—All rights reserved ©1967 by United Feature Syndicate, Inc.
10-19
BOOT!
OKAY, NOW YOU KICK IT BACK...
YOU'RE KIDDING!
SCHULZ

PEANUTS
10-20
BOOT!
Tm. Reg. U. S. Pat. Off.—All rights reserved ©1967 by United Feature Syndicate, Inc.
WHAT'S SO EXCITING ABOUT THE KICKOFF?
SCHULZ

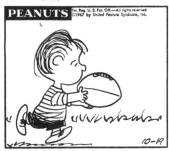

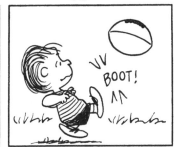

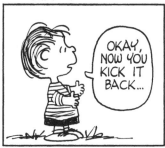

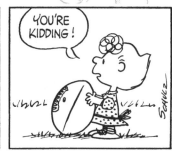

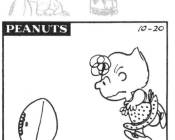

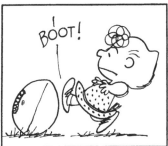

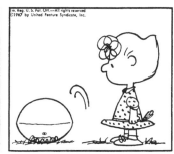

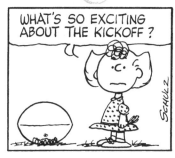

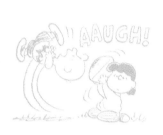

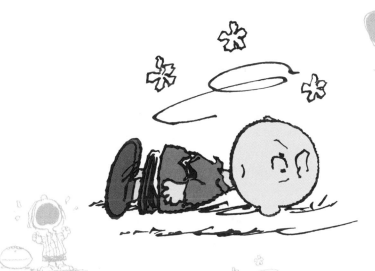

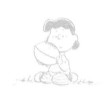

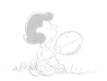

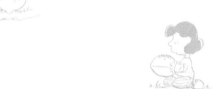

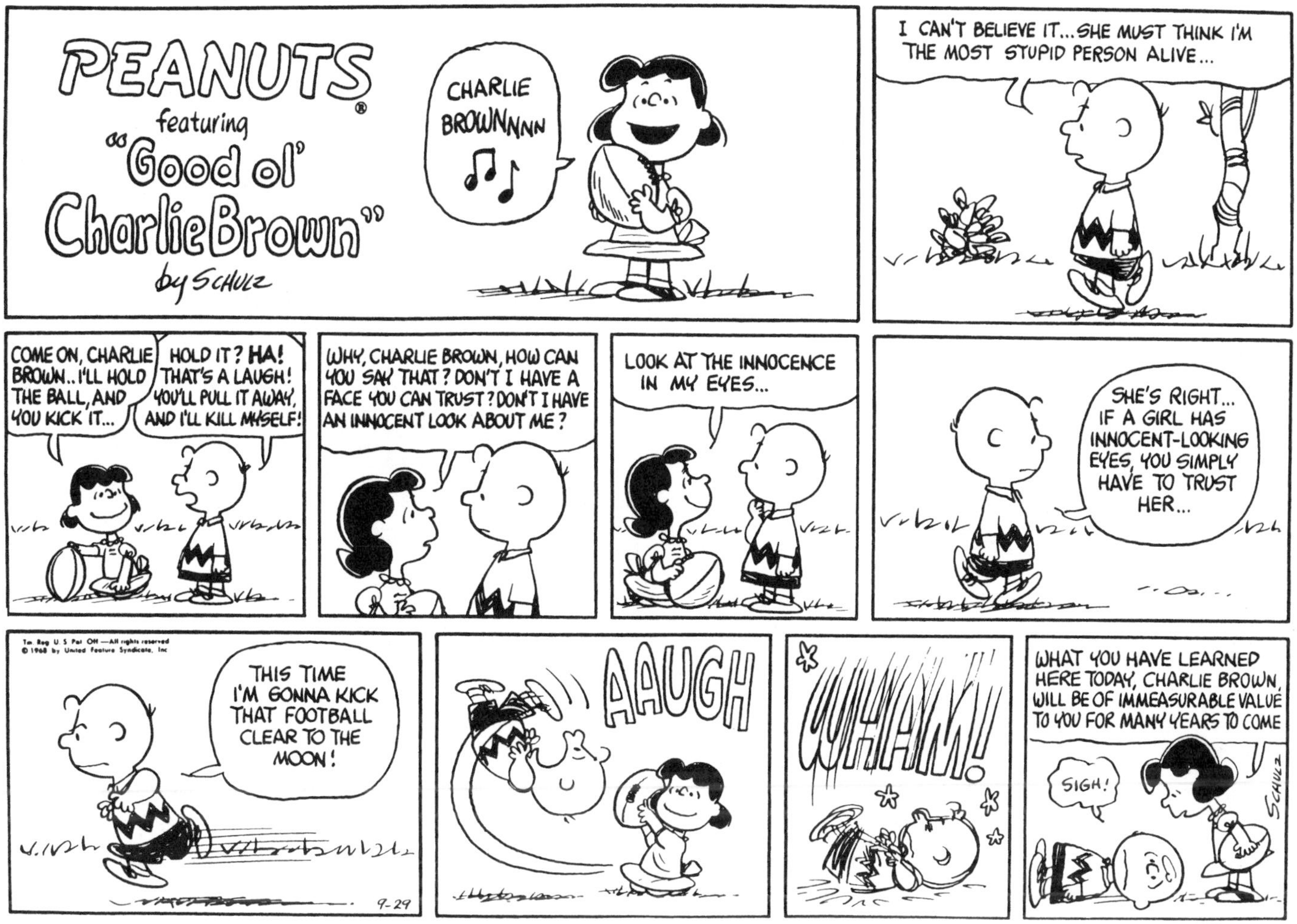
PEANUTS® featuring "Good ol' Charlie Brown" by SCHULZ
CHARLIE BROWNNNN
I CAN'T BELIEVE IT... SHE MUST THINK I'M THE MOST STUPID PERSON ALIVE...
COME ON, CHARLIE BROWN.. I'LL HOLD THE BALL, AND YOU KICK IT...
HOLD IT? HA! THAT'S A LAUGH! YOU'LL PULL IT AWAY, AND I'LL KILL MYSELF!
WHY, CHARLIE BROWN, HOW CAN YOU SAY THAT? DON'T I HAVE A FACE YOU CAN TRUST? DON'T I HAVE AN INNOCENT LOOK ABOUT ME?
LOOK AT THE INNOCENCE IN MY EYES...
SHE'S RIGHT... IF A GIRL HAS INNOCENT-LOOKING EYES, YOU SIMPLY HAVE TO TRUST HER...
Tm. Reg. U.S. Pat. Off.—All rights reserved © 1968 by United Feature Syndicate, Inc
THIS TIME I'M GONNA KICK THAT FOOTBALL CLEAR TO THE MOON!
9-29
AAUGH
WHAM!
WHAT YOU HAVE LEARNED HERE TODAY, CHARLIE BROWN, WILL BE OF IMMEASURABLE VALUE TO YOU FOR MANY YEARS TO COME
SIGH!
SCHULZ

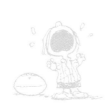

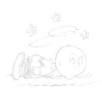

PEANUTS
SIX... ELEVEN.. NINE...
9-18
THIRTY-THREE...
Tm. Reg. U. S. Pat. Off.—All rights reserved © 1969 by United Feature Syndicate, Inc.
THUNK!
A LITTLE OFFSIDE THERE, MAC!
SCHULZ

PEANUTS
FORTY-ONE! SEVEN! FIFTEEN!
Tm. Reg. U. S. Pat. Off.—All rights reserved © 1969 by United Feature Syndicate, Inc.
9-20
MY CENTER HAS DIFFICULTY GETTING THE BALL BACK...
SCHULZ

PEANUTS
HELLO, CHUCK? THIS IS PEPPERMINT PATTY... I'M JUST CALLING ABOUT OUR FOOTBALL GAME
9-22
OUR TEAM HAS BEEN PRACTICING LIKE MAD... COUNTDOWNS, PASS PATTERNS, RED-DOGGING... YOU KNOW, THAT SORT OF THING...
Tm. Reg. U. S. Pat. Off.—All rights reserved © 1969 by United Feature Syndicate, Inc.
HOW'S YOUR TEAM DOING?
WELL, WE'VE JUST ABOUT GOT THE BALL INFLATED...
SCHULZ

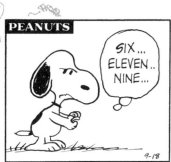

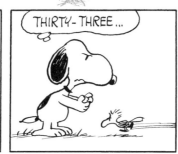

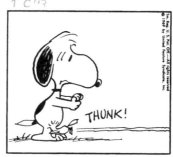

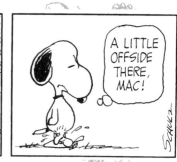

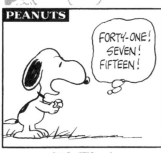

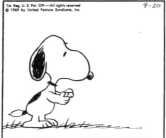

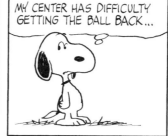

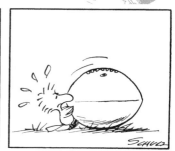

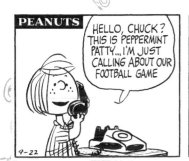

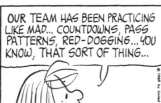

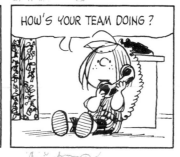

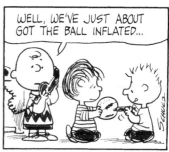

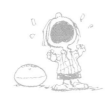

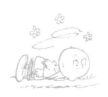

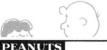

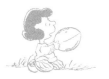

PEANUTS

9-23

THIS KICKOFF MAY TAKE A WHILE...

BOOT! BOOT! BOOT! BOOT!

SCHULZ

PEANUTS

WELL, COACH, WE'RE READY... WHERE'S THE OTHER TEAM?

I DON'T KNOW... I TOLD CHUCK TO GET HIS OUTFIT TOGETHER, AND BE HERE AT THREE...

9-24

HERE COMES A TEAM NOW...

SCHULZ

AAUGH!

PEANUTS

HI, CHUCK... SORRY YOU MISSED THE GAME YESTERDAY...

9-25

I SURE HAVE TO HAND IT TO YOU, THOUGH, CHUCK... THAT WAS SOME TEAM YOU SENT OVER... THEY CLOBBERED US, BUT GOOD!

TEAM?

THAT FUNNY LOOKING KID WITH THE BIG NOSE WAS GREAT, AND THOSE LITTLE GUYS HE HAD WITH HIM WERE ALL OVER THE FIELD!

SCHULZ

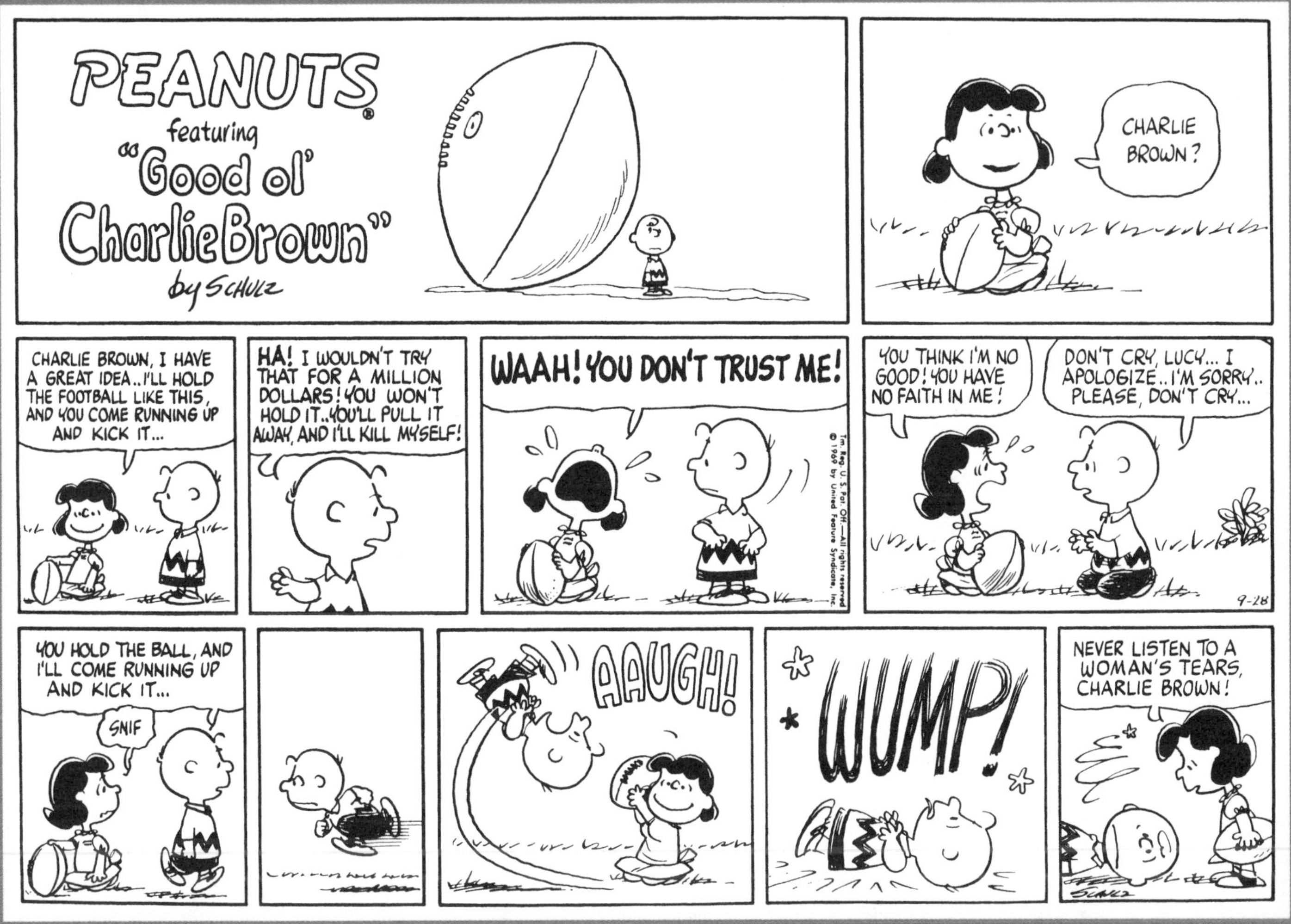
PEANUTS®
featuring
"Good ol' Charlie Brown"
by SCHULZ
CHARLIE BROWN?
CHARLIE BROWN, I HAVE A GREAT IDEA..I'LL HOLD THE FOOTBALL LIKE THIS, AND YOU COME RUNNING UP AND KICK IT...
HA! I WOULDN'T TRY THAT FOR A MILLION DOLLARS! YOU WON'T HOLD IT..YOU'LL PULL IT AWAY, AND I'LL KILL MYSELF!
WAAH! YOU DON'T TRUST ME!
Tm. Reg. U.S. Pat. Off.—All rights reserved © 1969 by United Feature Syndicate, Inc.
YOU THINK I'M NO GOOD! YOU HAVE NO FAITH IN ME!
DON'T CRY, LUCY... I APOLOGIZE..I'M SORRY.. PLEASE, DON'T CRY...
9-28
YOU HOLD THE BALL, AND I'LL COME RUNNING UP AND KICK IT...
SNIF
AAUGH!
WUMP!
NEVER LISTEN TO A WOMAN'S TEARS, CHARLIE BROWN!
SCHULZ

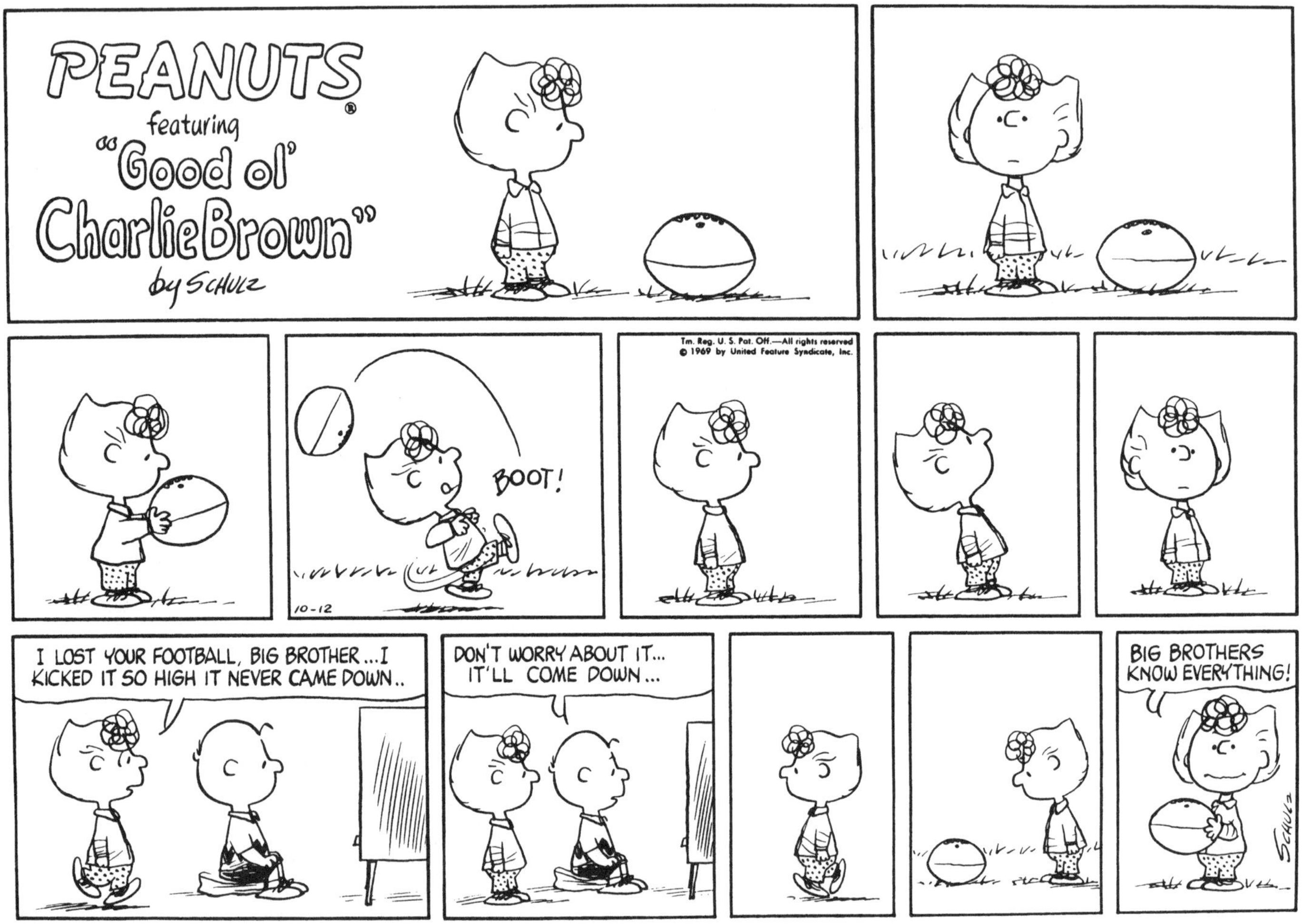
PEANUTS®
featuring
"Good ol' Charlie Brown"
by SCHULZ
Tm. Reg. U. S. Pat. Off.—All rights reserved © 1969 by United Feature Syndicate, Inc.
BOOT!
10-12
I LOST YOUR FOOTBALL, BIG BROTHER...I KICKED IT SO HIGH IT NEVER CAME DOWN..
DON'T WORRY ABOUT IT... IT'LL COME DOWN...
BIG BROTHERS KNOW EVERYTHING!
SCHULZ

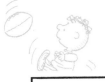

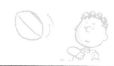

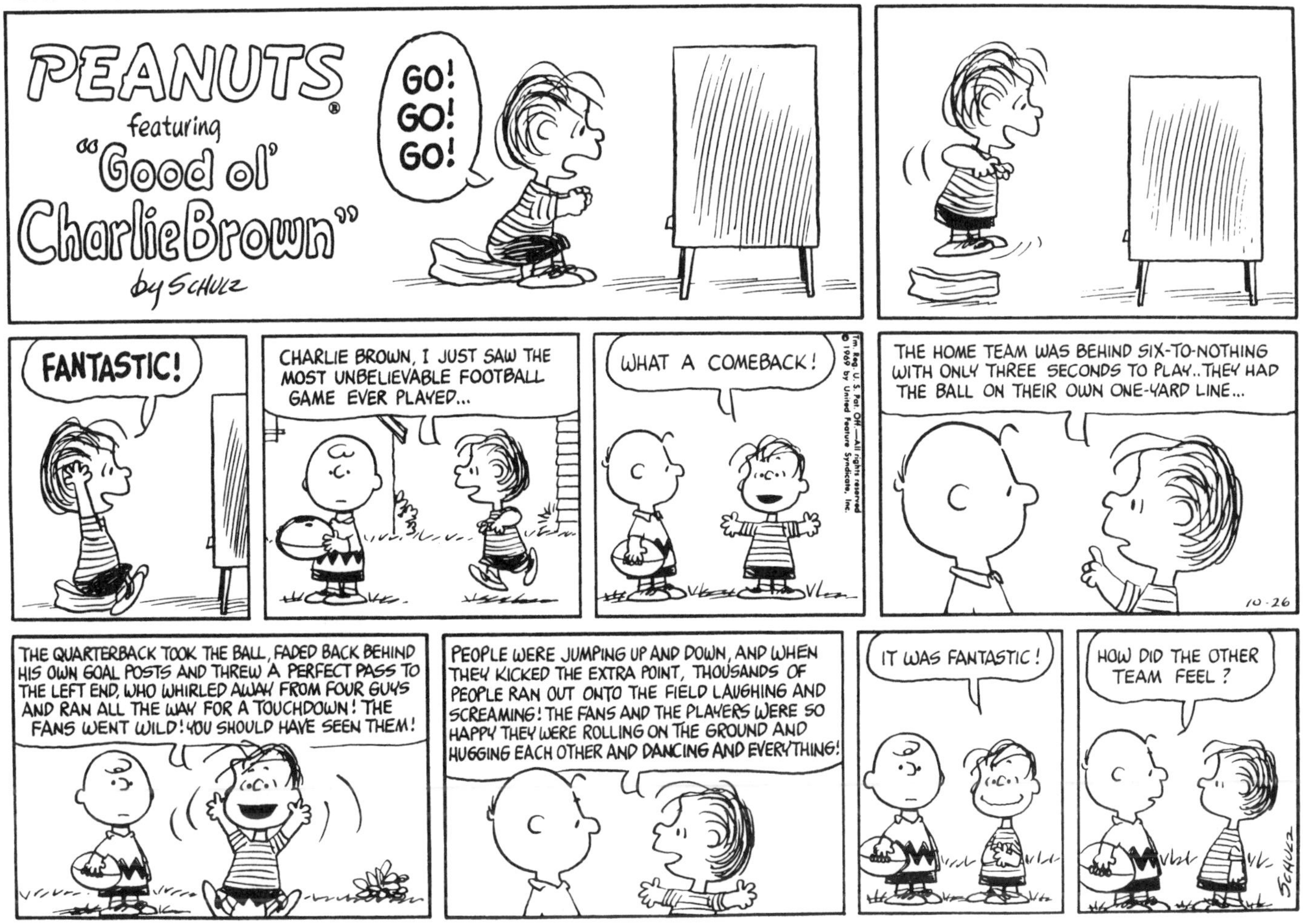
PEANUTS®
featuring "Good ol' Charlie Brown"
by SCHULZ
GO! GO! GO!
FANTASTIC!
CHARLIE BROWN, I JUST SAW THE MOST UNBELIEVABLE FOOTBALL GAME EVER PLAYED...
WHAT A COMEBACK!
Tm. Reg. U. S. Pat. Off.—All rights reserved © 1969 by United Feature Syndicate, Inc.
THE HOME TEAM WAS BEHIND SIX-TO-NOTHING WITH ONLY THREE SECONDS TO PLAY.. THEY HAD THE BALL ON THEIR OWN ONE-YARD LINE...
10-26
THE QUARTERBACK TOOK THE BALL, FADED BACK BEHIND HIS OWN GOAL POSTS AND THREW A PERFECT PASS TO THE LEFT END, WHO WHIRLED AWAY FROM FOUR GUYS AND RAN ALL THE WAY FOR A TOUCHDOWN! THE FANS WENT WILD! YOU SHOULD HAVE SEEN THEM!
PEOPLE WERE JUMPING UP AND DOWN, AND WHEN THEY KICKED THE EXTRA POINT, THOUSANDS OF PEOPLE RAN OUT ONTO THE FIELD LAUGHING AND SCREAMING! THE FANS AND THE PLAYERS WERE SO HAPPY THEY WERE ROLLING ON THE GROUND AND HUGGING EACH OTHER AND DANCING AND EVERYTHING!
IT WAS FANTASTIC!
HOW DID THE OTHER TEAM FEEL?
SCHULZ

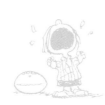

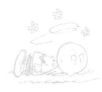

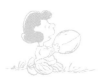

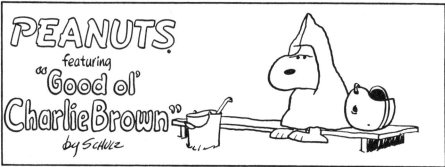

PEANUTS
featuring
"Good ol' Charlie Brown"
by SCHULZ
THREE MINUTES TO PLAY...
HERE'S THE WORLD FAMOUS QUARTERBACK COMING OFF THE BENCH TO WIN THE BIG GAME...
11-23
SIXTEEN! FORTY-TWO! SEVEN! HUT!!
HE FADES BACK, AND SPOTS AN OPEN RECEIVER...
HE HURLS THE BOMB!
Tm. Reg. U. S. Pat. Off.—All rights reserved © 1969 by United Feature Syndicate, Inc.
BONK!
BAD HANDS!
SCHULZ

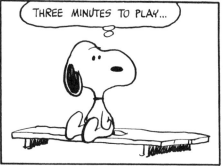

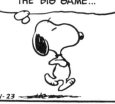

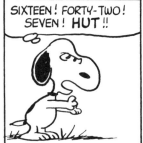

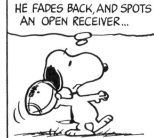

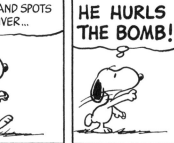

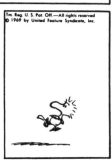

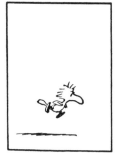

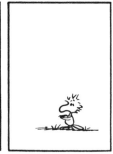

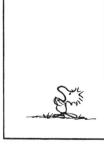

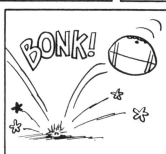

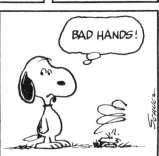

PEANUTS featuring "Good ol' Charlie Brown" by SCHULZ

SHE MUST BE KIDDING!

CHARLIE BROWN...

I CAN'T BELIEVE IT!

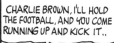

CHARLIE BROWN, I'LL HOLD THE FOOTBALL, AND YOU COME RUNNING UP AND KICK IT..

"HOW LONG, O LORD?"

YOU'RE QUOTING FROM THE SIXTH CHAPTER OF ISAIAH, AREN'T YOU, CHARLIE BROWN?

"UNTIL CITIES LIE WASTE WITHOUT INHABITANT, AND HOUSES WITHOUT MEN, AND THE LAND IS UTTERLY DESOLATE.."

10-11

ACTUALLY, THERE IS A NOTE OF PROTEST IN THE QUESTION AS ASKED BY ISAIAH, FOR WE MIGHT SAY HE WAS UNWILLING TO ACCEPT THE FINALITY OF THE LORD'S JUDGMENT...

AUGHH!

WUMP!

HOW LONG? ALL YOUR LIFE, CHARLIE BROWN.. ALL YOUR LIFE..

SCHULZ

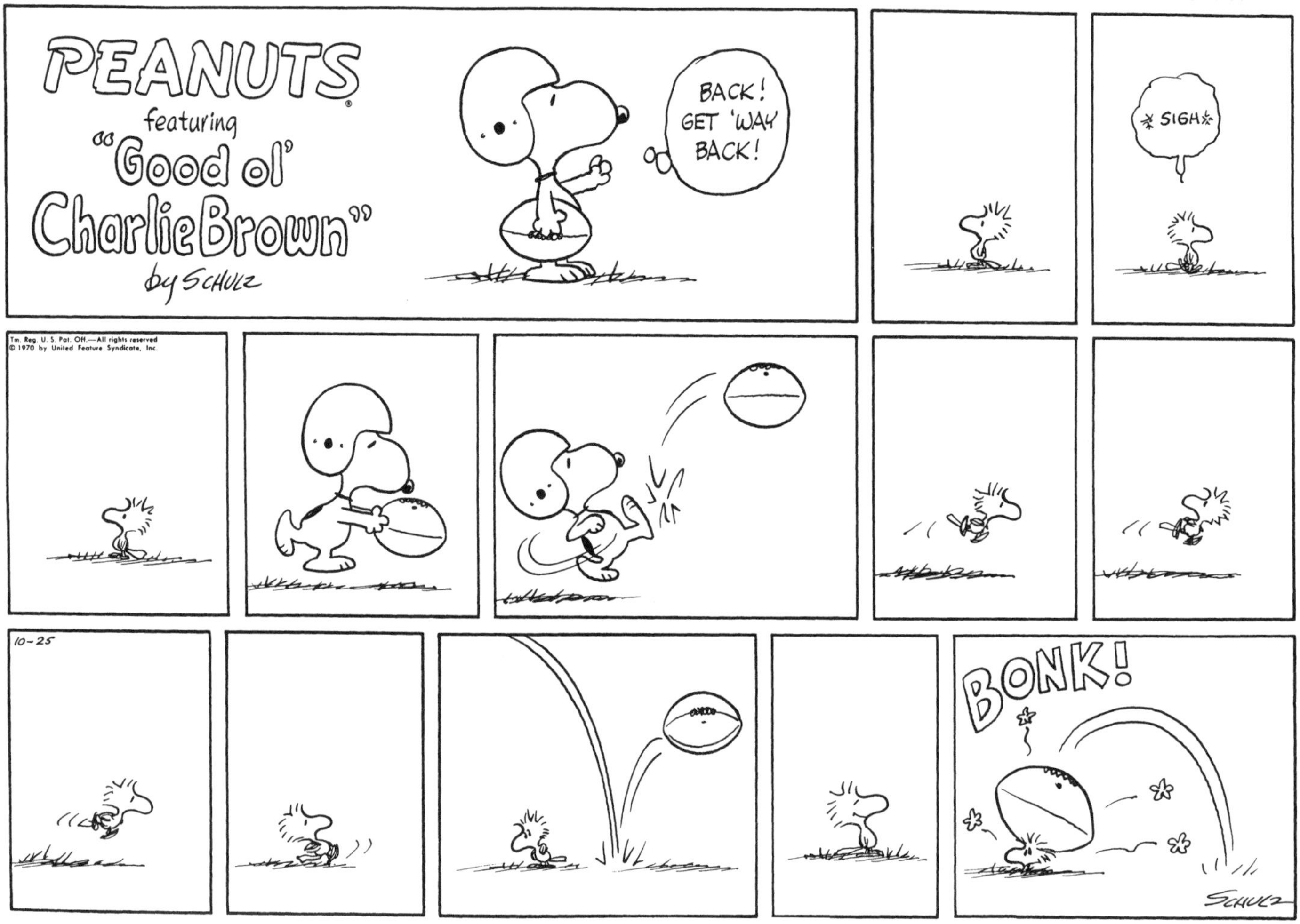

PEANUTS
featuring
"Good ol'
Charlie Brown"
by SCHULZ

10-24

OOF!

BOOT!

PEANUTS
featuring
"Good ol' CharlieBrown"
by SCHULZ

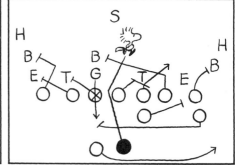

11-21

boot!

boot!
boot!
boot!

boomp!

boot!
boot!
boot!
boot!
boot!

boot! *boot!*
boot!
boot!

boot! boot!
boot! boot!
boot!
boot!

BANG!

THAT WAS AN EXCITING
FIRST QUARTER..

PEANUTS

boot

boot boot boot boot boot boot boot boot boot boot

I'M GLAD I CAN'T HEAR WHAT HOWARD COSELL IS SAYING ABOUT THIS...

9-1

AAUGH!

81

PEANUTS
9-2
KLUNK!
Tm. Reg. U.S. Pat. Off.—All rights reserved
© 1972 by United Feature Syndicate, Inc.
THAT'S WHAT IS CALLED "COMING IN OFF THE BENCH"
SCHULZ

PEANUTS
Tm. Reg. U.S. Pat. Off.—All rights reserved
© 1972 by United Feature Syndicate, Inc.
STOMP!
9-5
RAH?
SCHULZ

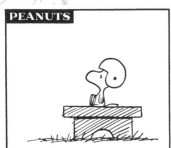

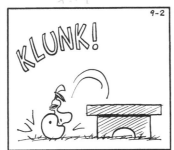

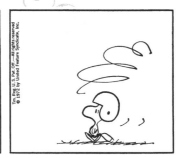

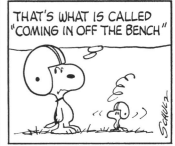

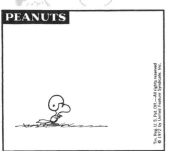

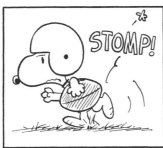

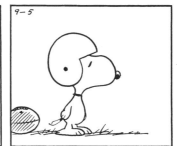

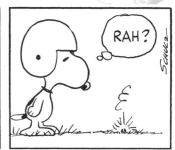

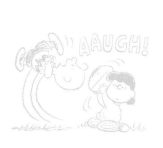

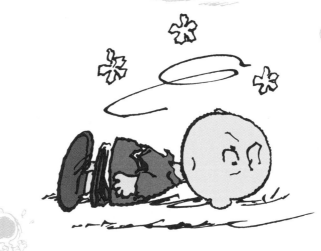

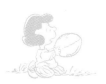

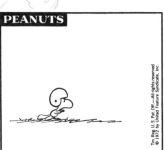

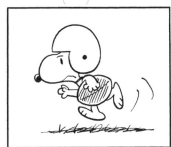

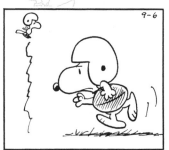

PEANUTS
Tm. Reg. U.S. Pat. Off.—All rights reserved © 1972 by United Feature Syndicate, Inc.
9-6
SCHULZ

PEANUTS
9-7
Tm. Reg. U.S. Pat. Off.—All rights reserved © 1972 by United Feature Syndicate, Inc.
BONK!
WOODSTOCK HAS DIFFICULTY RECOVERING FUMBLES...
SCHULZ

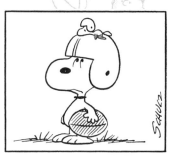

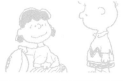

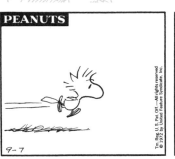

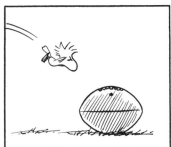

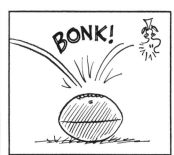

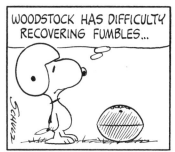

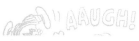

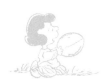

PEANUTS
9-8
THAT STUPID WOODSTOCK... HE LOST HIS BOOK WITH ALL OUR SECRET PLAYS!
Tm. Reg. U.S. Pat. Off.—All rights reserved © 1972 by United Feature Syndicate, Inc.
TWENTY THOUSAND LAPS AROUND THE FIELD!
SCHULZ

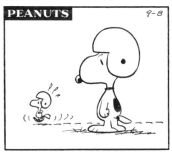

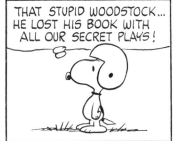

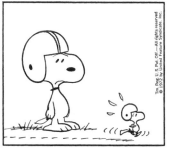

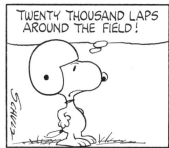

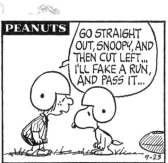

PEANUTS
GO STRAIGHT OUT, SNOOPY, AND THEN CUT LEFT... I'LL FAKE A RUN, AND PASS IT...
9-23
DO YOU THINK THAT'S A GOOD PLAY?
SMAK!
Tm. Reg. U.S. Pat. Off.—All rights reserved © 1972 by United Feature Syndicate, Inc.
HE THINKS IT'S A GOOD PLAY!
SCHULZ

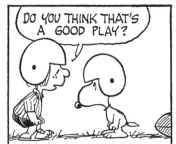

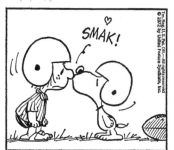

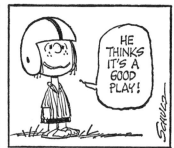

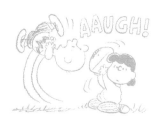

PEANUTS
ALL RIGHT, TEAM, LET'S PAY ATTENTION
WE'RE HERE TODAY TO TRY TO EVALUATE OUR PERFORMANCES ON THE FIELD...EACH OF US CAN STAND A LITTLE IMPROVEMENT...
EACH OF US CAN LEARN SOMETHING IF WE'RE WILLING TO ACCEPT CRITICISM...
9-30
SCHULZ
Tm. Reg. U.S. Pat. Off.—All rights reserved © 1972 by United Feature Syndicate, Inc.
YOUR NOSE IS TOO BIG!

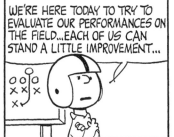

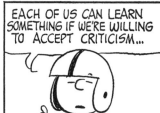

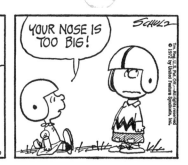

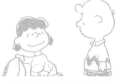

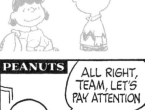

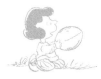

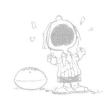

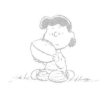

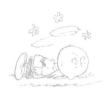

AAUGH!

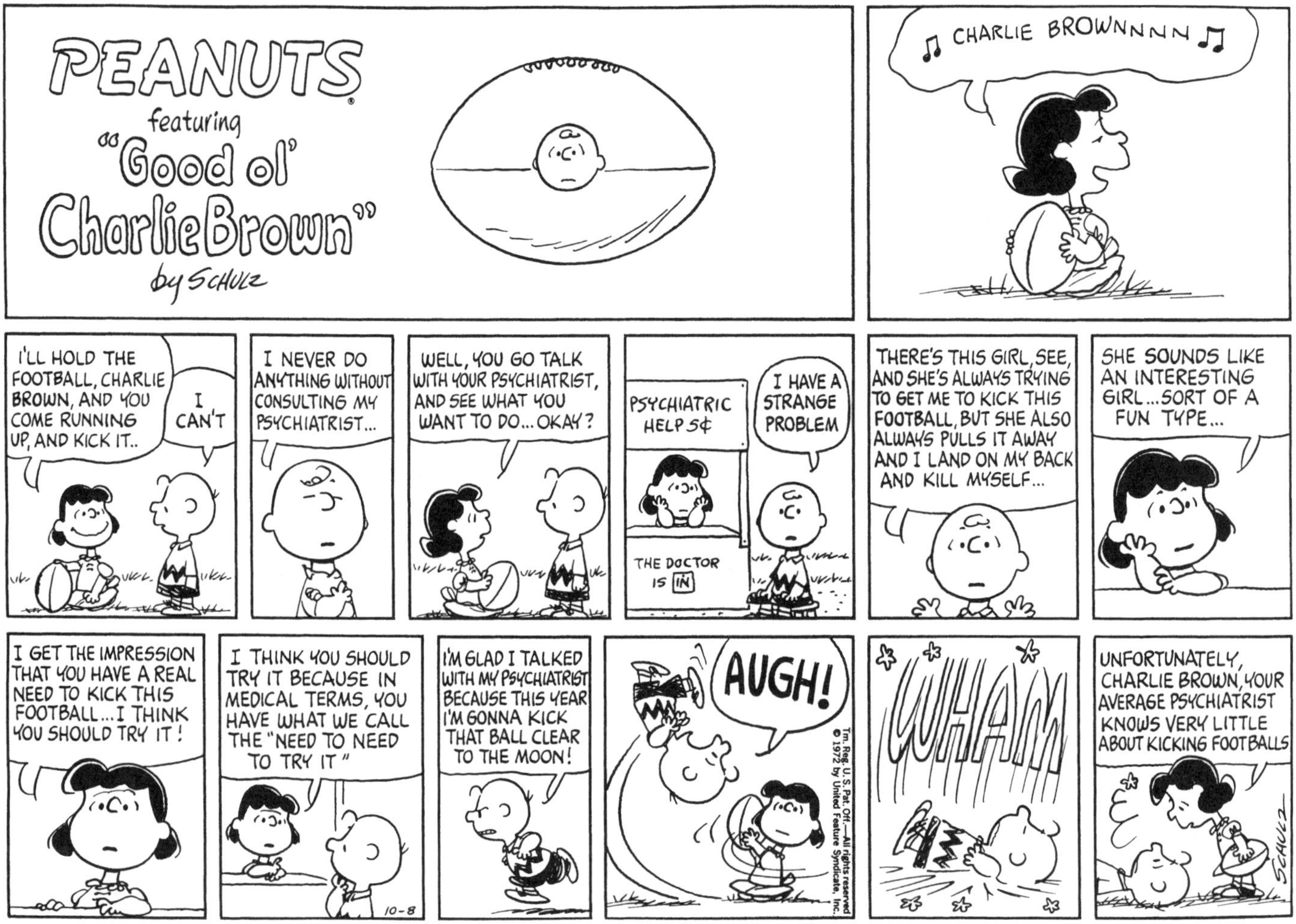
PEANUTS®
featuring "Good ol' Charlie Brown"
by SCHULZ
♫ CHARLIE BROWNNNNN ♫
I'LL HOLD THE FOOTBALL, CHARLIE BROWN, AND YOU COME RUNNING UP, AND KICK IT..
I CAN'T
I NEVER DO ANYTHING WITHOUT CONSULTING MY PSYCHIATRIST...
WELL, YOU GO TALK WITH YOUR PSYCHIATRIST, AND SEE WHAT YOU WANT TO DO...OKAY?
PSYCHIATRIC HELP 5¢
THE DOCTOR IS IN
I HAVE A STRANGE PROBLEM
THERE'S THIS GIRL, SEE, AND SHE'S ALWAYS TRYING TO GET ME TO KICK THIS FOOTBALL, BUT SHE ALSO ALWAYS PULLS IT AWAY AND I LAND ON MY BACK AND KILL MYSELF...
SHE SOUNDS LIKE AN INTERESTING GIRL...SORT OF A FUN TYPE...
I GET THE IMPRESSION THAT YOU HAVE A REAL NEED TO KICK THIS FOOTBALL...I THINK YOU SHOULD TRY IT!
I THINK YOU SHOULD TRY IT BECAUSE IN MEDICAL TERMS, YOU HAVE WHAT WE CALL THE "NEED TO NEED TO TRY IT"
10-8
I'M GLAD I TALKED WITH MY PSYCHIATRIST BECAUSE THIS YEAR I'M GONNA KICK THAT BALL CLEAR TO THE MOON!
AUGH!
Tm. Reg. U.S. Pat. Off.—All rights reserved © 1972 by United Feature Syndicate, Inc.
WHAM
UNFORTUNATELY, CHARLIE BROWN, YOUR AVERAGE PSYCHIATRIST KNOWS VERY LITTLE ABOUT KICKING FOOTBALLS
SCHULZ

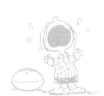

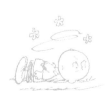

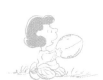

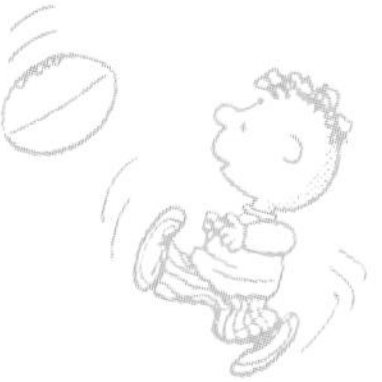
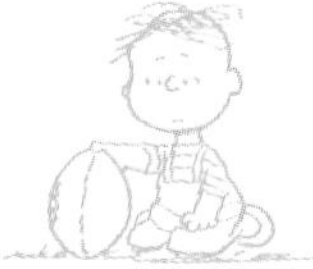
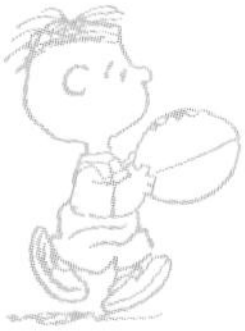
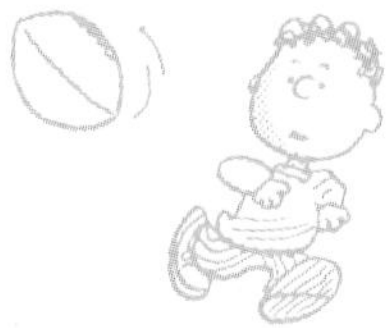

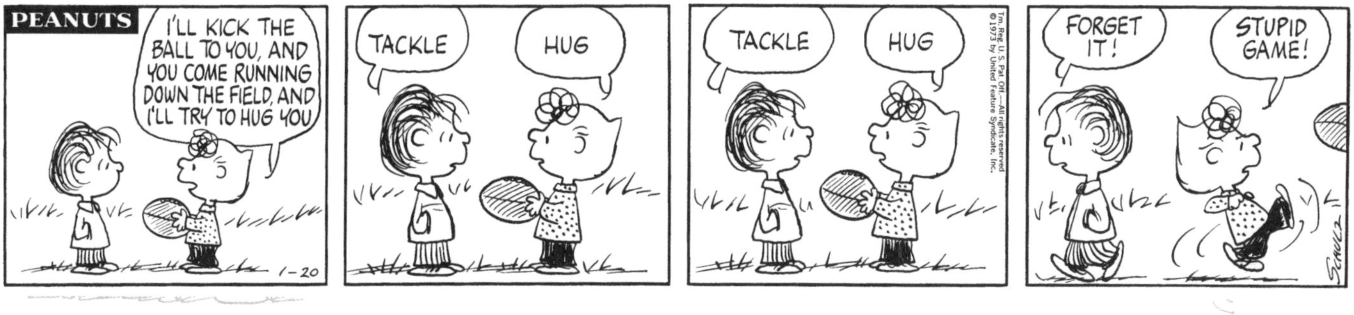
PEANUTS
I'LL KICK THE BALL TO YOU, AND YOU COME RUNNING DOWN THE FIELD, AND I'LL TRY TO HUG YOU
1-20
TACKLE
HUG
TACKLE
HUG
Tm. Reg. U.S. Pat. Off.—All rights reserved
© 1973 by United Feature Syndicate, Inc.
FORGET IT!
STUPID GAME!
SCHULZ

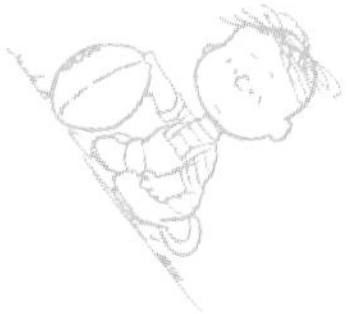
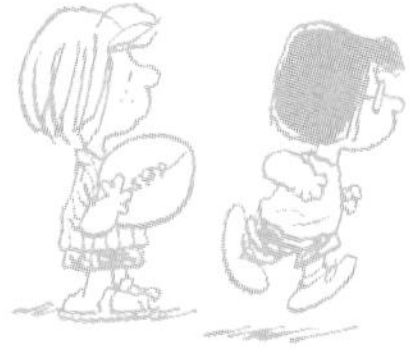
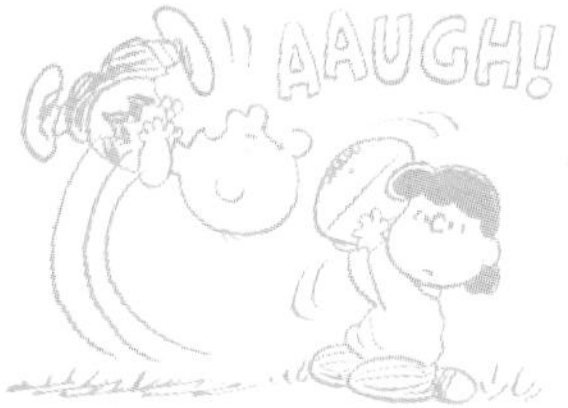
AAUGH!
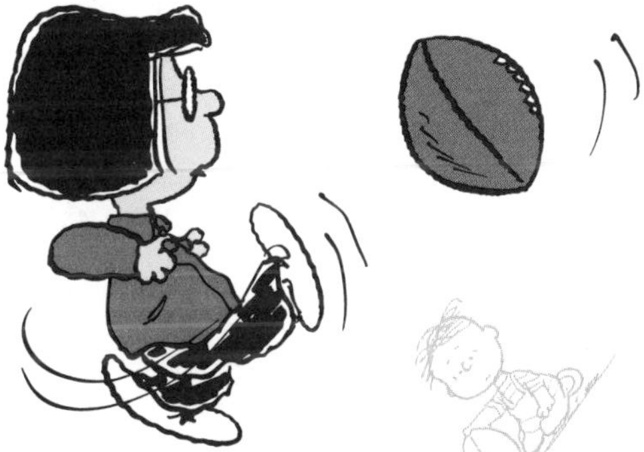
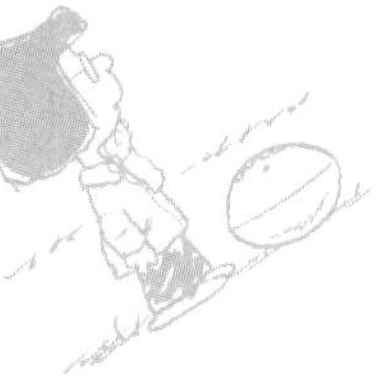
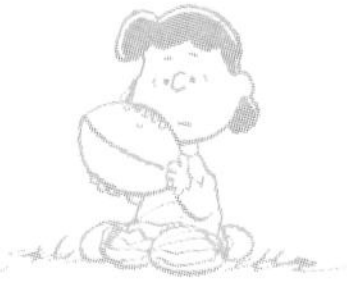
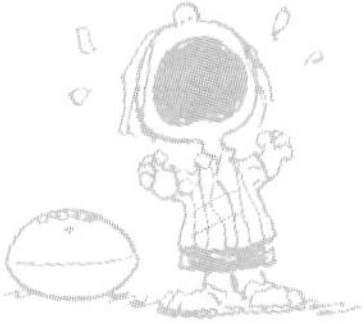
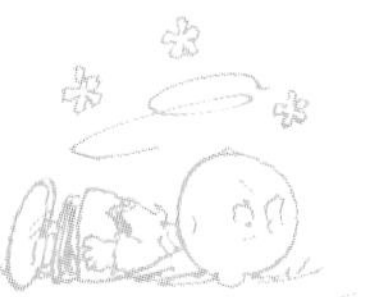
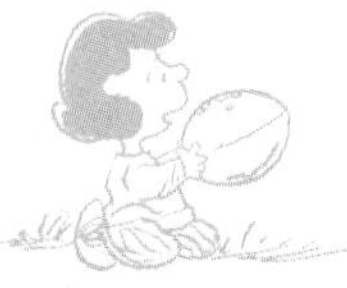
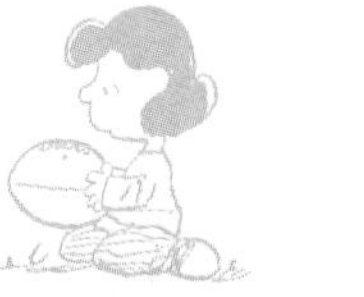

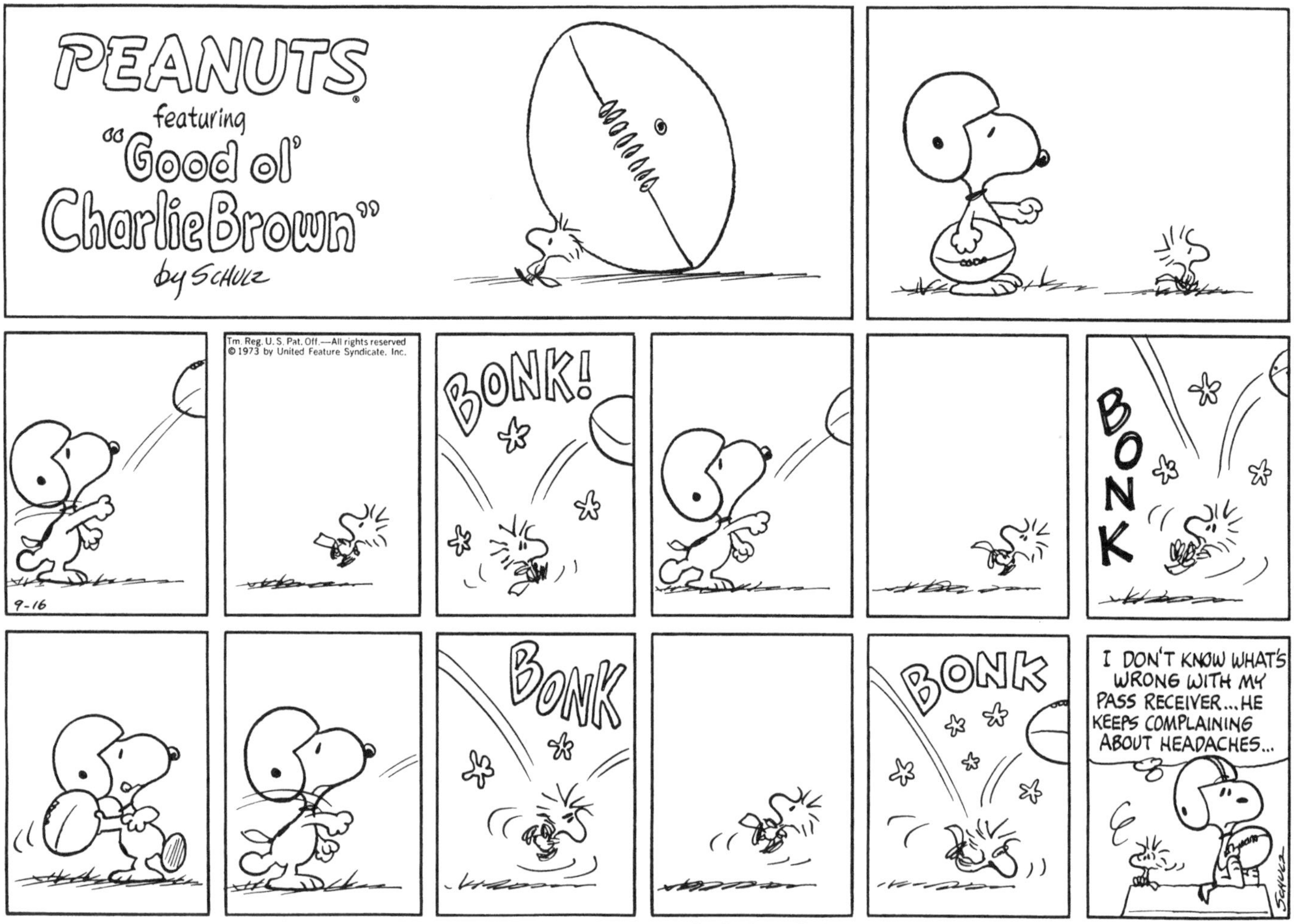
PEANUTS®
featuring
"Good ol' Charlie Brown"
by SCHULZ
9-16
Tm. Reg. U. S. Pat. Off.—All rights reserved
© 1973 by United Feature Syndicate, Inc.
BONK!
BONK
BONK
BONK
I DON'T KNOW WHAT'S WRONG WITH MY PASS RECEIVER... HE KEEPS COMPLAINING ABOUT HEADACHES...
SCHULZ

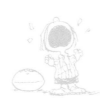

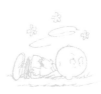

PEANUTS
featuring
"Good ol' Charlie Brown"
by SCHULZ
POW!
EVERYTHING ALL RIGHT BACK THERE?
LOOK OUT, CHUCK, HERE I COME!
10-14
POW!
GET READY, CHUCK! HERE I COME AGAIN!
SMASH!
THIS IS GREAT PRACTICE, HUH, CHUCK? GET READY 'CAUSE HERE I COME AGAIN!
Tm. Reg. U.S. Pat. Off.—All rights reserved
© 1973 by United Feature Syndicate, Inc.
CRASH!!
FUMBLE!
I FUMBLED THE BALL, CHUCK..WHY DIDN'T YOU JUMP ON IT?
I THOUGHT IT WAS MY HEAD!
SCHULZ

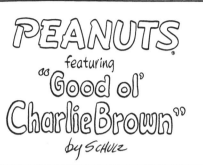

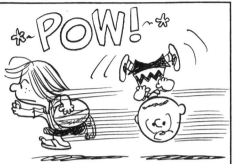

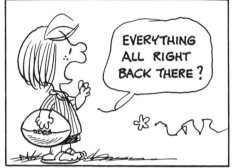

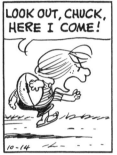

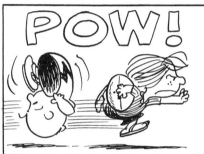

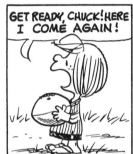

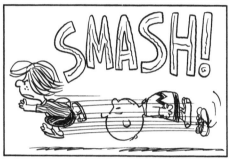

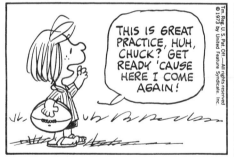

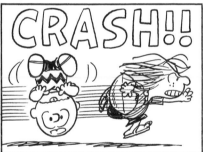

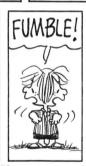

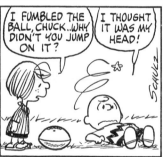

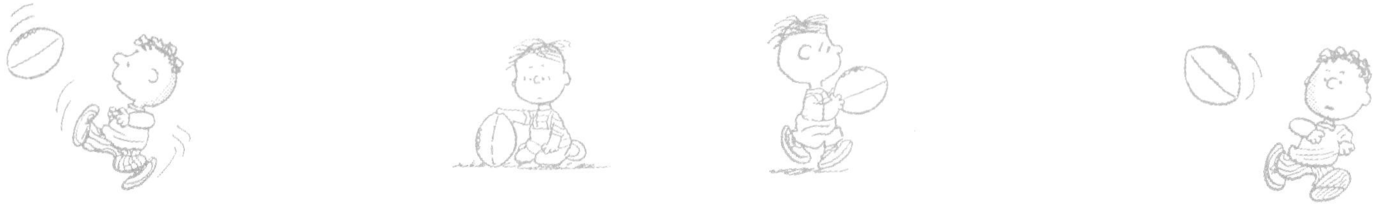

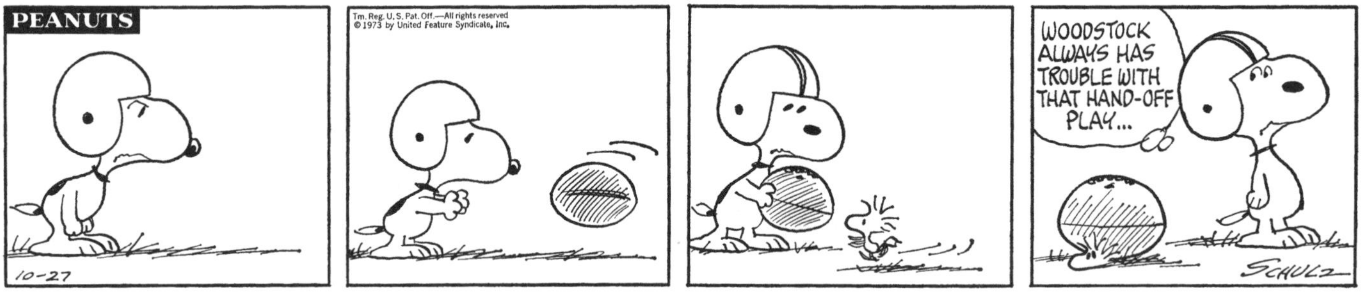
PEANUTS
Tm. Reg. U.S. Pat. Off.—All rights reserved
© 1973 by United Feature Syndicate, Inc.
10-27
WOODSTOCK ALWAYS HAS TROUBLE WITH THAT HAND-OFF PLAY...
SCHULZ

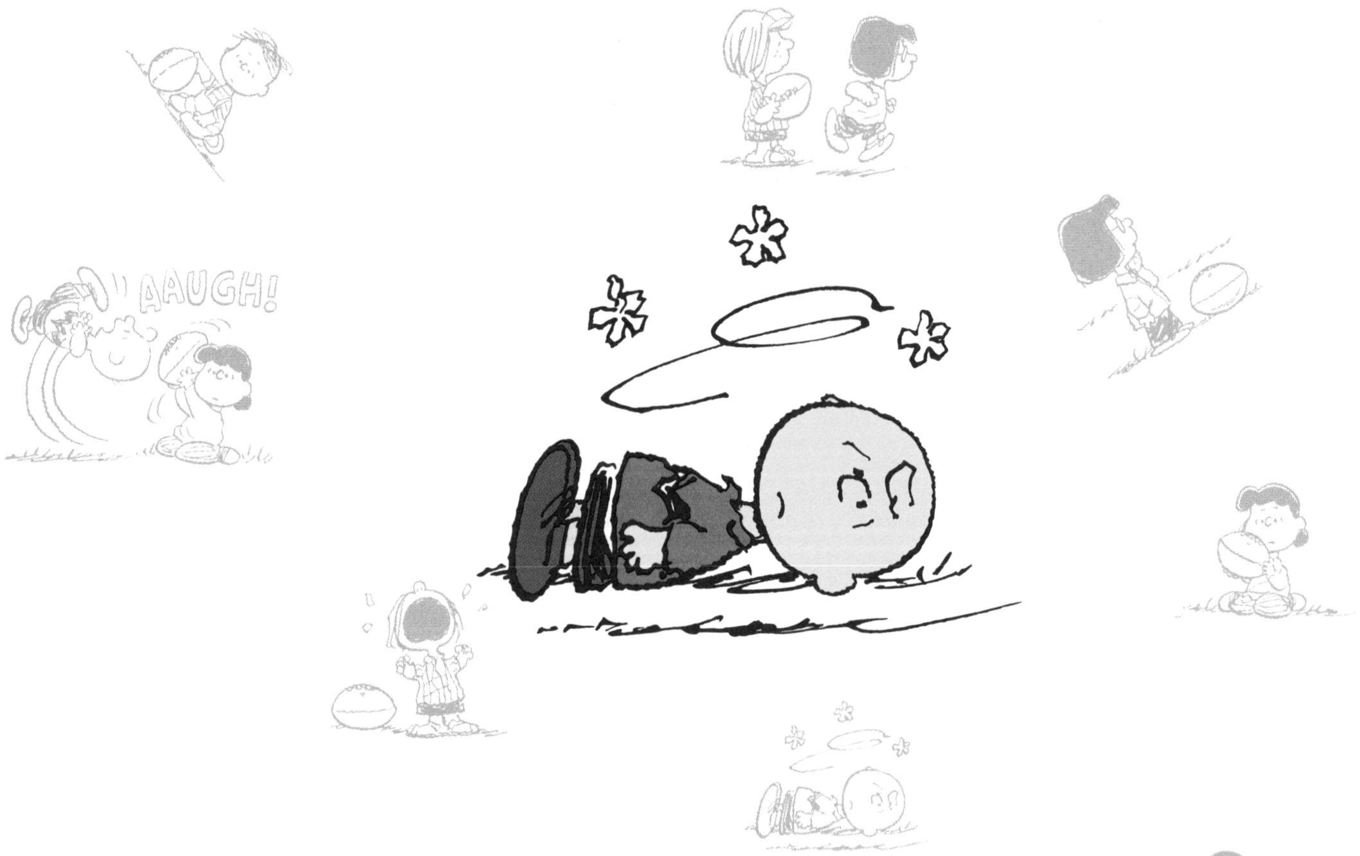
AAUGH!

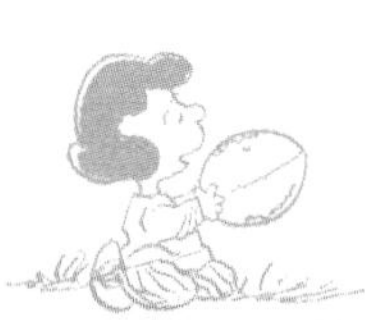

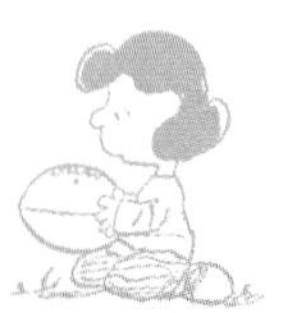

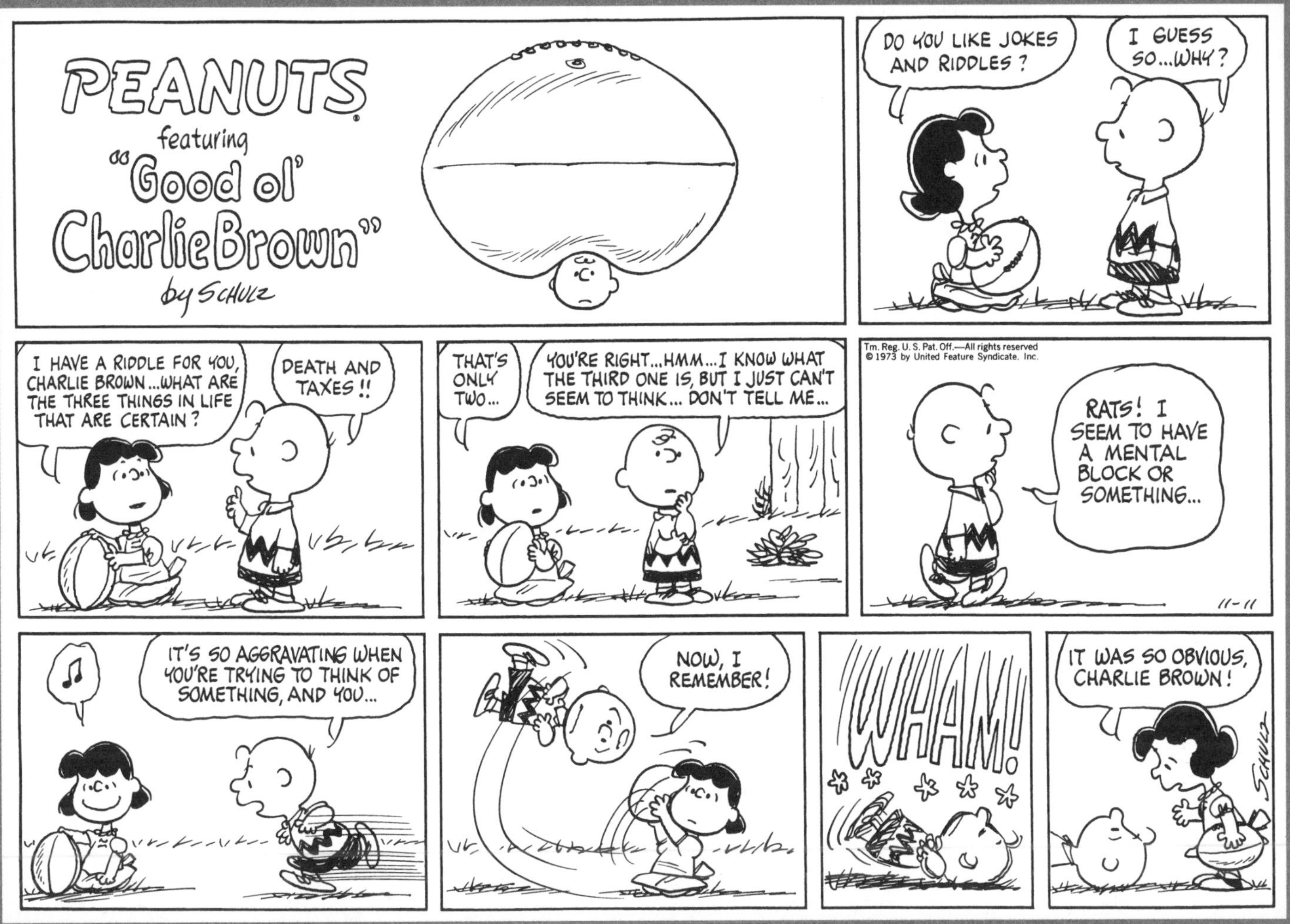
PEANUTS
featuring
"Good ol' CharlieBrown"
by SCHULZ
DO YOU LIKE JOKES AND RIDDLES ?
I GUESS SO...WHY ?
I HAVE A RIDDLE FOR YOU, CHARLIE BROWN...WHAT ARE THE THREE THINGS IN LIFE THAT ARE CERTAIN ?
DEATH AND TAXES !!
THAT'S ONLY TWO...
YOU'RE RIGHT...HMM...I KNOW WHAT THE THIRD ONE IS, BUT I JUST CAN'T SEEM TO THINK... DON'T TELL ME...
Tm. Reg. U. S. Pat. Off.—All rights reserved
© 1973 by United Feature Syndicate, Inc.
RATS! I SEEM TO HAVE A MENTAL BLOCK OR SOMETHING...
11-11
♫
IT'S SO AGGRAVATING WHEN YOU'RE TRYING TO THINK OF SOMETHING, AND YOU...
NOW, I REMEMBER!
WHAM!
IT WAS SO OBVIOUS, CHARLIE BROWN!
SCHULZ

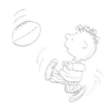

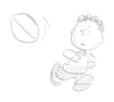

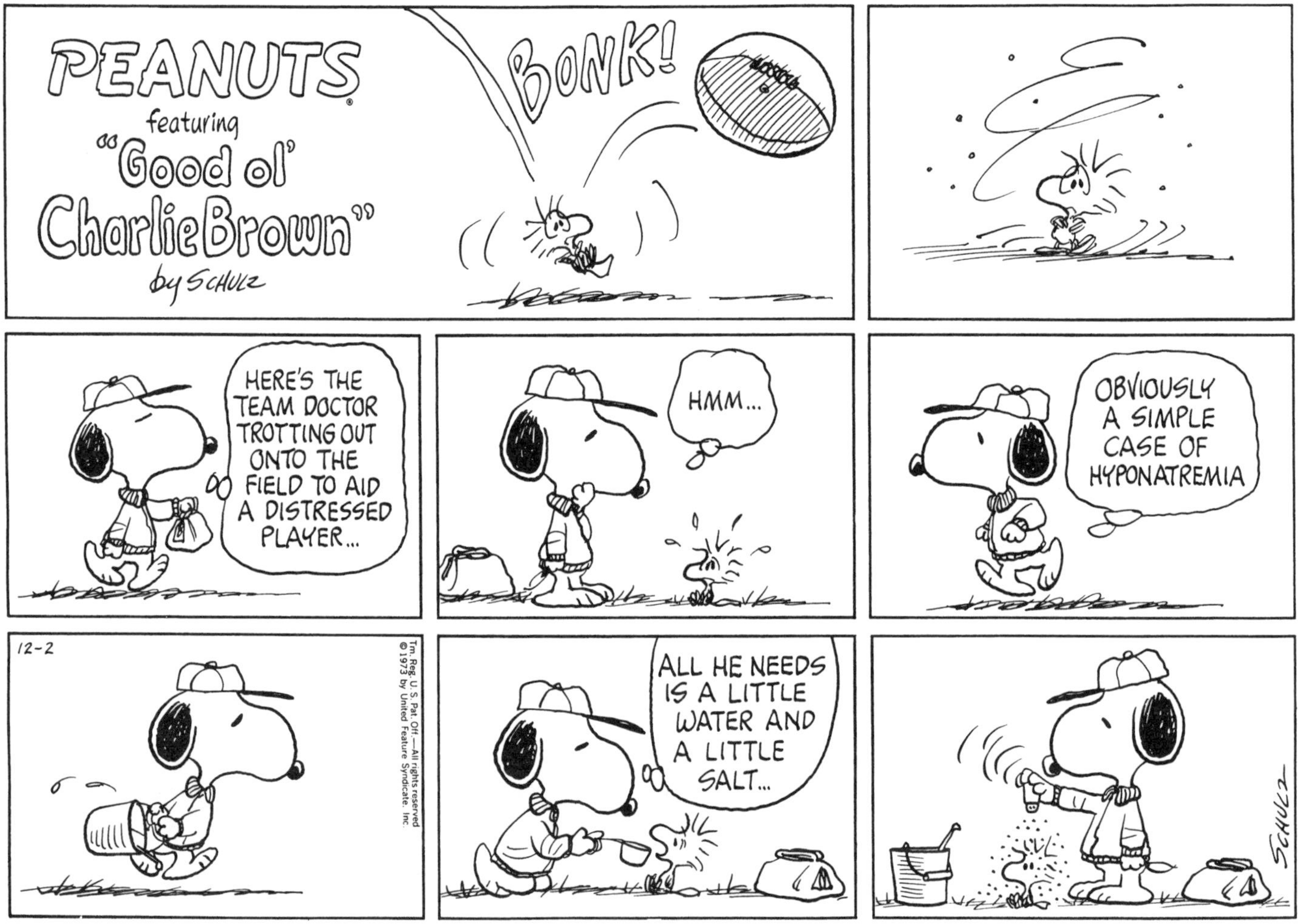
PEANUTS featuring "Good ol' Charlie Brown" by SCHULZ
BONK!
HERE'S THE TEAM DOCTOR TROTTING OUT ONTO THE FIELD TO AID A DISTRESSED PLAYER...
HMM...
OBVIOUSLY A SIMPLE CASE OF HYPONATREMIA
12-2
Tm. Reg. U.S. Pat. Off.—All rights reserved © 1973 by United Feature Syndicate, Inc.
ALL HE NEEDS IS A LITTLE WATER AND A LITTLE SALT...
SCHULZ

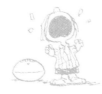

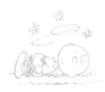

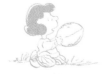

PEANUTS
9-28
Tm Reg U S Pat Off – All rights reserved
©1974 by United Feature Syndicate Inc.
BOOT!!
SCHULZ

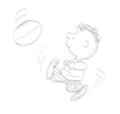

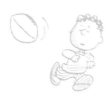

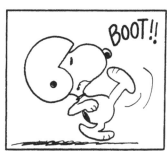

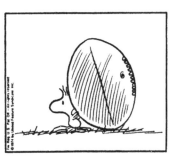

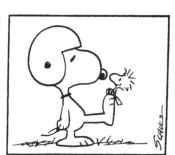

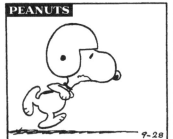

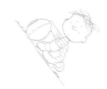

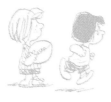

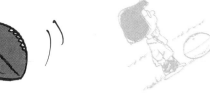

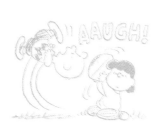

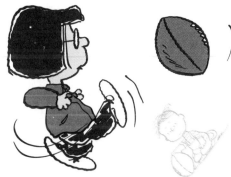

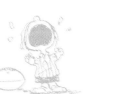

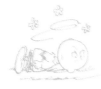

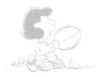

PEANUTS featuring "Good ol' Charlie Brown" by Schulz

GO, CHUCK, GO!!

9-29

BONK

COORDINATION AND COMMUNICATION... THOSE ARE YOUR PROBLEMS, CHUCK!

YOUR MIND TELLS YOUR BODY TO DO SOMETHING, BUT YOUR BODY DOESN'T OBEY...YOUR MIND AND YOUR BODY HAVE TO WORK TOGETHER...

MY MIND AND MY BODY HATE EACH OTHER!

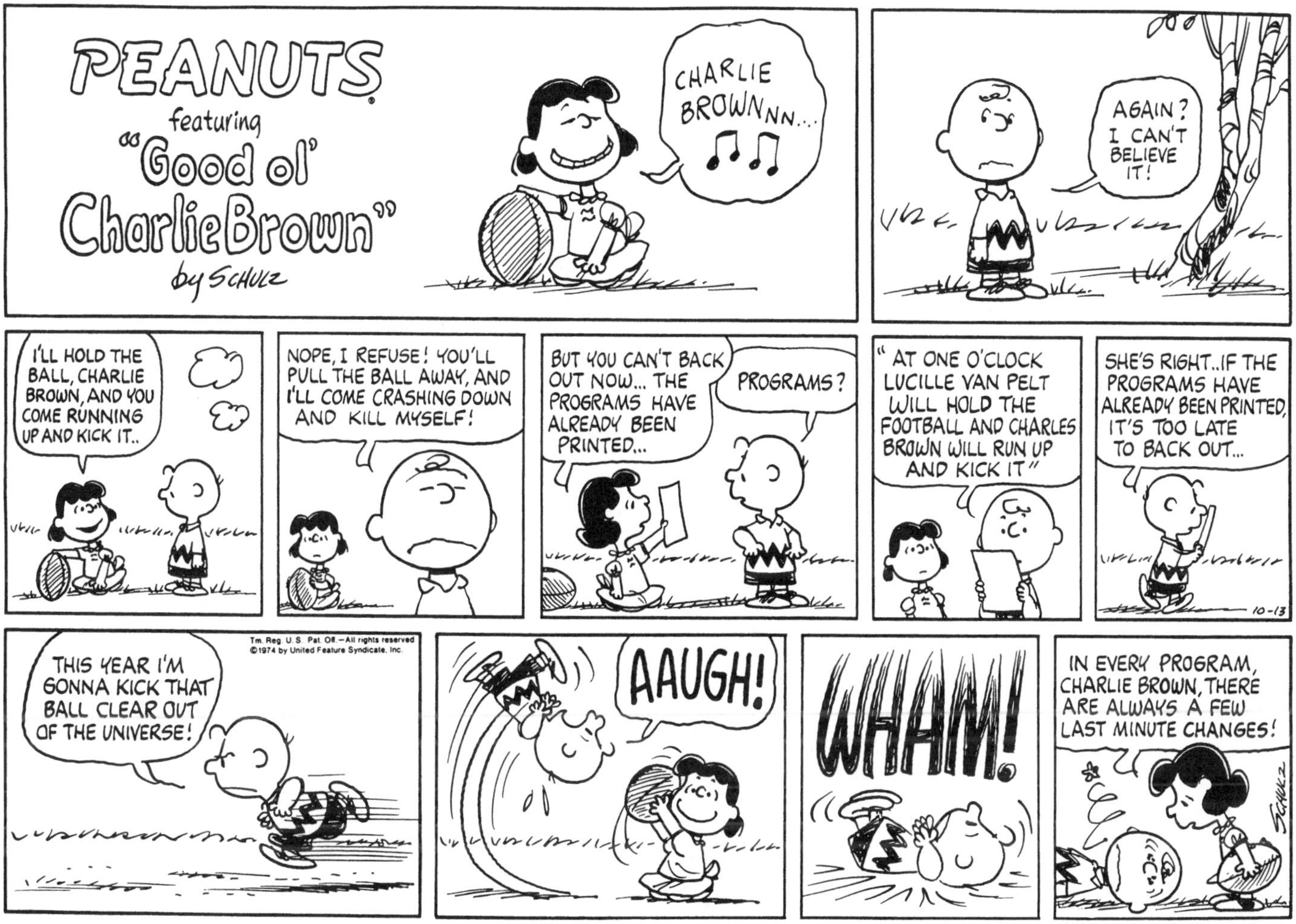

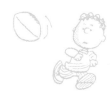

PEANUTS
featuring "Good ol' CharlieBrown"
by SCHULZ
CHARLIE BROWNNN...
AGAIN? I CAN'T BELIEVE IT!
I'LL HOLD THE BALL, CHARLIE BROWN, AND YOU COME RUNNING UP AND KICK IT..
NOPE, I REFUSE! YOU'LL PULL THE BALL AWAY, AND I'LL COME CRASHING DOWN AND KILL MYSELF!
BUT YOU CAN'T BACK OUT NOW... THE PROGRAMS HAVE ALREADY BEEN PRINTED...
PROGRAMS?
"AT ONE O'CLOCK LUCILLE VAN PELT WILL HOLD THE FOOTBALL AND CHARLES BROWN WILL RUN UP AND KICK IT"
SHE'S RIGHT..IF THE PROGRAMS HAVE ALREADY BEEN PRINTED, IT'S TOO LATE TO BACK OUT...
10-13
Tm. Reg. U.S. Pat. Off.—All rights reserved ©1974 by United Feature Syndicate, Inc.
THIS YEAR I'M GONNA KICK THAT BALL CLEAR OUT OF THE UNIVERSE!
AAUGH!
WHAM!
IN EVERY PROGRAM, CHARLIE BROWN, THERE ARE ALWAYS A FEW LAST MINUTE CHANGES!
SCHULZ

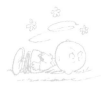

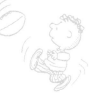

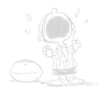

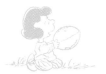

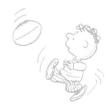

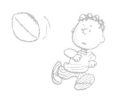

PEANUTS
9-6
Tm Reg U S Pat Off—All rights reserved
©1975 by United Feature Syndicate, Inc
BONK!
I KNEW IT WOULD HAPPEN...HIS KNEES ARE STARTING TO GO!
SCHULZ

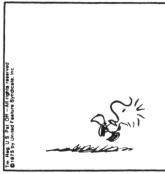

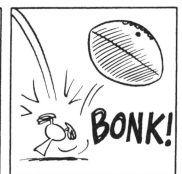

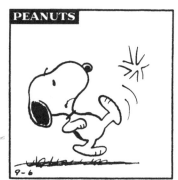

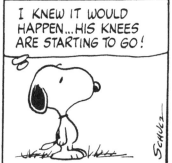

AAUGH!

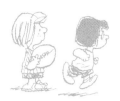

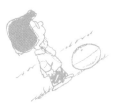

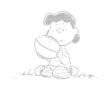

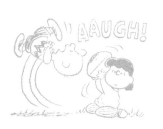

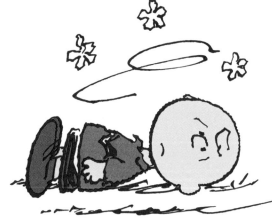

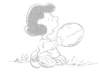

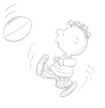

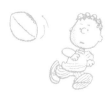

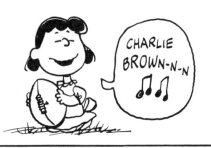

PEANUTS
featuring "Good ol' Charlie Brown"
by SCHULZ
CHARLIE BROWN-N-N
I CAN'T BELIEVE IT..
I'LL HOLD THE BALL, AND YOU RUN UP AND KICK IT
YOU NEVER HOLD IT! YOU ALWAYS PULL IT AWAY, AND I LAND FLAT ON MY BACK AND KILL MYSELF!
THAT'S MISTRUST! THAT'S MISTRUST OF ME AS AN ATHLETE, A PERSON AND A WOMAN! DO YOU MISTRUST ALL WOMEN? DO YOU MISTRUST EVEN YOUR MOTHER?
I DON'T MISTRUST MY MOTHER...GOOD GRIEF, NO!! IF THERE'S ANYONE IN THIS WORLD I DO TRUST, IT'S MY MOTHER!
10-19
Tm. Reg. U.S. Pat. Off.—All rights reserved
©1975 by United Feature Syndicate, Inc.
AUGH!
WAM!
I'M NOT YOUR MOTHER, CHARLIE BROWN!
SCHULZ

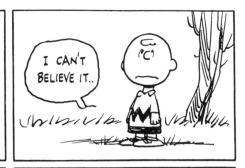

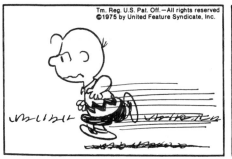

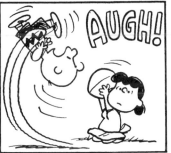

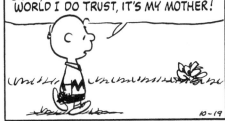

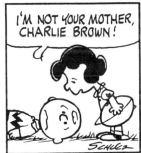

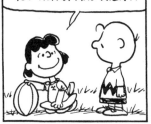

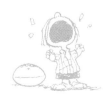

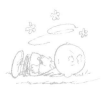

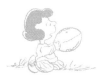

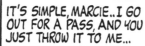

PEANUTS

I DON'T KNOW ANYTHING ABOUT FOOTBALL, SIR.

IT'S SIMPLE, MARCIE..I GO OUT FOR A PASS, AND YOU JUST THROW IT TO ME...

BONK!

LET ME GET A LITTLE FURTHER DOWN THE FIELD, MARCIE!

12-8

PEANUTS

I'VE BEEN READING UP ON FOOTBALL, SIR...

WHEN YOU FIRST ASKED ME TO PLAY, I DIDN'T KNOW ANYTHING ABOUT IT

THAT'S ALL CHANGED

NOW, I'M READY TO GET OUT THERE, AND KICK AROUND THE OL' HOGSKIN!

12-9

AAUGH!

PEANUTS

WHAT IF I KICK IT OVER YOUR HEAD, SIR?

WHAT IF SOME MAJOR LEAGUE SCOUT SPOTS ME, AND HIRES ME FOR HIS TEAM, AND I HAVE TO GO TO THE SUPER BOWL? WHAT WOULD I DO ABOUT SCHOOL?

JUST SHUT UP, MARCIE, AND KICK THE BALL!

DON'T BE IMPATIENT WITH ME, SIR...

12-10

PEANUTS

OKAY, BALL, BEFORE I KICK YOU, I WANT TO APOLOGIZE...

I WANT YOU TO KNOW THERE'S NOTHING PERSONAL IN THIS, THAT I INTEND YOU NO HARM, THAT I HOPE THIS KICK DOES YOU NO INJURY, AND THAT...

12-11

KICK THE BALL, MARCIE!!

PATIENCE, SIR! THESE ARE THINGS WHICH MUST BE SAID!

PEANUTS

OKAY, SIR, HERE IT COMES!

STAND BACK! HEADS UP! ARE YOU READY? THIS IS IT! HERE WE GO! FORE! DOWN THE FIELD! IN THE AIR! HERE IT COMES!

12-12

MARCIE, WILL YOU HURRY UP, AND KICK THAT FOOTBALL?!!

WITHOUT PRELIMINARIES?

SCHULZ

PEANUTS

GIMME THAT BALL, MARCIE!

12-13

I COULD STAND OUT THERE FOR THE REST OF MY LIFE WAITING FOR YOU TO KICK IT!

WUMP! ?!

YOU WERE TRYING A TRICK PLAY ON ME, WEREN'T YOU, SIR?

SCHULZ

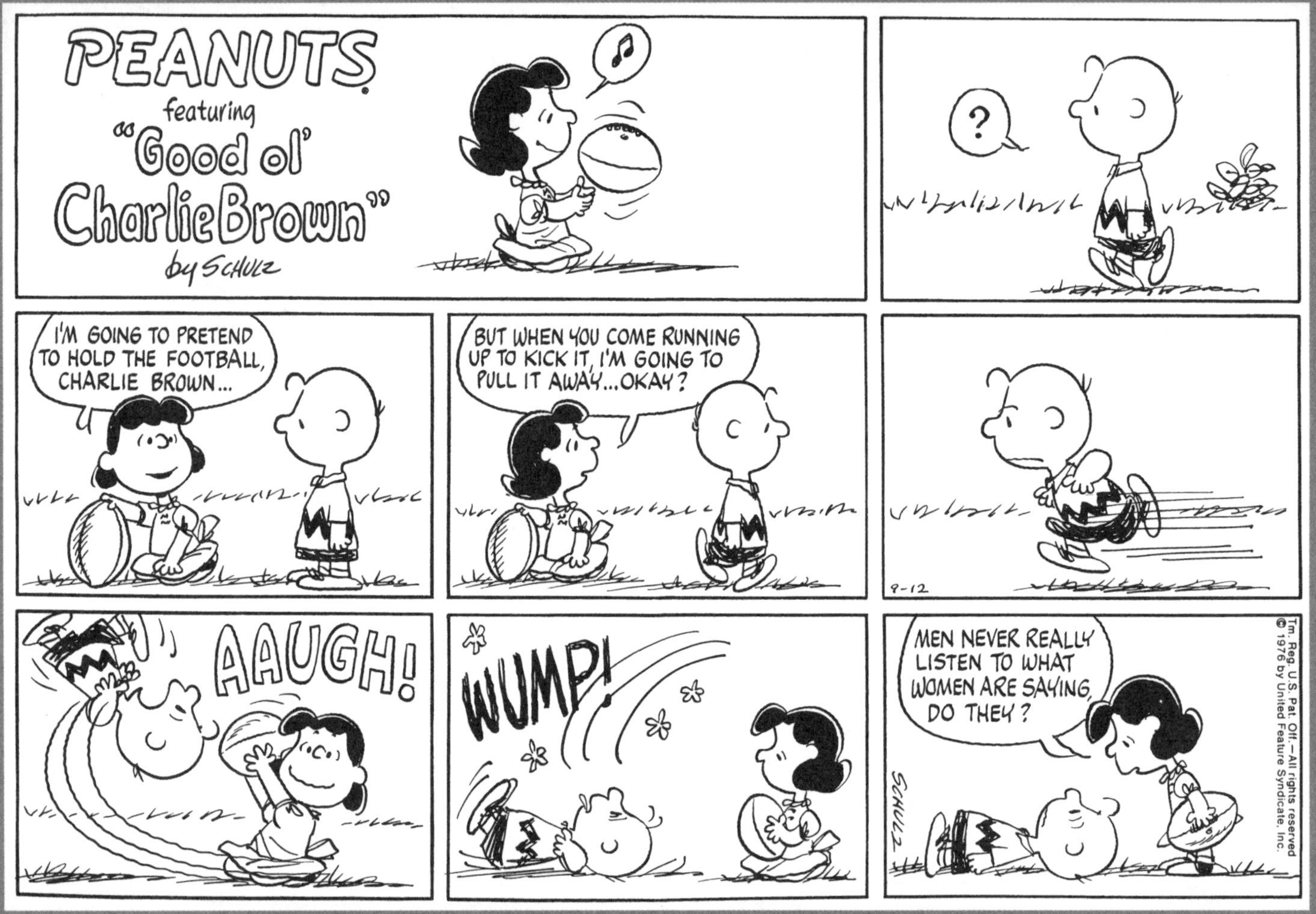
PEANUTS
featuring
"Good ol' CharlieBrown"
by SCHULZ
?
I'M GOING TO PRETEND TO HOLD THE FOOTBALL, CHARLIE BROWN...
BUT WHEN YOU COME RUNNING UP TO KICK IT, I'M GOING TO PULL IT AWAY...OKAY?
9-12
AAUGH!
WUMP!
MEN NEVER REALLY LISTEN TO WHAT WOMEN ARE SAYING, DO THEY?
SCHULZ
Tm. Reg. U.S. Pat. Off.—All rights reserved © 1976 by United Feature Syndicate, Inc.

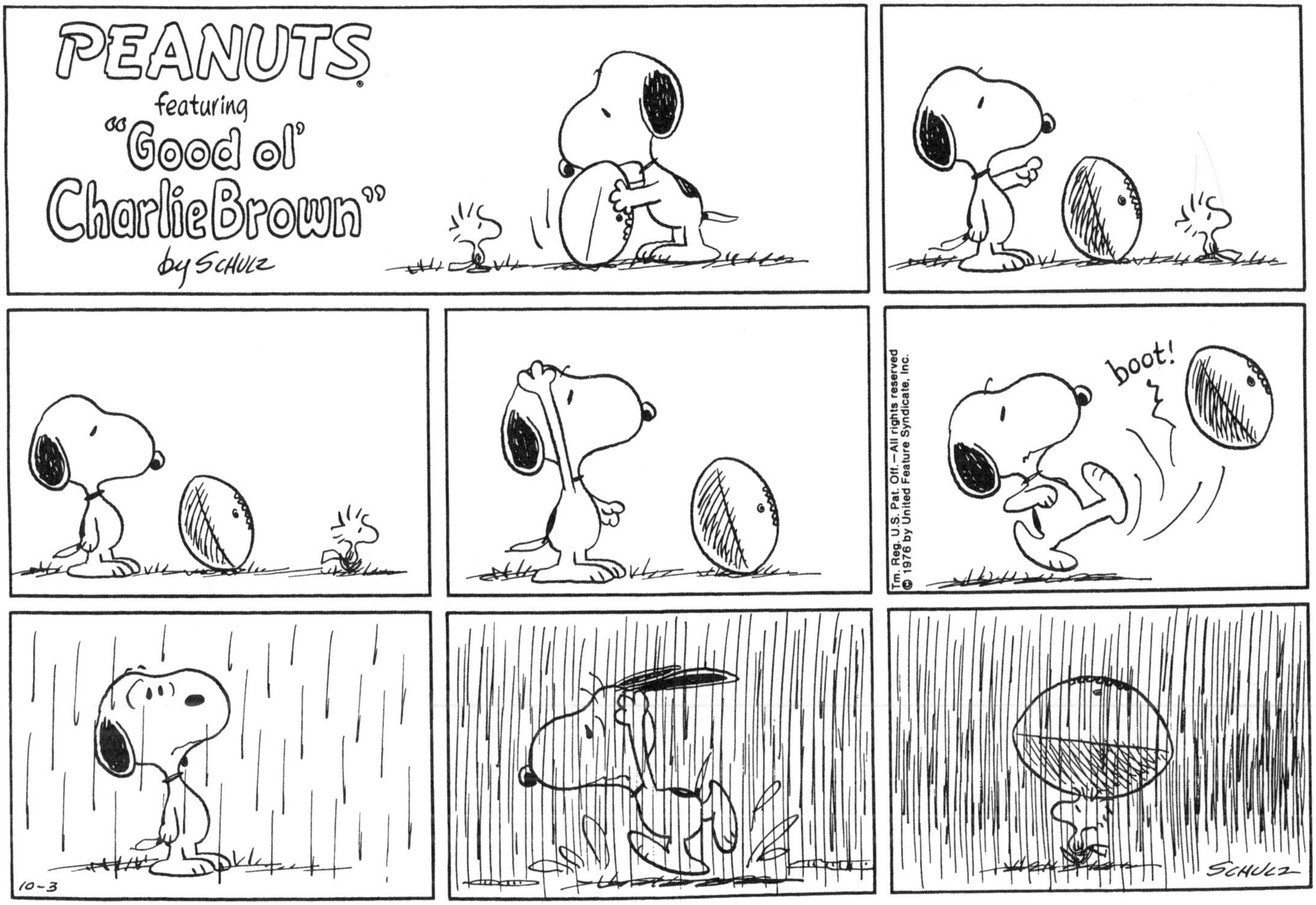
PEANUTS
featuring
"Good ol' CharlieBrown"
by SCHULZ
Tm. Reg. U.S. Pat. Off.—All rights reserved
© 1976 by United Feature Syndicate, Inc.
boot!
10-3
SCHULZ

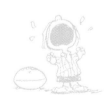

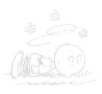

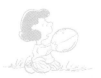

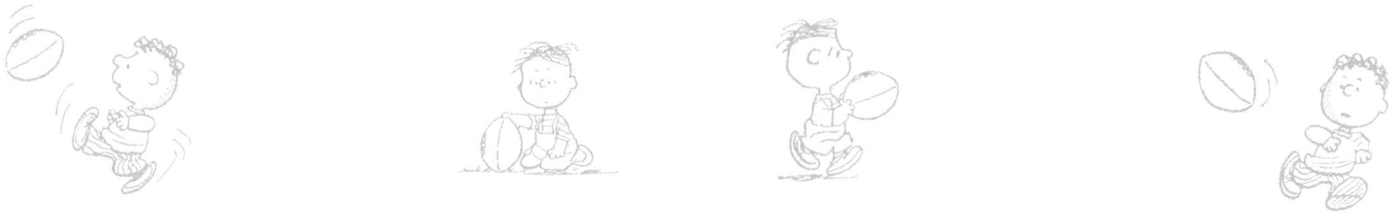

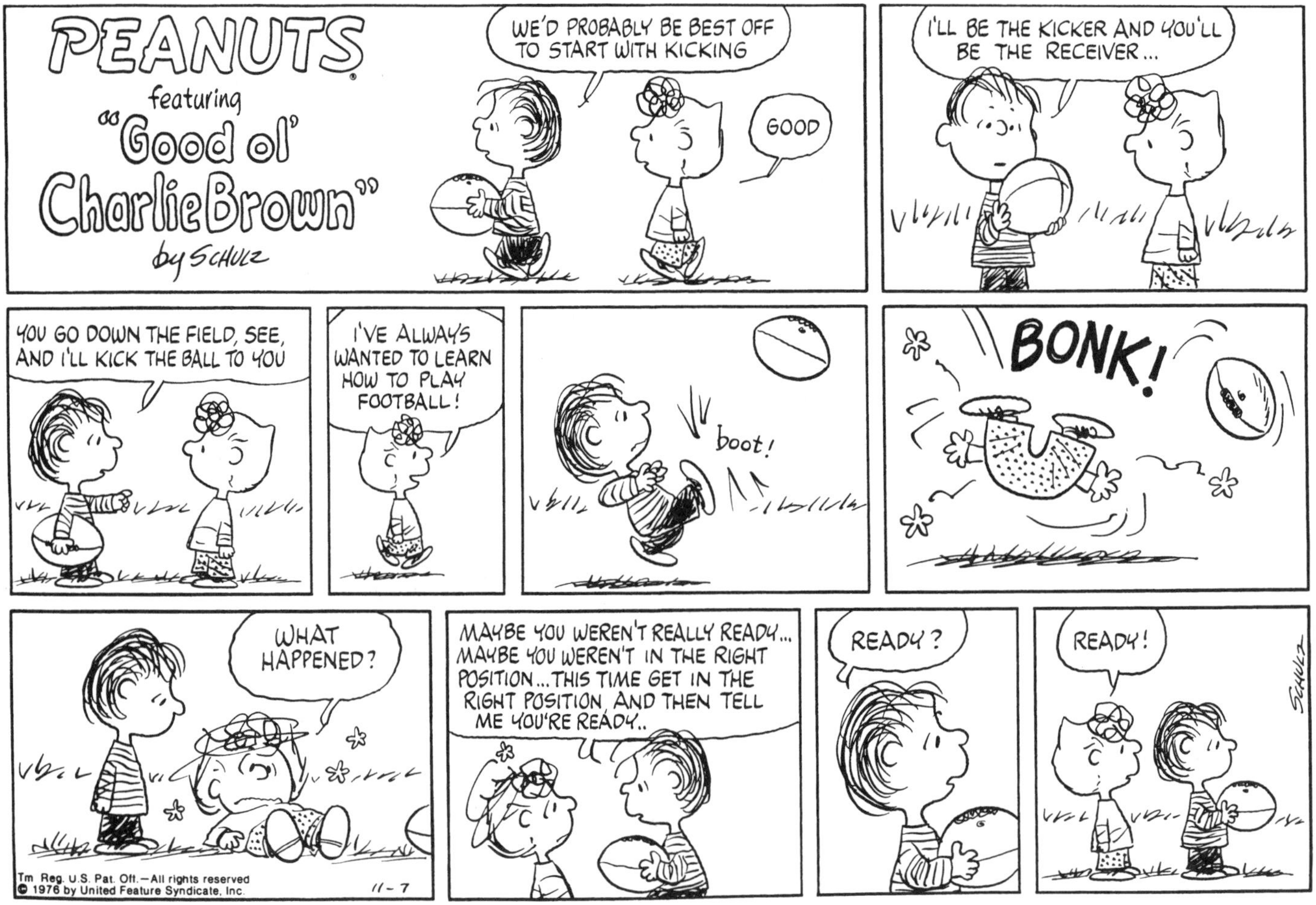
PEANUTS
featuring
"Good ol' CharlieBrown"
by SCHULZ
WE'D PROBABLY BE BEST OFF TO START WITH KICKING
GOOD
I'LL BE THE KICKER AND YOU'LL BE THE RECEIVER...
YOU GO DOWN THE FIELD, SEE, AND I'LL KICK THE BALL TO YOU
I'VE ALWAYS WANTED TO LEARN HOW TO PLAY FOOTBALL!
boot!
BONK!
WHAT HAPPENED?
Tm Reg. U.S. Pat. Off.—All rights reserved
© 1976 by United Feature Syndicate, Inc.
11-7
MAYBE YOU WEREN'T REALLY READY... MAYBE YOU WEREN'T IN THE RIGHT POSITION...THIS TIME GET IN THE RIGHT POSITION, AND THEN TELL ME YOU'RE READY..
READY?
READY!
SCHULZ

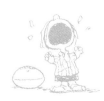

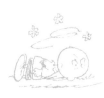

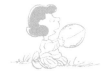

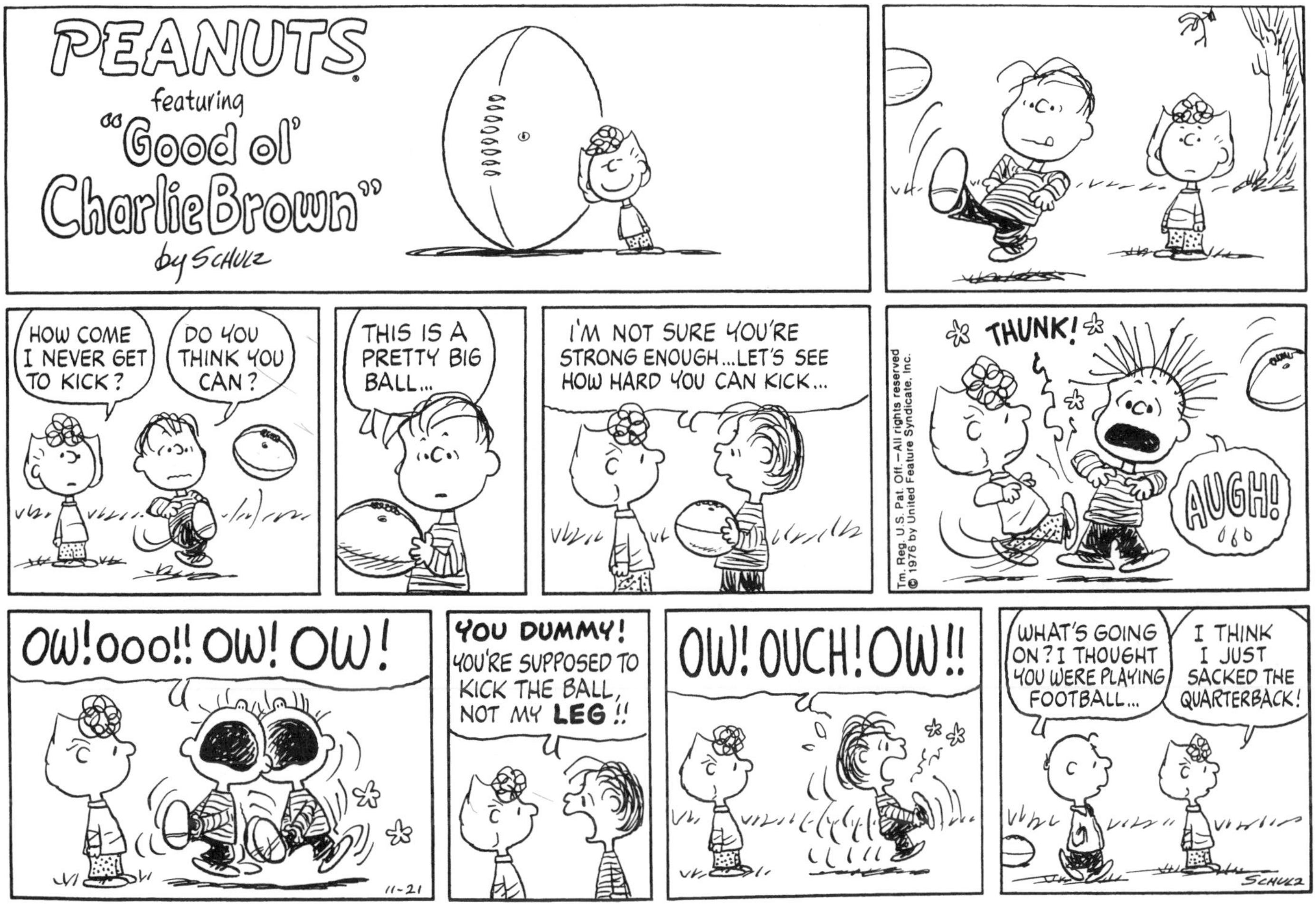
PEANUTS
featuring
"Good ol' Charlie Brown"
by SCHULZ
HOW COME I NEVER GET TO KICK?
DO YOU THINK YOU CAN?
THIS IS A PRETTY BIG BALL...
I'M NOT SURE YOU'RE STRONG ENOUGH...LET'S SEE HOW HARD YOU CAN KICK...
Tm. Reg. U.S. Pat. Off.—All rights reserved
© 1976 by United Feature Syndicate, Inc.
THUNK!
AUGH!
OW! OOO!! OW! OW!
11-21
YOU DUMMY! YOU'RE SUPPOSED TO KICK THE BALL, NOT MY LEG!!
OW! OUCH! OW!!
WHAT'S GOING ON? I THOUGHT YOU WERE PLAYING FOOTBALL...
I THINK I JUST SACKED THE QUARTERBACK!
SCHULZ

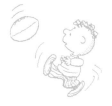

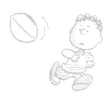

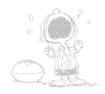

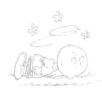

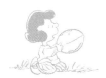

WATCH SNOOPY... I THINK HE'S GOING TO PULL THE OLD STATUE OF LIBERTY PLAY...
HOW DO YOU KNOW?
9-12
SOMEHOW I JUST SENSE IT...
SCHULZ
© 1977 United Feature Syndicate, Inc

ALL I HAVE TO DO IS KICK IT, RIGHT?
RIGHT
9-21
WHAT IF IT KICKS ME BACK?
SCHULZ
© 1977 United Feature Syndicate, Inc

9-22
I'VE DECIDED I DON'T WANT TO KICK IT
WHY NOT?
© 1977 United Feature Syndicate, Inc
WHAT DID IT EVER DO TO ME?
SCHULZ

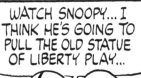

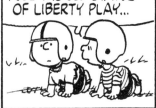

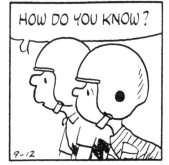

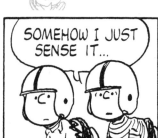

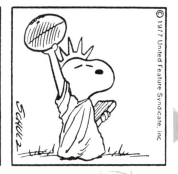

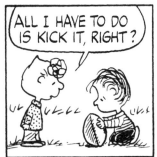

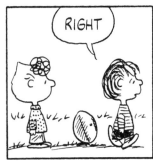

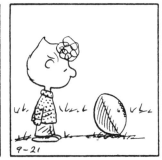

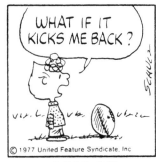

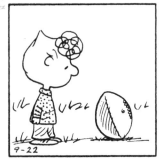

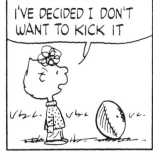

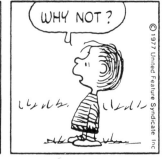

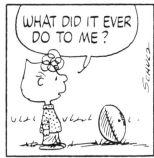

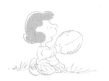

THIS BALL IS HISSING AT ME
SSSS
© 1977 United Feature Syndicate, Inc.
MAYBE SOME OF THE AIR IS LEAKING OUT
NO, I THINK IT'S HISSING AT ME
SSSSSS
THIS BALL HATES ME!
SSSSSS

I'M NOT GOING TO STAND HERE WHILE SOME STUPID BALL HISSES AT ME!
SSSSS
WELL, THEN, KICK IT!
I THINK I SCARED IT...
© 1977 United Feature Syndicate, Inc.
IT JUST PASSED OUT!

© 1977 United Feature Syndicate, Inc.

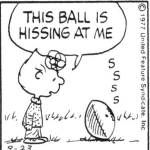

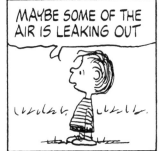

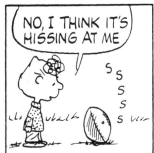

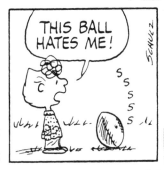

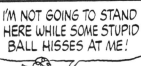

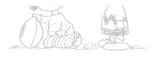

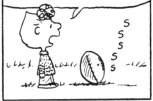

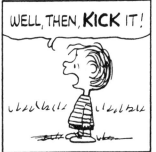

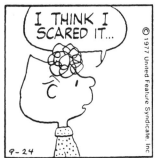

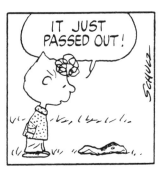

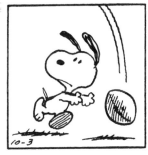

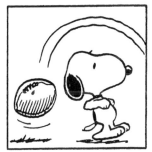

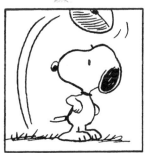

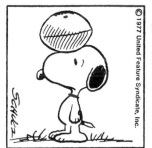

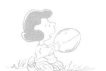

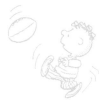

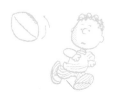

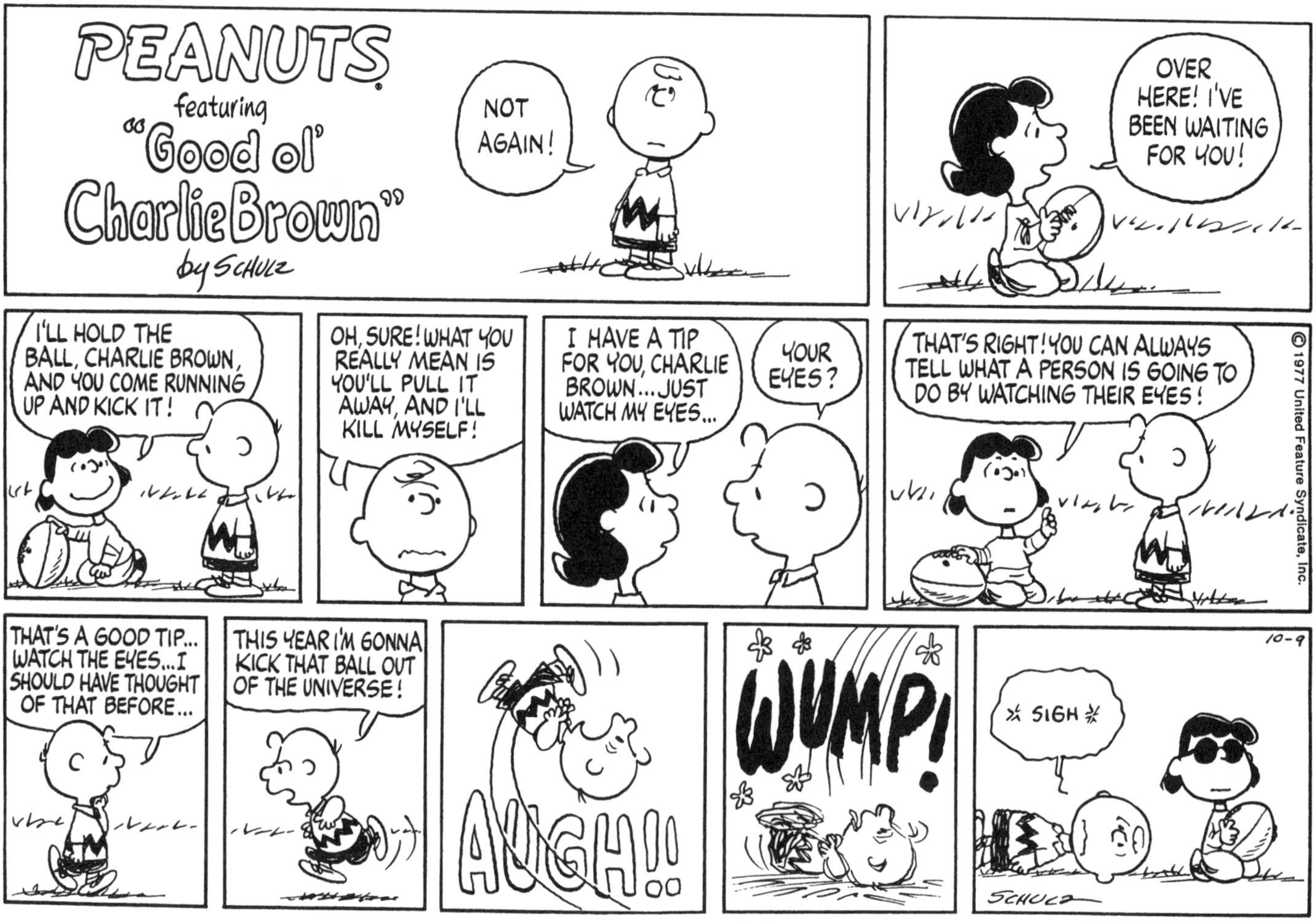
PEANUTS
featuring "Good ol' CharlieBrown"
by SCHULZ
NOT AGAIN!
OVER HERE! I'VE BEEN WAITING FOR YOU!
I'LL HOLD THE BALL, CHARLIE BROWN, AND YOU COME RUNNING UP AND KICK IT!
OH, SURE! WHAT YOU REALLY MEAN IS YOU'LL PULL IT AWAY, AND I'LL KILL MYSELF!
I HAVE A TIP FOR YOU, CHARLIE BROWN...JUST WATCH MY EYES...
YOUR EYES?
THAT'S RIGHT! YOU CAN ALWAYS TELL WHAT A PERSON IS GOING TO DO BY WATCHING THEIR EYES!
© 1977 United Feature Syndicate, Inc.
THAT'S A GOOD TIP... WATCH THE EYES...I SHOULD HAVE THOUGHT OF THAT BEFORE...
THIS YEAR I'M GONNA KICK THAT BALL OUT OF THE UNIVERSE!
AUGH!!
WUMP!
10-9
☼ SIGH ☼
SCHULZ

PEANUTS featuring "Good ol' Charlie Brown" by Schulz

OKAY, THIS IS WHAT WE'LL DO...

YOU GO DOWN TO THE END OF THE FIELD, AND I'LL KICK THE BALL TO YOU

I'LL BE ALL ALONE DOWN THERE...

YOU WON'T BE ALONE..THE BALL WILL BE WITH YOU!

WHAT IF IT DOESN'T SHOW UP?

IT'LL BE THERE... I'M GOING TO KICK IT TO YOU

WHAT IF I GO ALL THE WAY DOWN THERE, AND I GET MUGGED?

HOW CAN YOU GET MUGGED? WE'RE THE ONLY ONES AROUND HERE!

THAT'S WHAT YOU SAY!

10-16

ANOTHER THING...SO I WALK ALL THE WAY DOWN THERE... HOW DO I KNOW YOU WON'T RUN OFF AND LEAVE ME?

OKAY, FORGET IT!

NO, THAT'S ALL RIGHT... I'LL DO IT

© 1977 United Feature Syndicate, Inc.

MY MOTHER WARNED ME THAT FOOTBALL WAS A RISKY GAME

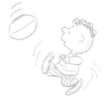

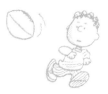

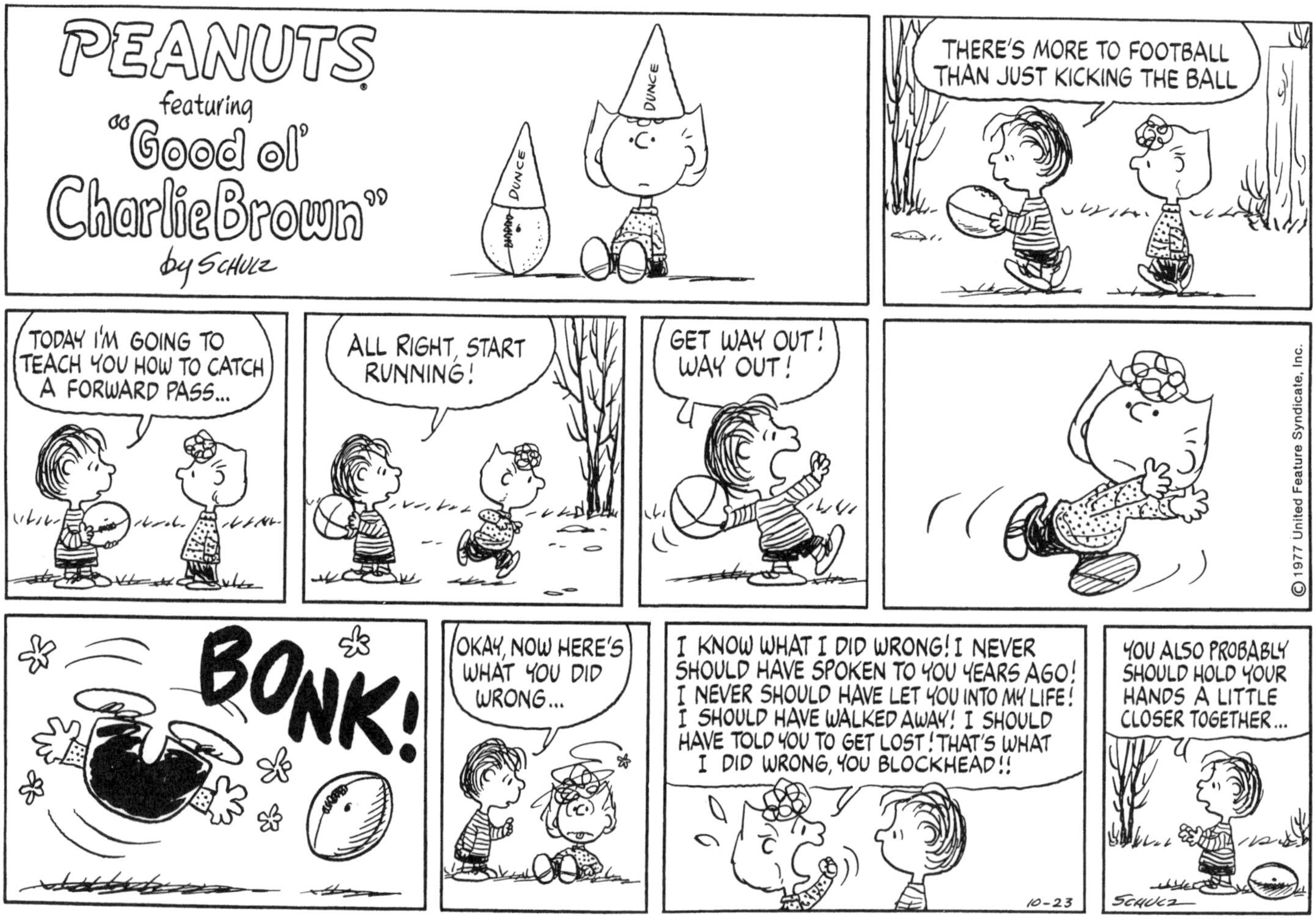
PEANUTS
featuring
"Good ol' Charlie Brown"
by SCHULZ
DUNCE
DUNCE
THERE'S MORE TO FOOTBALL THAN JUST KICKING THE BALL
TODAY I'M GOING TO TEACH YOU HOW TO CATCH A FORWARD PASS...
ALL RIGHT, START RUNNING!
GET WAY OUT! WAY OUT!
BONK!
OKAY, NOW HERE'S WHAT YOU DID WRONG...
I KNOW WHAT I DID WRONG! I NEVER SHOULD HAVE SPOKEN TO YOU YEARS AGO! I NEVER SHOULD HAVE LET YOU INTO MY LIFE! I SHOULD HAVE WALKED AWAY! I SHOULD HAVE TOLD YOU TO GET LOST! THAT'S WHAT I DID WRONG, YOU BLOCKHEAD!!
YOU ALSO PROBABLY SHOULD HOLD YOUR HANDS A LITTLE CLOSER TOGETHER...
10-23
SCHULZ

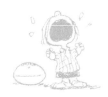

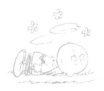

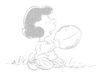

PEANUTS
featuring
"Good ol' Charlie Brown"
by SCHULZ

OVER HERE!

I DON'T BELIEVE IT...

© 1978 United Feature Syndicate, Inc.

I HAVE A BONUS FOR YOU, CHARLIE BROWN...

A BONUS?

I AM NOT ONLY GOING TO HOLD THE BALL FOR YOU SO YOU CAN KICK IT, BUT I AM ALSO GOING TO GIVE YOU A BANANA!

A BANANA...WHY WOULD SHE GIVE ME A BANANA?

OH, WELL, IF SOMEONE GIVES YOU A BANANA, I GUESS YOU HAVE TO TRUST HER

GET READY, BALL! YOU'RE GOING TO THE MOON!

10-1

AAUGH!

WHAM!

BANANAS ARE HIGH IN POTASSIUM, CHARLIE BROWN, WHICH PROMOTES HEALING OF MUSCLES!

SCHULZ

Panel 1: KICK ME THE OL' PIGSKIN, SIR!

Panel 2: I HATE TO DISILLUSION YOU, MARCIE...

Panel 3: THIS BALL ISN'T MADE OUT OF PIGSKIN... IT'S PLASTIC..

Panel 4: KICK ME THE OL' PLASTIC, SIR!

Panel 5: LET'S TRY SOMETHING DIFFERENT FOR THE KICKOFF...

Panel 6: INSTEAD OF HAVING SOMEONE HOLD THE BALL WITH HIS FINGER, LET'S USE A KICKING TEE...

Panel 7: A KICKING TEE...RIGHT!

GO ALL THE WAY DOWN THE FIELD, MARCIE...
I'LL HIT YOU WITH A PASS
© 1978 United Feature Syndicate, Inc.
11-9
WE'VE ALWAYS BEEN FRIENDS, SIR...WHY WOULD YOU WANT TO HIT ME?
SCHULZ

BOOT!
11-11
© 1978 United Feature Syndicate, Inc.
BONK!
SCHULZ
THAT'S GONNA CUT DOWN ON THE ENDORSEMENTS

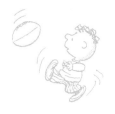

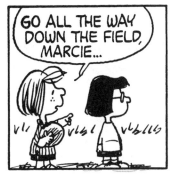

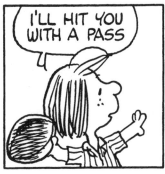

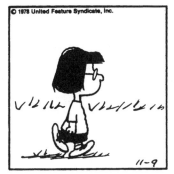

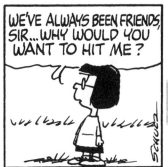

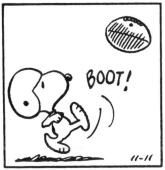

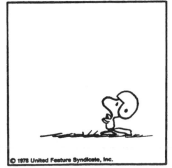

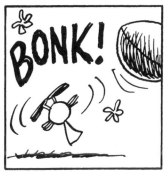

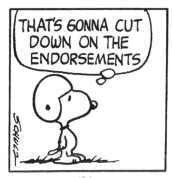

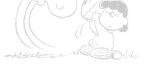

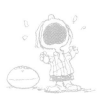

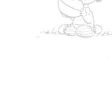

KNOCK KNOCK KNOCK
7-30
© 1979 United Feature Syndicate, Inc.
CHARLIE BROWN! YOU'RE BACK!! YOU'RE WELL!
I HEARD SOMETHING ABOUT A PROMISE..
OH, GOOD GRIEF!
SCHULZ

YOU HOLD THE BALL, AND I'LL COME RUNNING UP AND KICK IT
© 1979 United Feature Syndicate, Inc.
REMEMBER, YOU PROMISED THAT IF I GOT WELL, YOU'D NEVER PULL THE FOOTBALL AWAY AGAIN
7-31
CAN'T I CHANGE MY MIND?
NO, YOU CAN'T BREAK A PROMISE TO A SICK FRIEND
HA! NOW, WHAT ARE YOU GONNA DO?
QUIET! I'M THINKING!
SCHULZ

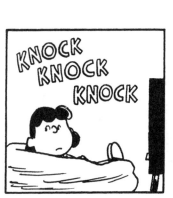

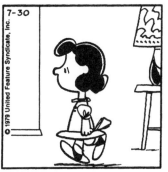

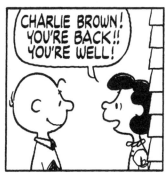

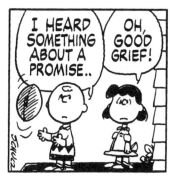

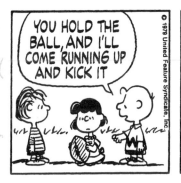

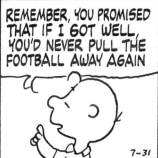

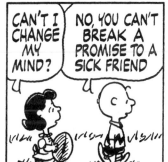

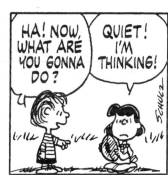

THIS TIME I'M REALLY GONNA KICK THAT FOOTBALL!

© 1979 United Feature Syndicate, Inc.

YOU'RE CRAZY, CHARLIE BROWN! SHE'LL PULL IT AWAY LIKE SHE ALWAYS DOES! DON'T TRUST HER!

BUT SHE PROMISED SHE'D NEVER PULL IT AWAY AGAIN IF I GOT WELL..

8-1

I FEEL GREAT! HERE I GO!!

I CAN'T LOOK..

SCHULZ

© 1979 United Feature Syndicate, Inc.

8-2

AAUGH!

MY FINGER! MY HAND! MY ARM!

?

YOU MISSED THE BALL, YOU BLOCKHEAD! YOU KICKED MY FINGER! YOU KICKED MY HAND!!

OW! OW! OW!

?

SCHULZ

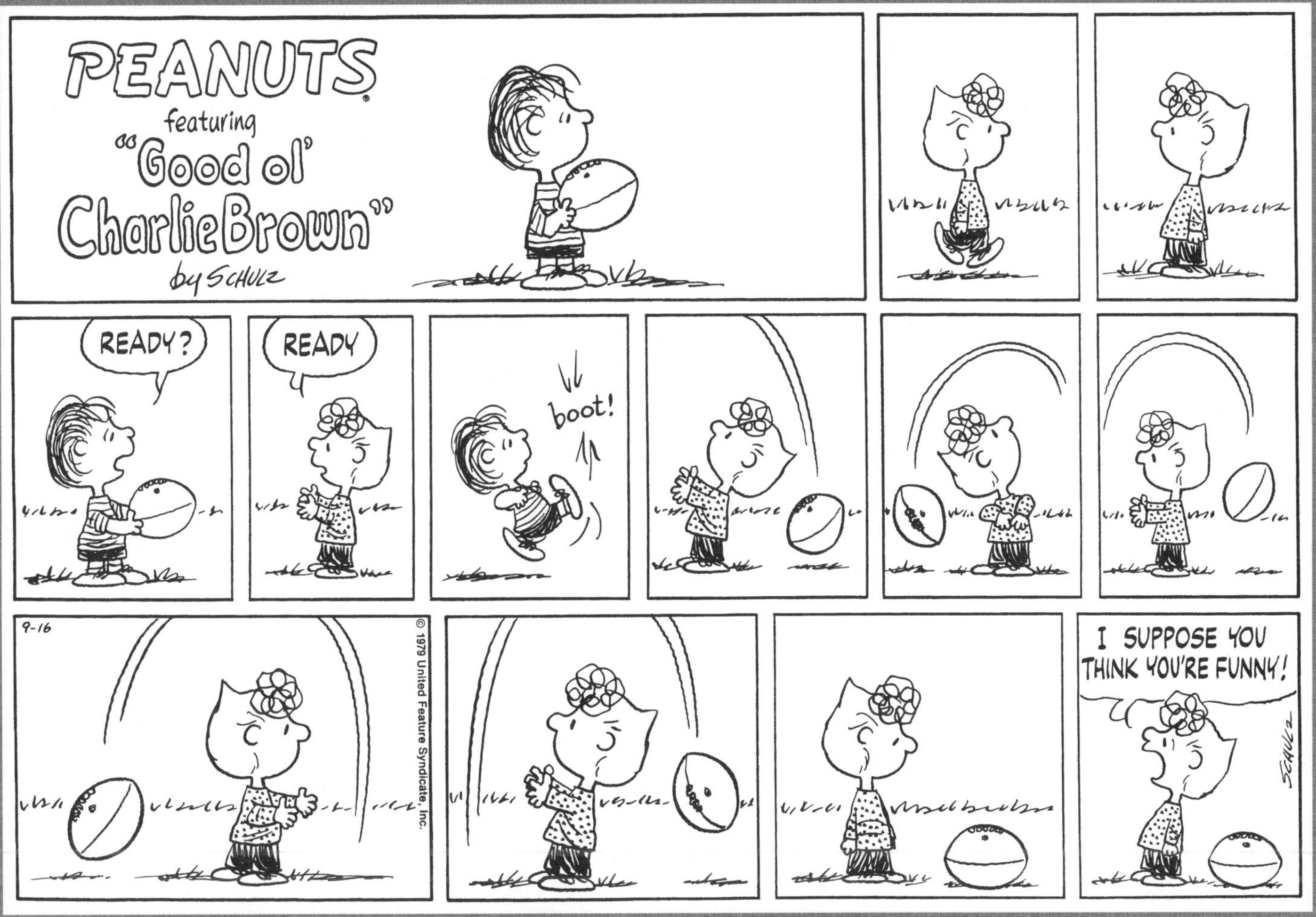
PEANUTS
featuring
"Good ol' Charlie Brown"
by SCHULZ
READY?
READY
boot!
9-16
© 1979 United Feature Syndicate, Inc.
I SUPPOSE YOU THINK YOU'RE FUNNY!
SCHULZ

boot!
© 1979 United Feature Syndicate, Inc.
BONK!
9-24
EXPLAIN TITLE IX TO ME AGAIN, WILL YOU?
SCHULZ

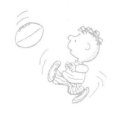

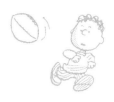

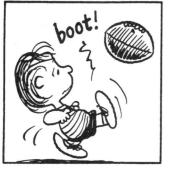

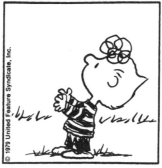

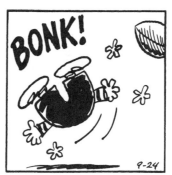

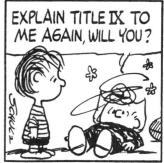

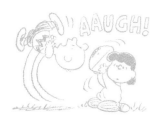

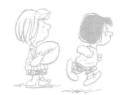

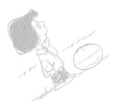

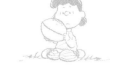

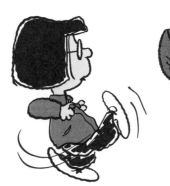

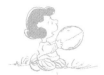

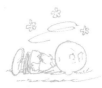

PEANUTS featuring "Good ol' Charlie Brown" *by Schulz*

I THINK WE SHOULD PRACTICE SOMETHING DIFFERENT THIS TIME..

NOT TOO DIFFERENT, SIR...

THIS IS THE PLAY, MARCIE... YOU GO STRAIGHT OUT, CUT LEFT, CUT BACK, GO STRAIGHT, CUT BACK, GO RIGHT AND THEN OUT...

HAVE YOU GOT THAT?

I THINK SO, SIR...I GO OUT LEFT, CUT STRAIGHT, CUT RIGHT, CUT BACK, GO LEFT, CUT BACK, GO STRAIGHT, CUT LEFT AND RUN RIGHT...

NO, MARCIE, THAT'S ALL WRONG! YOU GO STRAIGHT OUT, CUT LEFT, CUT BACK, GO STRAIGHT, CUT BACK, GO RIGHT AND THEN OUT!

MAYBE I SHOULD THROW THE BALL, SIR, AND YOU GO OUT...

THAT'S A GOOD IDEA...I'LL GO OUT LEFT, CUT BACK, GO RIGHT, CUT LEFT AND THEN STRAIGHT OUT..

GO OUT RIGHT, CUT LEFT, CUT BACK, GO STRAIGHT AND CUT RIGHT...

NO, MARCIE! I'LL GO OUT LEFT, CUT BACK, GO RIGHT, CUT LEFT AND THEN STRAIGHT OUT!

I HAVE ANOTHER IDEA, SIR..

I'LL GO LEFT, CUT BACK, GO STRAIGHT, CUT RIGHT, GO BACK, CUT LEFT AND THEN GO HOME FOR DINNER!

I CAN'T STAND IT...

9-21

PEANUTS featuring "Good ol' Charlie Brown" *by Schulz*

FOOTBALL?

 HOW CAN I KICK A FOOTBALL IF YOU DON'T TEACH ME?

 YOU HAVE A POINT... I SUPPOSE THE FIRST THING WE HAVE TO FIND OUT IS WHAT FOOT YOU KICK WITH

 I'VE NEVER THOUGHT ABOUT IT... I IMAGINE I KICK WITH MY RIGHT FOOT...

10-19

 HOW'S THIS?

AAUGH! MY SHIN!

 OR MAYBE I'M BETTER WITH MY LEFT..IS THIS BETTER?

OW! MY LEG!!

© 1980 United Feature Syndicate, Inc.

 OW! OOO! OW!

 GOOD GRIEF!

 IT SAYS HERE THAT ALTHOUGH A CAREER IN ATHLETICS CAN BE REWARDING, COACHING OR TEACHING CAN BE JUST AS GRATIFYING..

I DOUBT THAT

Schulz

PEANUTS
featuring "Good ol' CharlieBrown"
by SCHULZ

ECCLESIASTES.. THIRD CHAPTER..

AH! JUST THE PERSON I WANTED TO SEE...

"TO EVERY THING THERE IS A SEASON," CHARLIE BROWN...

"A TIME TO BE BORN, AND A TIME TO DIE"

"A TIME TO PLANT, AND A TIME TO PLUCK UP THAT WHICH IS PLANTED"

11-16

"A TIME TO WEEP, AND A TIME TO LAUGH.. A TIME TO MOURN, AND A TIME TO DANCE.."

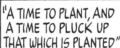
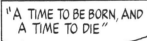

© 1980 United Feature Syndicate, Inc.

"A TIME TO LOVE, AND A TIME TO HATE.. A TIME OF WAR, AND A TIME OF PEACE"

AAUGH!

WHAM!

AND A TIME TO PULL AWAY THE FOOTBALL

SCHULZ

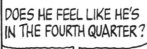

Panel 1: MY GRANDFATHER SAYS LIFE IS A LOT LIKE A FOOTBALL GAME...

3-7

Panel 2: DOES HE FEEL LIKE HE'S IN THE FOURTH QUARTER?

Panel 3: WORSE THAN THAT...

© 1981 United Feature Syndicate, Inc.

Panel 4: HE'S AFRAID HE DOESN'T HAVE ANY MORE "TIME OUTS"

SCHULZ

120

PEANUTS
featuring
"Good ol' CharlieBrown"
by SCHULZ

WELL, SURE..TRY IT IF YOU THINK IT'LL HELP...

BOOT!

9-27
© 1981 United Feature Syndicate, Inc.

BONK!

BUMP!

BONK!

THEN AGAIN, MAYBE YOU SHOULDN'T USE QUITE SO MUCH "STICKUM"

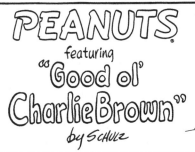

PEANUTS featuring *"Good ol' CharlieBrown"* by SCHULZ

I'M READY.. THE BALL'S READY.. ARE YOU READY?

YES, MARCIE, I'M READY! I'VE BEEN READY FOR TWENTY MINUTES!

© 1982 United Feature Syndicate, Inc.

DO FOOTBALLS MIND BEING KICKED, SIR? DO YOU THINK IT CAUSES THEM TO BE TRAUMATIZED?

PLEASE, MARCIE..JUST KICK THE BALL!

LOOK WHAT HAPPENED, SIR.. I KICKED THE BALL, AND MY SHOE CAME OFF!

AND NOW LOOK WHAT HAPPENED, SIR! HEE HEE! I ACCIDENTALLY TIED MY SHOE WITH THE LACES ON THE FOOTBALL!

9-12

IS THAT MY MOTHER CALLING ME? IT MUST BE SUPPERTIME

I GUESS I'LL JUST HAVE TO HOP ALL THE WAY HOME

I HATE PLAYING WITH YOU, MARCIE!!

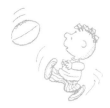

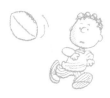

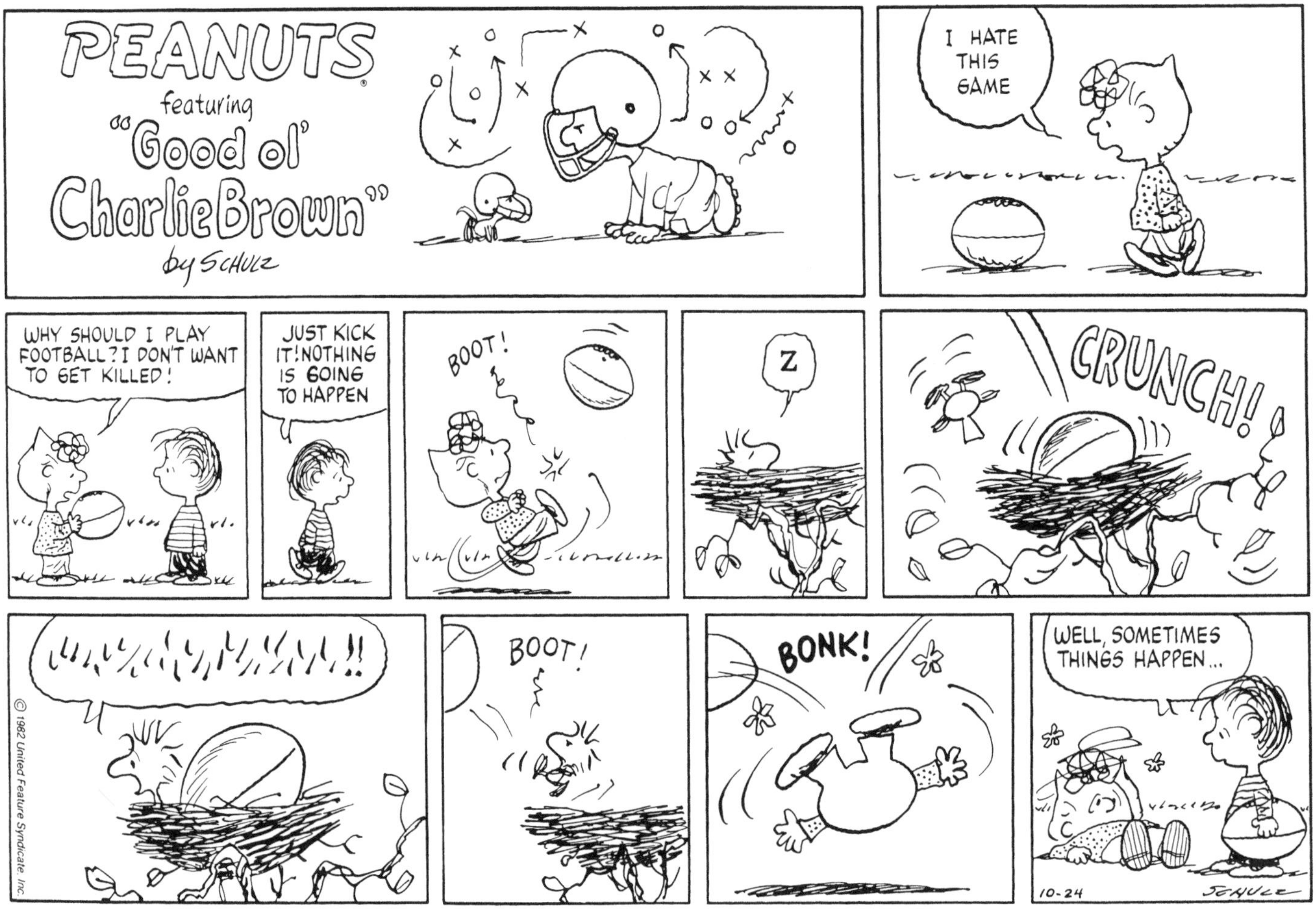
PEANUTS
featuring
"Good ol' CharlieBrown"
by SCHULZ
I HATE THIS GAME
WHY SHOULD I PLAY FOOTBALL? I DON'T WANT TO GET KILLED!
JUST KICK IT! NOTHING IS GOING TO HAPPEN
BOOT!
Z
CRUNCH!
!!
© 1982 United Feature Syndicate, Inc.
BOOT!
BONK!
WELL, SOMETIMES THINGS HAPPEN...
10-24
SCHULZ

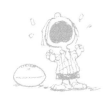

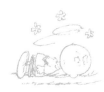

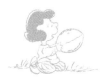

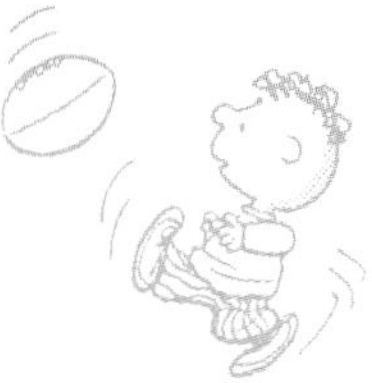
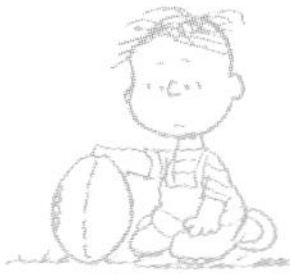
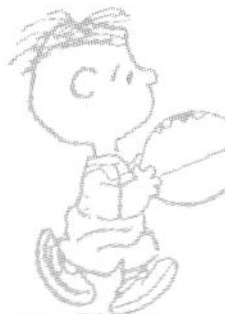
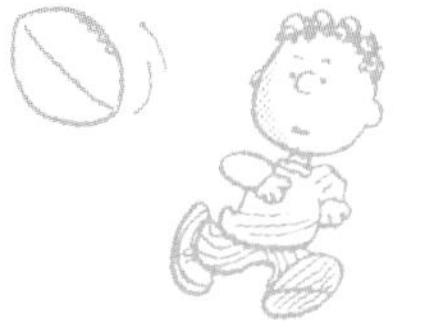

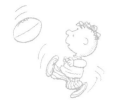

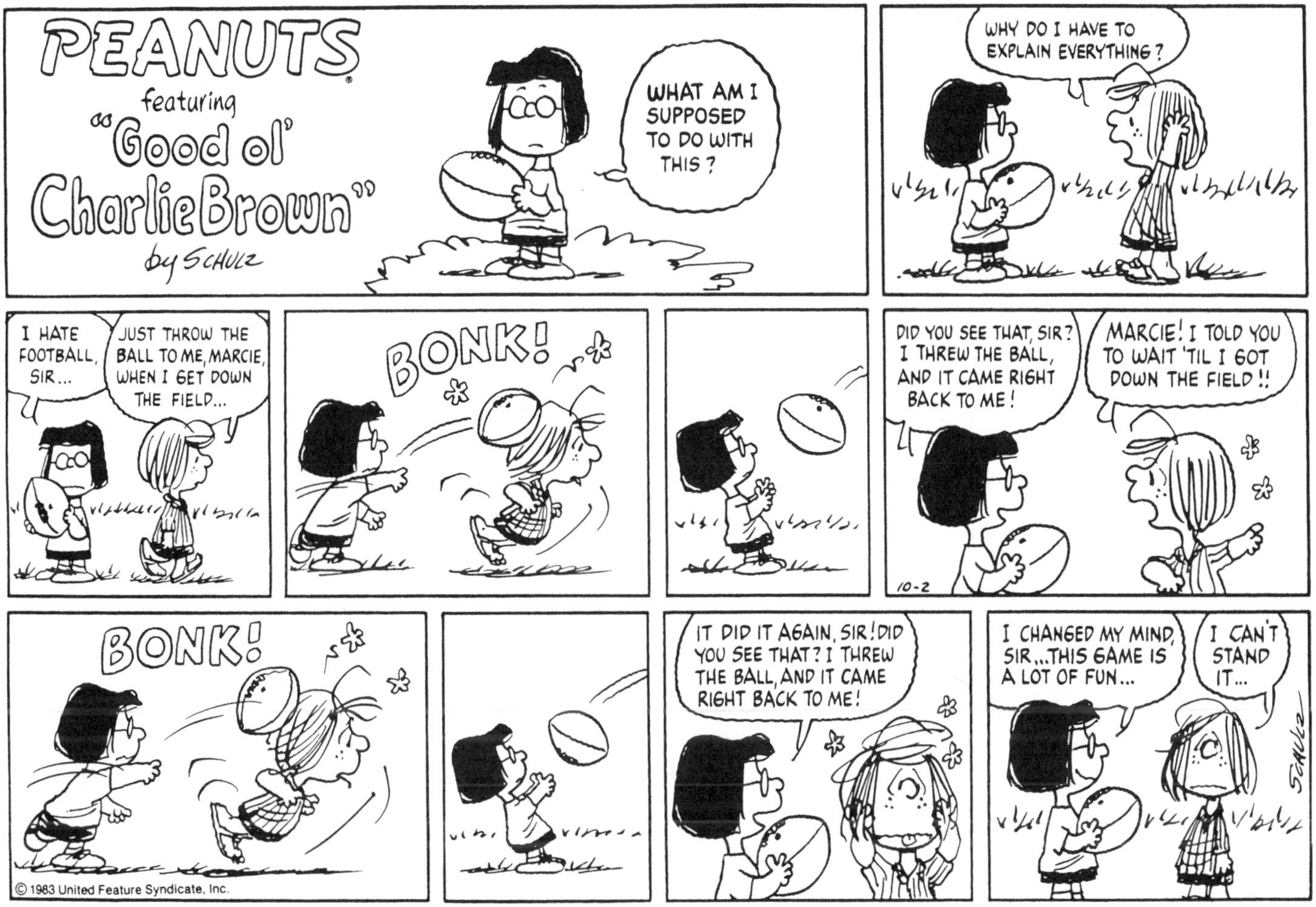
PEANUTS
featuring "Good ol' Charlie Brown"
by SCHULZ
WHAT AM I SUPPOSED TO DO WITH THIS?
WHY DO I HAVE TO EXPLAIN EVERYTHING?
I HATE FOOTBALL, SIR...
JUST THROW THE BALL TO ME, MARCIE, WHEN I GET DOWN THE FIELD...
BONK!
DID YOU SEE THAT, SIR? I THREW THE BALL, AND IT CAME RIGHT BACK TO ME!
MARCIE! I TOLD YOU TO WAIT 'TIL I GOT DOWN THE FIELD!!
10-2
BONK!
IT DID IT AGAIN, SIR! DID YOU SEE THAT? I THREW THE BALL, AND IT CAME RIGHT BACK TO ME!
I CHANGED MY MIND, SIR... THIS GAME IS A LOT OF FUN...
I CAN'T STAND IT...
SCHULZ
© 1983 United Feature Syndicate, Inc.

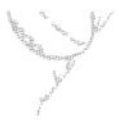
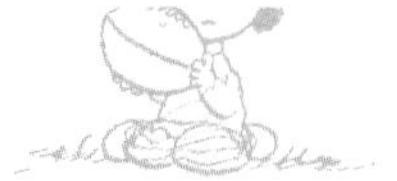
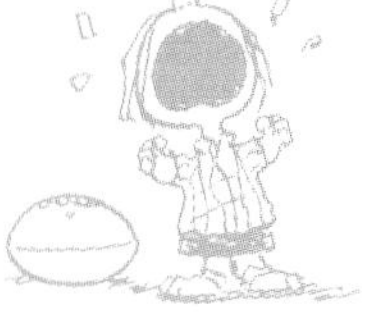
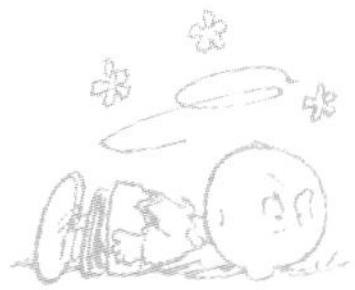
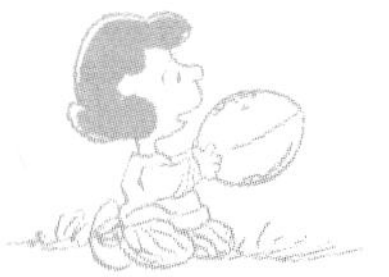
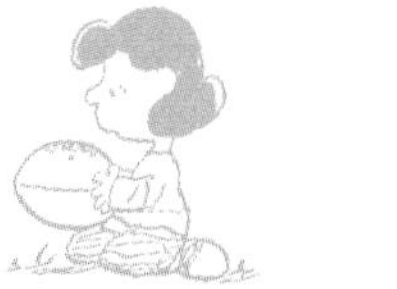

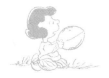

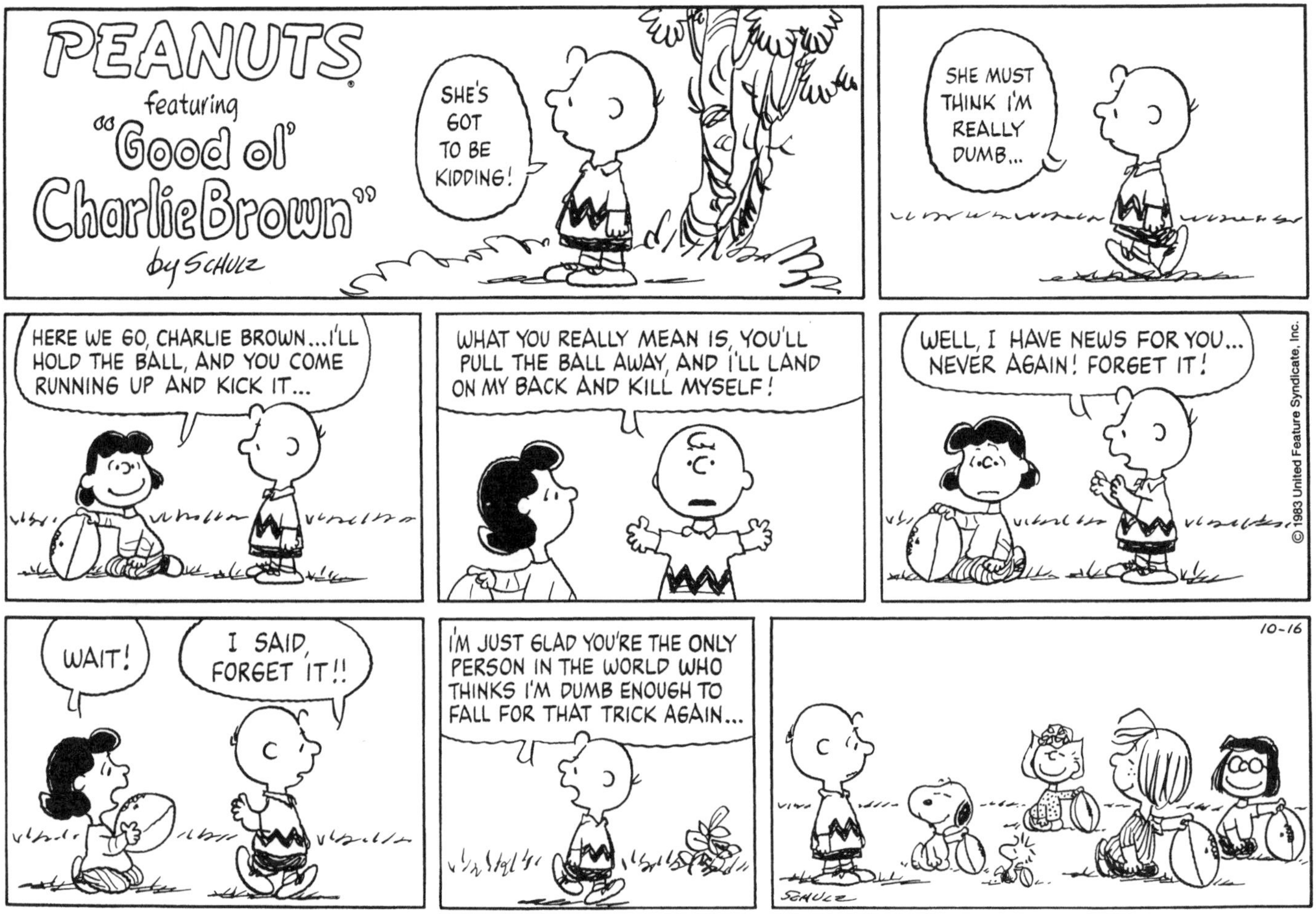
PEANUTS
featuring "Good ol' CharlieBrown"
by SCHULZ
SHE'S GOT TO BE KIDDING!
SHE MUST THINK I'M REALLY DUMB...
HERE WE GO, CHARLIE BROWN...I'LL HOLD THE BALL, AND YOU COME RUNNING UP AND KICK IT...
WHAT YOU REALLY MEAN IS, YOU'LL PULL THE BALL AWAY, AND I'LL LAND ON MY BACK AND KILL MYSELF!
WELL, I HAVE NEWS FOR YOU... NEVER AGAIN! FORGET IT!
© 1983 United Feature Syndicate, Inc.
WAIT!
I SAID, FORGET IT!!
I'M JUST GLAD YOU'RE THE ONLY PERSON IN THE WORLD WHO THINKS I'M DUMB ENOUGH TO FALL FOR THAT TRICK AGAIN...
10-16
SCHULZ

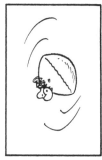

Panel 1: I'VE BEEN WATCHING AN EXCITING FOOTBALL GAME..THE CONGREGATION IS GOING WILD...

Panel 2: FOOTBALL GAMES HAVE FANS.. CHURCHES HAVE CONGREGATIONS..CONCERTS HAVE AUDIENCES...

Panel 3: COURTROOMS HAVE SPECTATORS.. RIOTS HAVE MOBS AND ACCIDENTS HAVE ONLOOKERS...

Panel 4: THE CONGREGATION JUST TORE DOWN THE GOAL POSTS!

11-17 © 1983 United Feature Syndicate, Inc.

Panel 1: Dear Brother Snoopy, Life here on the desert is good.

3-20

Panel 2: I read a lot and go on long walks.

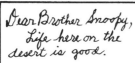

Panel 3: When there is nothing else to do, I practice a few field goals.

© 1984 United Feature Syndicate, Inc.

Panel 4:

SCHULZ

Panel 1: I USED TO WONDER WHY I HATED THE KICKOFF..NOW I KNOW

Panel 2: © 1984 United Feature Syndicate, Inc. 9-26

Panel 3: boot! boot! boot! boot! boot!

Panel 4: MY ARMS GET TIRED!

Panel 1: YOU NEED TO PRACTICE YOUR TACKLING, MARCIE

Panel 2: I'LL COME RUNNING BY YOU, AND YOU TRY TO GRAB ME BEFORE I GET TO THE GOAL LINE...

Panel 3: 10-10 © 1984 United Feature Syndicate, Inc.

Panel 4: I HATE PLAYING WITH YOU, MARCIE!

Panel 1: MARCIE, YOU DON'T TACKLE ANOTHER PLAYER BY GRABBING HER HAIR!

Panel 2: WHAT DO I GRAB, SIR? / JUST DON'T GRAB MY HAIR!

Panel 3: OKAY, TRY IT AGAIN... HERE I COME! 10-11

Panel 4: © 1984 United Feature Syndicate, Inc.

Panel 5: MARCIE, YOU CAN'T PLAY FOOTBALL WHILE YOU'RE WEARING GLASSES..

Panel 6: I'LL TAKE THEM OFF AND PUT THEM RIGHT HERE...HOW'S THAT?

Panel 7: OKAY, HERE I COME AGAIN... SEE IF YOU CAN TACKLE ME... 10-12

Panel 8: GOTCHA, SIR!

© 1984 United Feature Syndicate, Inc.

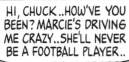

Panel 1: HI, CHUCK..HOW'VE YOU BEEN? MARCIE'S DRIVING ME CRAZY..SHE'LL NEVER BE A FOOTBALL PLAYER..

Panel 2: SOME PEOPLE JUST NEVER LEARN, DO THEY, CHUCK?

Panel 3: CHARLIE BROWN...♪♫ C'MON OUTSIDE...I'LL HOLD THE BALL, AND YOU KICK IT...

10-13

Panel 4: NO, WE DON'T

SCHULZ

Panel 5: WHERE'S THE FOOTBALL GAME?

Panel 6: I THOUGHT THERE WAS FOOTBALL ON THURSDAY NIGHTS

Panel 7: THIS IS WEDNESDAY

1-2-85

Panel 8: THAT'S NO EXCUSE!

SCHULZ

PEANUTS featuring "Good ol' Charlie Brown"
by SCHULZ

WE'LL PRETEND IT'S THE KICKOFF, OKAY?

9-22

I'LL COME RUNNING DOWN THE FIELD, AND YOU TRY TO TACKLE ME...

: SIGH :

TOUCHDOWN!

I GUESS I WAS WRONG.. YOU'RE TOO SMALL TO PLAY FOOTBALL

MAYBE WE CAN FIND A PLACE FOR YOU IN THE BAND...

THIS TIME, MARCIE, I'LL PUNT, AND YOU BE THE ONE WHO TRIES TO BLOCK IT...

READY, SIR? HERE I COME!

11-29

THUMP!

YOUR STYLE, MARCIE, LEAVES A LOT TO BE DESIRED!

KICK THE BALL, MARCIE!

IT'LL HATE ME, SIR..

11-30

FOOTBALLS DON'T HATE, MARCIE!

HOW NICE OF YOU..

WHAT HAPPENED? DID I MISS ANYTHING?

HE MADE A TOUCHDOWN, AND THE GREAT CROWD GAVE HIM A BIG HAND...

OR MAYBE THE BIG CROWD GAVE HIM A GREAT HAND...I DON'T KNOW..

12-2

WHATEVER.. WHO CARES?

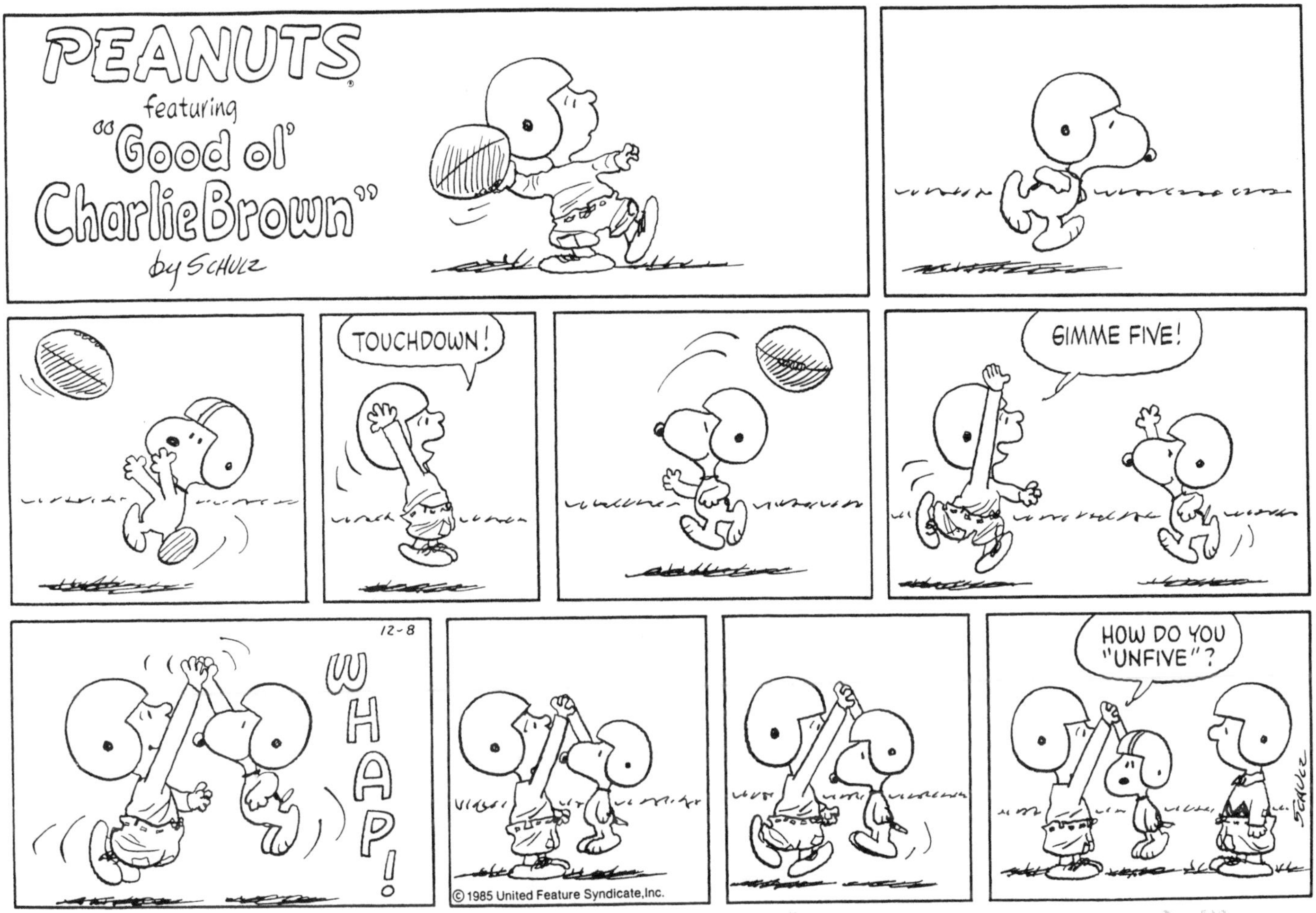
PEANUTS
featuring
"Good ol' Charlie Brown"
by SCHULZ
TOUCHDOWN!
GIMME FIVE!
12-8
WHAP!
© 1985 United Feature Syndicate, Inc.
HOW DO YOU "UNFIVE"?
SCHULZ

Panel 1: (Snoopy looking at Woodstock with a thought bubble) | | ? |

Panel 2: NO!

Panel 3: I SAID WE'RE GOING OUT TO KICK AROUND THE OL' PIGSKIN..

Panel 4: I DIDN'T SAY "BEAGLESKIN"!

10-1

Panel 5: WE SHOULD ORGANIZE A FOOTBALL TEAM, MARCIE

10-14

Panel 6: WE CAN'T, SIR..WE DON'T HAVE COSTUMES

Panel 7: UNIFORMS

Panel 8: WHATEVER

Panel 9: I DON'T WANT TO PLAY FOOTBALL, SIR..IT'S NOT FEMININE ENOUGH!

Panel 10: NOT FEMININE ENOUGH?!!

Panel 11: WHAT DO YOU WANT TO DO, TIE A RIBBON AROUND THE BALL OR SOMETHING?

10-15

Panel 12: LOOKS CUTE, DOESN'T IT?

Panel 1: I'LL HOLD THE BALL, SIR, AND YOU KICK IT...

Panel 2: MARCIE, I'M NOT GONNA KICK A BALL THAT HAS A CUTE RIBBON TIED AROUND IT!

10-16

Panel 3: I'LL BET THE ICEBOX WOULD

Panel 4: "REFRIGERATOR"

WHATEVER

Panel 5: AND MARCIE SAYS FOOTBALL ISN'T FEMININE, CHUCK.. ISN'T SHE SOMETHING?

Panel 6: IF I LIKE TO PLAY FOOTBALL, DOES THAT MEAN I'M NOT FEMININE, CHUCK?

Panel 7: WHAT DO YOU THINK, CHUCK? HUH? WHAT DO YOU THINK?

10-17

Panel 8: WE'RE SORRY.. THE NUMBER YOU HAVE REACHED IS NO LONGER IN SERVICE..

WAIT 'TIL I GET DOWN NEAR THAT TREE, MARCIE..

THEN YOU KICK THE OL' PIGSKIN TO ME...

WHY WOULD I WANT TO DO THAT?

POOR PIGGY..

MR. BROWN, MY NAME IS LELAND..WE'D LIKE TO PLAY FOR YOUR FOOTBALL TEAM

I DON'T HAVE A FOOTBALL TEAM, LELAND

IF YOU DID, WE'D SURE LIKE TO PLAY FOR YOU..

WHY DO YOU KEEP SAYING "WE"?

THERE'S MORE THAN ONE OF US UNDER HERE!

HEY, CHUCK, DO YOU KNOW A LITTLE KID NAMED LELAND?

HE SAYS THEY WANT TO PLAY ON MY FOOTBALL TEAM..

THEY'RE SO LITTLE, CHUCK, THERE'S TWO OF 'EM UNDER ONE HELMET...

THREE!

I'M SORRY, LELAND... I CAN'T USE YOU GUYS ON MY TEAM..

LET'S FACE IT.. YOU'RE RIDICULOUS!

WHOEVER HEARD OF THREE PLAYERS UNDER ONE HELMET?

10-10

YOU SHOULD SEE US WITH THE SHOULDER PADS!

 **AAUGH!**

IT'S EXCITEMENT TIME AS THE TEAMS TROT OUT ONTO THE FIELD!

IT'S THE KICKOFF!

boot!

IT'S EXCITEMENT TIME..
boot! boot!
boot! boot!
boot! boot!

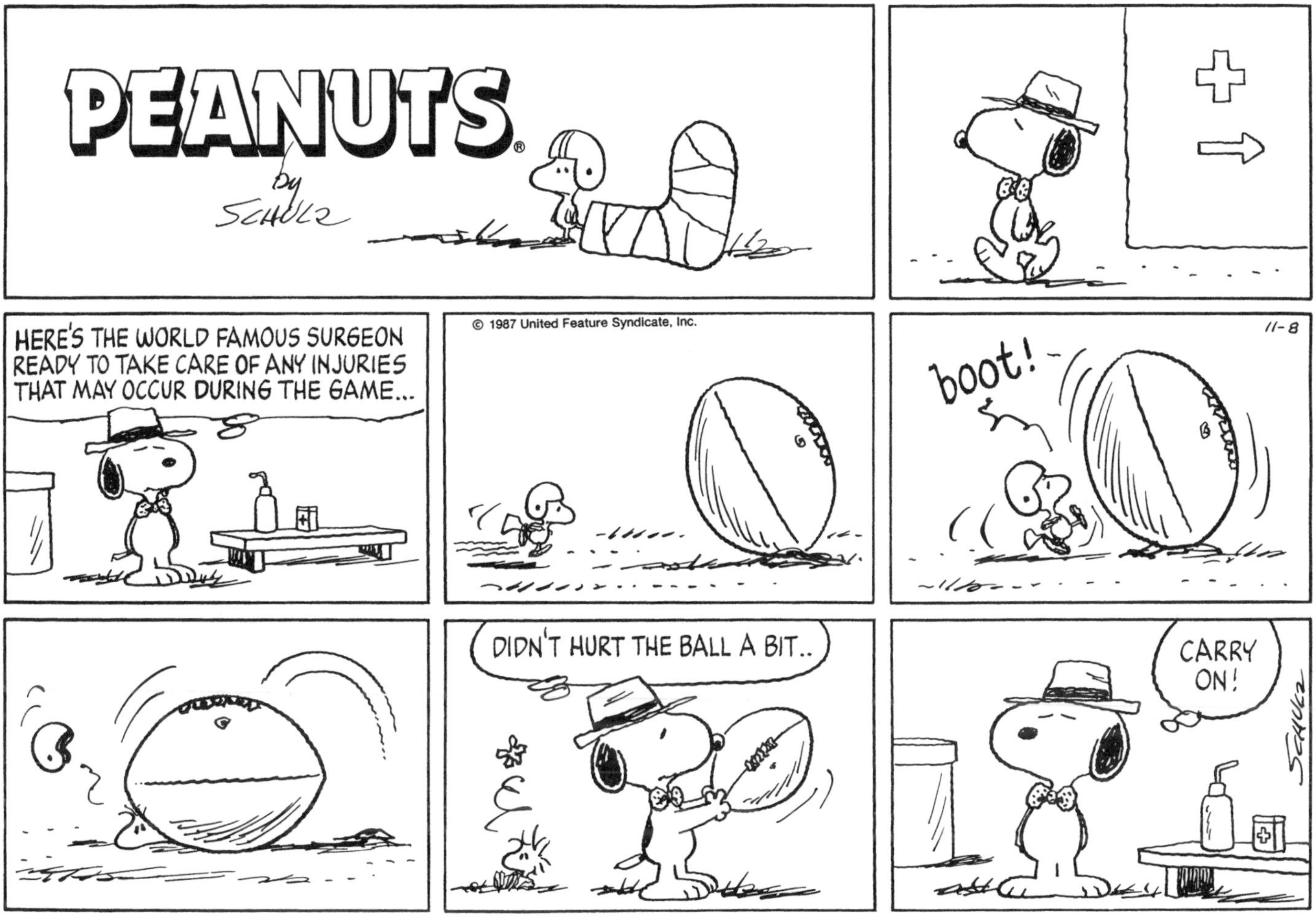
PEANUTS
by SCHULZ
© 1987 United Feature Syndicate, Inc.
11-8
HERE'S THE WORLD FAMOUS SURGEON READY TO TAKE CARE OF ANY INJURIES THAT MAY OCCUR DURING THE GAME...
boot!
DIDN'T HURT THE BALL A BIT..
CARRY ON!
SCHULZ

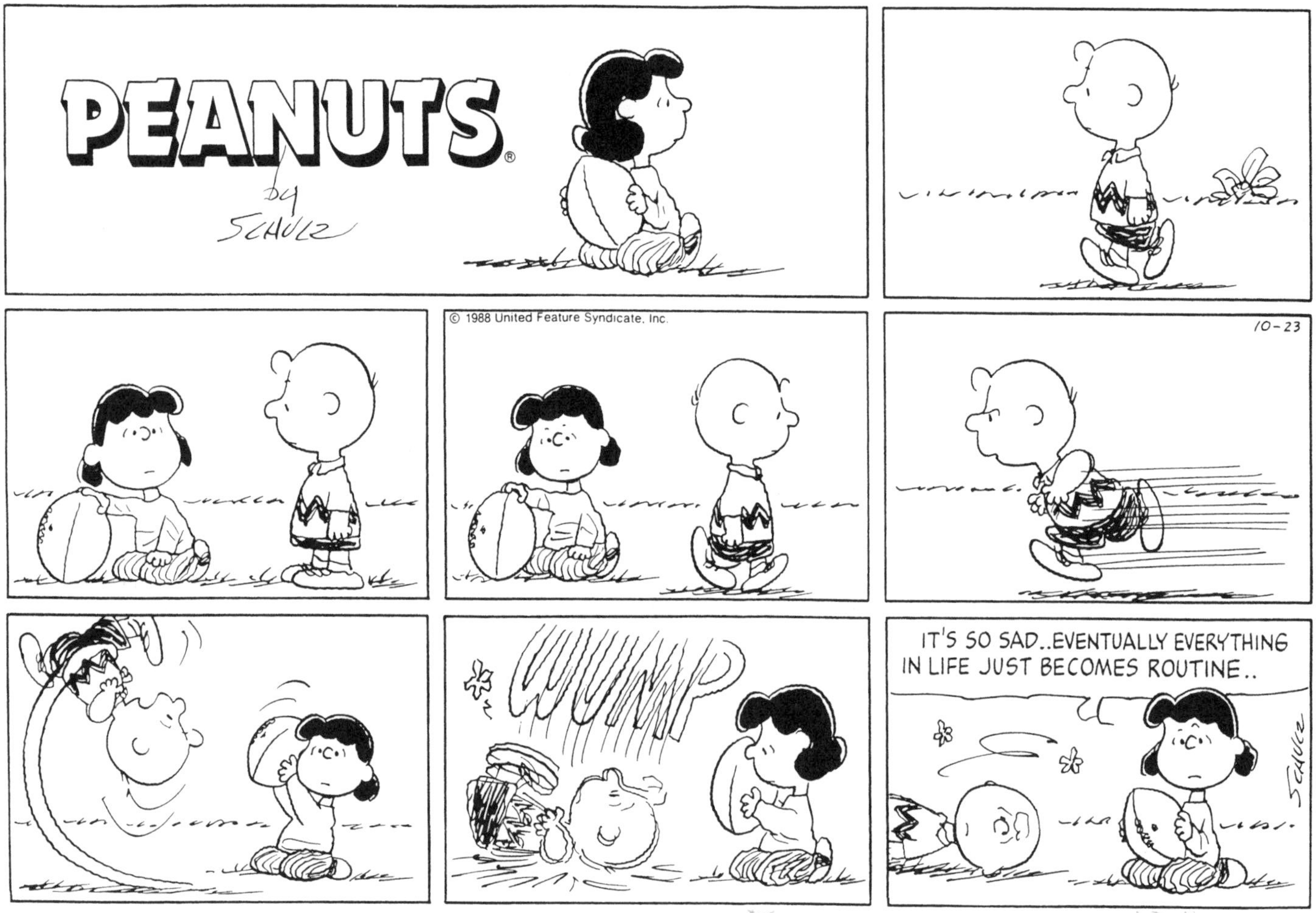
PEANUTS®
by SCHULZ
© 1988 United Feature Syndicate, Inc.
10-23
WUUMP
IT'S SO SAD..EVENTUALLY EVERYTHING IN LIFE JUST BECOMES ROUTINE..
SCHULZ

Panel 1: YOU SHOULD BRING YOUR FOOTBALL TEAM OVER, CHUCK, AND WE COULD HAVE A GAME..

Panel 2: I DON'T HAVE A FOOTBALL TEAM.. I ONLY HAVE A BASEBALL TEAM... 9-19

Panel 3: YOU ONLY **THINK** YOU HAVE A BASEBALL TEAM, CHUCK..

Panel 4: YOU HOLD THE BALL, MARCIE, AND I'LL COME RUNNING UP AND KICK IT...

Panel 5: BONK! 9-20

Panel 6: WHILE I WAS WAITING, SIR, I THOUGHT I'D PRACTICE A FEW PASSES..

Panel 7: I CAN'T PLAY FOOTBALL TODAY, SIR..I'M TAKING WATERCOLOR LESSONS..

Panel 8: THAT'S GREAT, MARCIE..I HOPE YOU SPILL COBALT BLUE ALL OVER YOUR SHOES! 9-21

Panel 9: THANK YOU, SIR.. AND I HOPE YOU SACK THE HATCHBACK...

YEAH, CHUCK, I'M CALLING YOU BECAUSE I NEED SOMEBODY TO PLAY FOOTBALL WITH...MARCIE IS JUST TOO WEIRD...

ASK HIM IF HE STILL LOVES ME

SO LONG, CHUCK

YOU DIDN'T ASK HIM

HE NEVER WOULD HAVE UNDERSTOOD THE QUESTION, MARCIE

9-22

THANKS FOR COMING, GUYS..

I'M GLAD SOMEBODY IS STILL INTERESTED IN PLAYING FOOTBALL..

JUST TRY NEVER TO BRING UP THE SUBJECT OF KNEE SURGERY..

9-23

© 1989 United Feature Syndicate, Inc.

AAUGH!

MY GRAMPA AND GRAMMA HAVE BEEN MARRIED FOR FIFTY YEARS...

THEY'RE LUCKY, AREN'T THEY?

9-27

© 1989 United Feature Syndicate, Inc.

GRAMPA SAYS IT ISN'T LUCK.. IT'S SKILL!

LOOK WHAT I FOUND OVER IN THE REC ROOM, BROWNIE CHARLES...A FOOTBALL!

I HAVE A GOOD IDEA..I'LL HOLD THE BALL, AND YOU COME RUNNING UP AND KICK IT...

WHAT DO YOU THINK?

I THINK I NEED TO MAKE A PHONE CALL

7-31

LINUS, WHAT AM I GOING TO DO?

SHE'S WAITING OUT THERE WITH A FOOTBALL, AND EXPECTS ME TO GO RUNNING UP AND KICK IT...

DO YOU THINK SHE'LL PULL IT AWAY LIKE YOUR STUPID SISTER ALWAYS DOES?

8-1

WHO'S STUPID?

SORRY, WRONG NUMBER..

I'M WAITING, BROWNIE CHARLES! I'M HOLDING THE BALL! ALL YOU HAVE TO DO IS KICK IT!

IF YOU CAN'T TRUST THE PRETTIEST LITTLE GIRL YOU'VE EVER SEEN, WHO CAN YOU TRUST?

8-2

SCREECH!!

THAT WAS JUST A PRACTICE RUN, OKAY?

TOUCHDOWN!

BETTER LUCK NEXT TIME, CHARLES..

10-14

RING!

HEY, CHUCK.. HOW ABOUT TELLING ONE OF YOUR GUYS HERE THAT THE GAME'S OVER

© 1990 United Feature Syndicate, Inc.

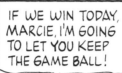

Panel 1: IF WE WIN TODAY, MARCIE, I'M GOING TO LET YOU KEEP THE GAME BALL!

Panel 2: IT'S ALREADY MY BALL, SIR.. MY DAD GAVE IT TO ME FOR MY BIRTHDAY..

11-9

Panel 3:

Panel 4: OH..

SCHULZ

AAUGH!

PEANUTS by SCHULZ

CHARLIE BROWNNN! ♪♪♪

I'LL HOLD THE BALL, CHARLIE BROWN, AND YOU COME RUNNING UP AND KICK IT...

CONGRATULATE ME! YOU HAVE JUST NOMINATED ME "MOST STUPID KID OF THE YEAR"

BUT LOOK, CHARLIE BROWN.. I'VE BEEN READING THIS BOOK ABOUT HOLDING THE BALL...

SEE? IT TELLS HOW TO HOLD IT FOR THE KICKOFF, FOR FIELD GOALS AND FOR EXTRA POINTS...

9-29

IF SOMEONE IS READING A BOOK ABOUT SOMETHING, I GUESS YOU HAVE TO TRUST HER..

THIS YEAR I'M GONNA KICK THAT BALL ALL THE WAY TO OMAHA!

AAUGH!

WHAM!

I WROTE THE BOOK, CHARLIE BROWN!

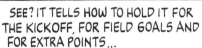

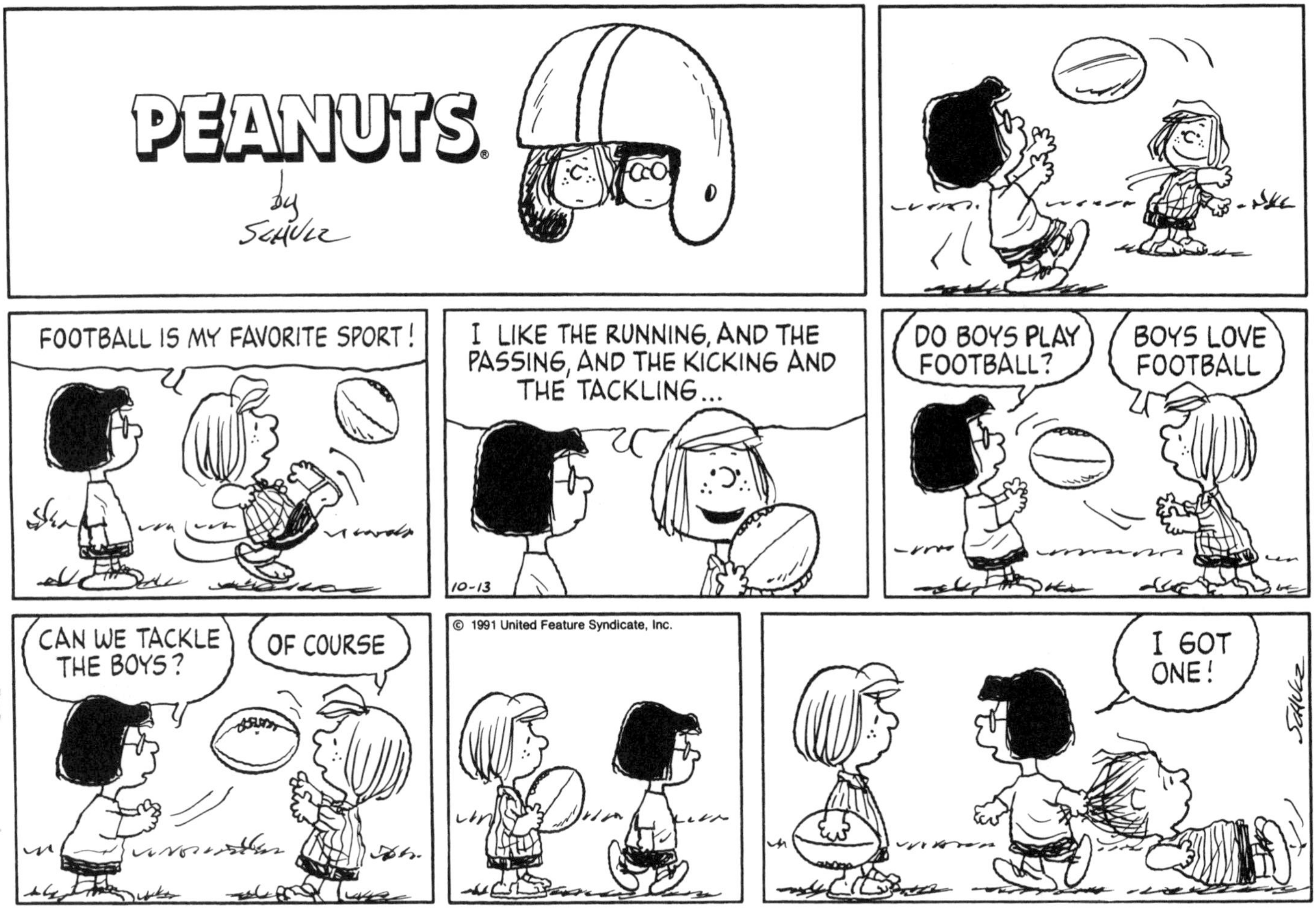
PEANUTS
by SCHULZ
FOOTBALL IS MY FAVORITE SPORT!
I LIKE THE RUNNING, AND THE PASSING, AND THE KICKING AND THE TACKLING...
10-13
DO BOYS PLAY FOOTBALL?
BOYS LOVE FOOTBALL
CAN WE TACKLE THE BOYS?
OF COURSE
© 1991 United Feature Syndicate, Inc.
I GOT ONE!
SCHULZ

YOU KICK THE BALL, MARCIE, AND I'LL CATCH IT..

11-13

WHERE WERE YOU?

OKAY, MARCIE..I'LL KICK THE BALL, AND YOU CATCH IT!

WHAT IF IT HITS ME IN THE STOMACH?

IT WON'T HIT YOU IN THE STOMACH IF YOU'RE CAREFUL...

11-14

MARCIE, HOW CAN YOU CATCH THE BALL IF YOU'RE STANDING BEHIND A TREE?

I DON'T WANT TO GET HIT IN THE STOMACH WITH THE BALL...

11-15

PRETTY GOOD CATCH, HUH, SIR?

MARCIE, I DON'T THINK YOU HAVE WHAT IT TAKES TO BE A FOOTBALL PLAYER..

DON'T BE TOO SURE... I COULD STILL TURN OUT TO BE ANOTHER JOE IOWA!

MONTANA!

WHATEVER

bonk!

WHAT HAPPENED TO MONDAY NOON FOOTBALL?

12-23

YOU MEAN MONDAY NIGHT FOOTBALL..

NO WONDER I NEVER SEE ANY GAMES..

Hockey

PEANUTS

1-31

OKAY, I'M READY... THROW ME THE HOCKEY BALL!

YOU INVITED HER.. I DIDN'T

PEANUTS

I LOVE PLAYING HOCKEY BALL!

2-1

PEANUTS
NOW HERE'S THE WAY WE START THE GAME..
2-2
WE HAVE A "FACE-OFF," SEE... WE LEAN OVER AND TAP OUR STICKS TOGETHER THREE TIMES.... OKAY, LET'S GO...
SMAK!
Tm. Reg. U. S. Pat. Off.—All rights reserved © 1968 by United Feature Syndicate, Inc.
SCHULZ
PENALTY BOX

PEANUTS
Tm. Reg. U. S. Pat. Off.—All rights reserved © 1968 by United Feature Syndicate, Inc.
HERE'S THE WORLD-FAMOUS HOCKEY PLAYER SKATING OUT ONTO THE ICE..
10-8
I PICK UP THE PUCK NEAR THE BLUE LINE...
I SHOOT! THE GOALIE NEVER EVEN SEES THE PUCK!
THEY'RE NOT SLEEPING WELL IN MONTREAL TONIGHT...
SCHULZ

PEANUTS
I DON'T THINK YOU'RE A REAL HOCKEY PLAYER AT ALL..
Tm. Reg. U. S. Pat. Off.—All rights reserved © 1968 by United Feature Syndicate, Inc.
10-9
PROVE TO ME THAT YOU'RE A REAL HOCKEY PLAYER..
YOU'RE A REAL HOCKEY PLAYER!
SCHULZ

PEANUTS

IT'S THE THIRD PERIOD OF THE BIG HOCKEY GAME...

10-10

TEMPERS ARE RUNNING SHORT... A FAN AT RINKSIDE SHOUTS A DEROGATORY REMARK...

WHOP!

WE HOCKEY PLAYERS HATE DEROGATORY REMARKS!

PEANUTS

10-11

HERE'S THE WORLD-FAMOUS HOCKEY PLAYER WINDING UP FOR ONE OF HIS SPECTACULAR SLAP SHOTS...

POW!

SOME PEOPLE HAVE DOGS WHO BARK TOO MUCH... SOME PEOPLE HAVE DOGS WHO CHASE CHICKENS... SOME PEOPLE HAVE DOGS WHO DIG UP FLOWERS...

"GREAT SHOT!" THANK YOU, STAN.. THANK YOU, BOBBY.. THANK YOU, MAURICE...

PEANUTS

HERE'S THE WORLD FAMOUS HOCKEY PLAYER STANDING AT ATTENTION WHILE THEY PLAY THE NATIONAL ANTHEM

12-12

WHAT AN INSPIRING MOMENT !

BEAUTIFUL!

TEN MORE SECONDS, AND I CAN CLOBBER SOMEBODY !

164

165

PEANUTS

HERE'S THE WORLD-FAMOUS HOCKEY GOALIE GUARDING THE NET..

Tm. Reg. U.S. Pat. Off.—All rights reserved
© 1969 by United Feature Syndicate, Inc.

AAUGH!

NOBODY SCORES!

2-10

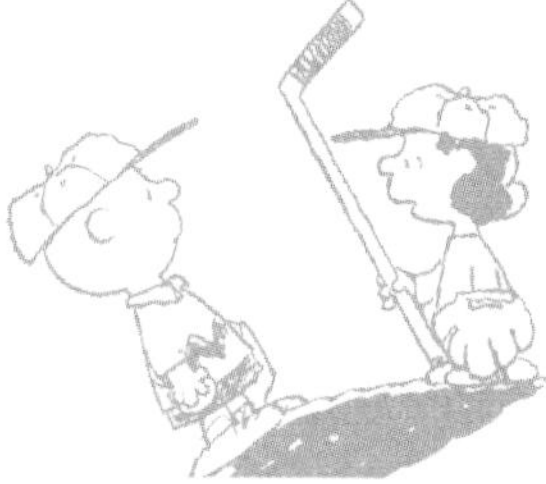
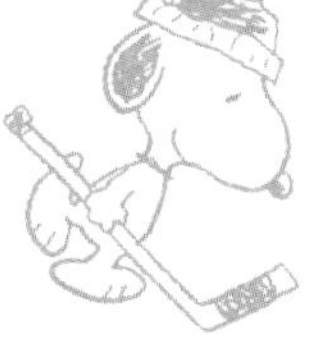
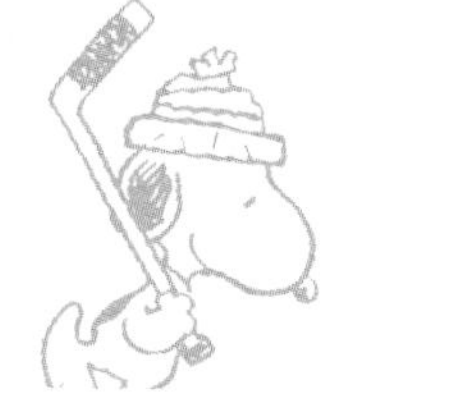

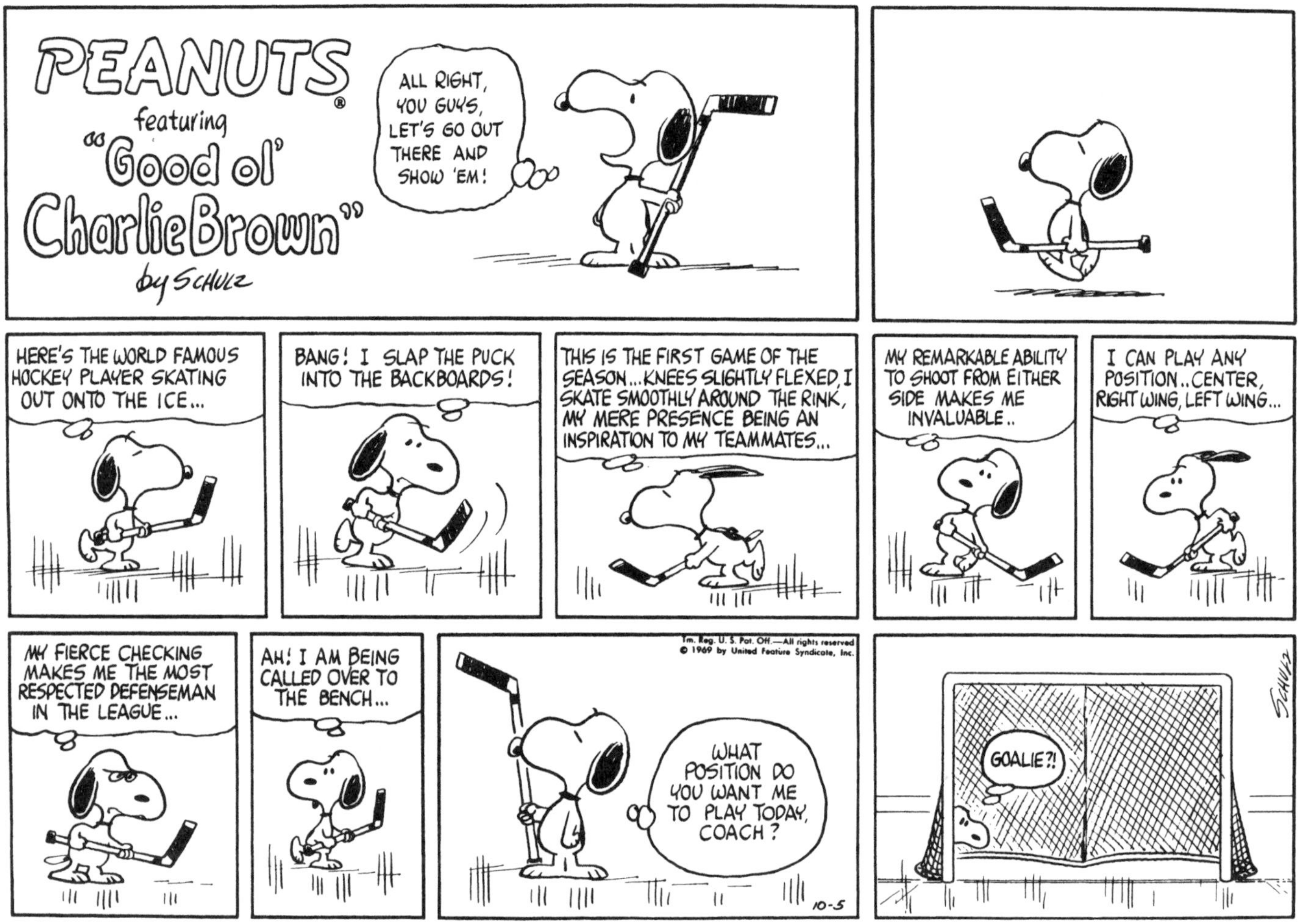
PEANUTS®
featuring "Good ol' Charlie Brown"
by SCHULZ
ALL RIGHT, YOU GUYS, LET'S GO OUT THERE AND SHOW 'EM!
HERE'S THE WORLD FAMOUS HOCKEY PLAYER SKATING OUT ONTO THE ICE...
BANG! I SLAP THE PUCK INTO THE BACKBOARDS!
THIS IS THE FIRST GAME OF THE SEASON...KNEES SLIGHTLY FLEXED, I SKATE SMOOTHLY AROUND THE RINK, MY MERE PRESENCE BEING AN INSPIRATION TO MY TEAMMATES...
MY REMARKABLE ABILITY TO SHOOT FROM EITHER SIDE MAKES ME INVALUABLE..
I CAN PLAY ANY POSITION..CENTER, RIGHT WING, LEFT WING...
MY FIERCE CHECKING MAKES ME THE MOST RESPECTED DEFENSEMAN IN THE LEAGUE...
AH! I AM BEING CALLED OVER TO THE BENCH...
Tm. Reg. U. S. Pat. Off.—All rights reserved © 1969 by United Feature Syndicate, Inc.
WHAT POSITION DO YOU WANT ME TO PLAY TODAY, COACH?
10-5
SCHULZ
GOALIE?!

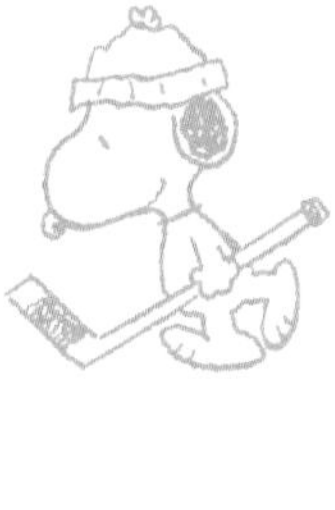
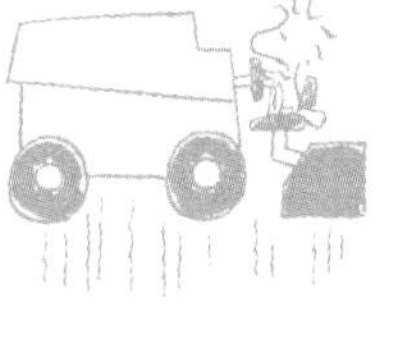
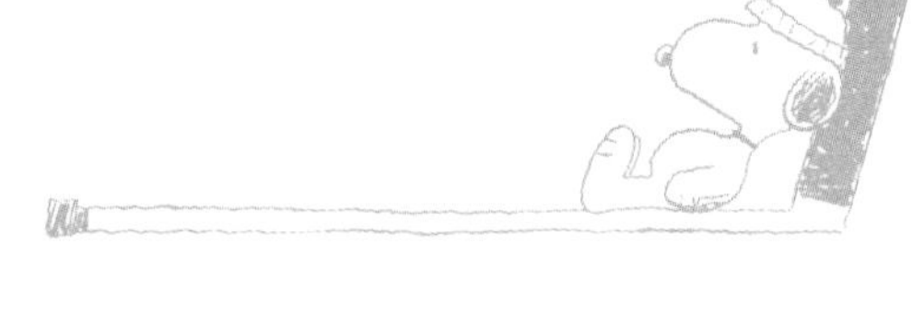

PEANUTS
HERE'S THE WORLD-FAMOUS HOCKEY PLAYER TAPING HIS STICK BEFORE THE GAME..
Tm. Reg. U. S. Pat. Off.—All rights reserved © 1969 by United Feature Syndicate, Inc.
11-3
WE HOCKEY PLAYERS ARE VERY FUSSY ABOUT THE WAY WE TAPE OUR STICKS
SOMETIMES, OF COURSE, WE HAVE A LITTLE TROUBLE WITH THE TAPE...
SCHULZ

PEANUTS
HERE'S THE WORLD-FAMOUS HOCKEY PLAYER SITTING IN THE PENALTY BOX
TWO MINUTES FOR SLASHING... FIVE MINUTES FOR FIGHTING.... TEN MINUTES MISCONDUCT...
I DON'T UNDERSTAND IT..
Tm. Reg. U. S. Pat. Off.—All rights reserved © 1969 by United Feature Syndicate, Inc.
11-5
I'M SO INNOCENT!
SCHULZ

PEANUTS
SHOOT! SHOOT!
BOOOOO! OFFSIDE! MAN IN THE CREASE!
11-7
BOOOOOOO!! HEY, REF, CAN'T YOU SEE?!! HOW ABOUT ICING?!?
SEASON-TICKET HOLDER!
Tm. Reg. U. S. Pat. Off.—All rights reserved © 1969 by United Feature Syndicate, Inc.
SCHULZ

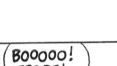

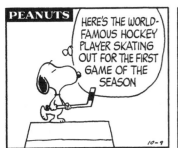

PEANUTS

HERE'S THE WORLD-FAMOUS HOCKEY PLAYER SKATING OUT FOR THE FIRST GAME OF THE SEASON

10-9

AH, THE NATIONAL ANTHEM!

IN A FEW SECONDS, THE GAME WILL START...THE REFEREE WILL DROP THE PUCK...

ONE MINUTE LATER I'LL BE IN THE PENALTY BOX!

SCHULZ

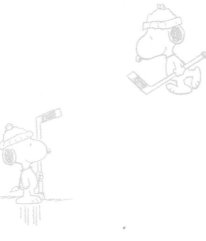

PEANUTS
featuring
"Good ol' Charlie Brown"
by SCHULZ

COOL AND CALM..

HERE'S THE WORLD FAMOUS HOCKEY PLAYER SKATING OUT FOR THE FACE-OFF...

GET THE PUCK!

PASS! SHOOT! CHECK 'IM!

KNOCK HIM DOWN! SHOOT! CLEAR IT! MOVE! SKATE WITH IT!

HIT HIM! SHOOT!!

SKATE! SKATE! ALLONS! ALLONS!

A WHISTLE!

WHO, ME??!

TWO MINUTES FOR TRIPPING, TWO MINUTES FOR ELBOWING, TWO MINUTES FOR SLASHING, TWO MINUTES FOR HIGH-STICKING, TWO MINUTES FOR CHARGING, TWO MINUTES FOR HOLDING, TWO MINUTES FOR CROSS CHECKING, FIVE MINUTES FOR BOARD CHECKING AND A TEN-MINUTE MISCONDUCT...

BUT I'M SUCH A NICE GUY...

12-13

172

PEANUTS featuring "Good ol' Charlie Brown" by SCHULZ

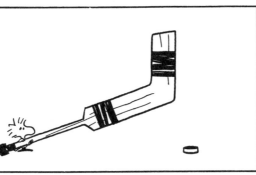

HERE'S THE FACE-OFF FOR THE START OF THE BIG HOCKEY GAME..

OW! HE HIT ME ON THE SHIN!

OW! OOOOO!! OW!

YOU STUPID BIRD! YOU KNEW I DIDN'T HAVE ANY SHIN PADS ON!

OW! OOOO! OW!! OW!! OOOOO!

NOW I HAVE TO SPEND THE NEXT HOUR SITTING IN MY WHIRLPOOL BATH...

SCHULZ

10-10

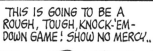

PEANUTS

HERE'S THE WORLD-FAMOUS HOCKEY PLAYER SKATING OUT FOR THE BIG GAME..

10-19

THIS IS GOING TO BE A ROUGH, TOUGH, KNOCK-'EM-DOWN GAME! SHOW NO MERCY..

..BUT REMEMBER NOW...

NO RAISING!

SCHULZ

PEANUTS

HERE'S THE WORLD FAMOUS HOCKEY PLAYER SKATING OUT ONTO THE ICE

TONIGHT'S GAME IS AGAINST DETROIT... WHERE'S GORDIE HOWE?

11-20

GORDIE HOWE ISN'T PLAYING ?! GORDIE HOWE HAS RETIRED ?!?

RATS! I WAS GOING TO GIVE HIM AN ELBOW!

SCHULZ

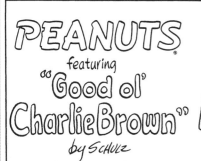

PEANUTS featuring "Good ol' Charlie Brown" by Schulz

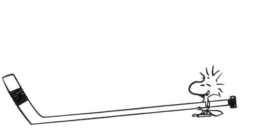

HERE WE ARE SKATING OUT ONTO WOODSTOCK'S HOME ICE FOR THE BIG HOCKEY GAME...

AND HERE COME THE OFFICIALS...

THE REFEREE

THE LINESMEN

11-25

THE GOAL JUDGES AND THE PENALTY TIMEKEEPER

THE OFFICIAL SCORER AND THE GAME TIMEKEEPER!

WHICH BRINGS UP A SLIGHT PROBLEM...

WHERE DO WE PUT THE ORGAN FOR THE NATIONAL ANTHEM?

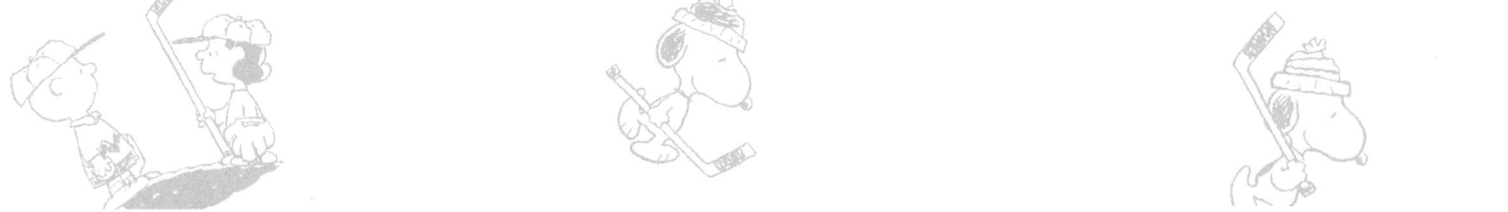

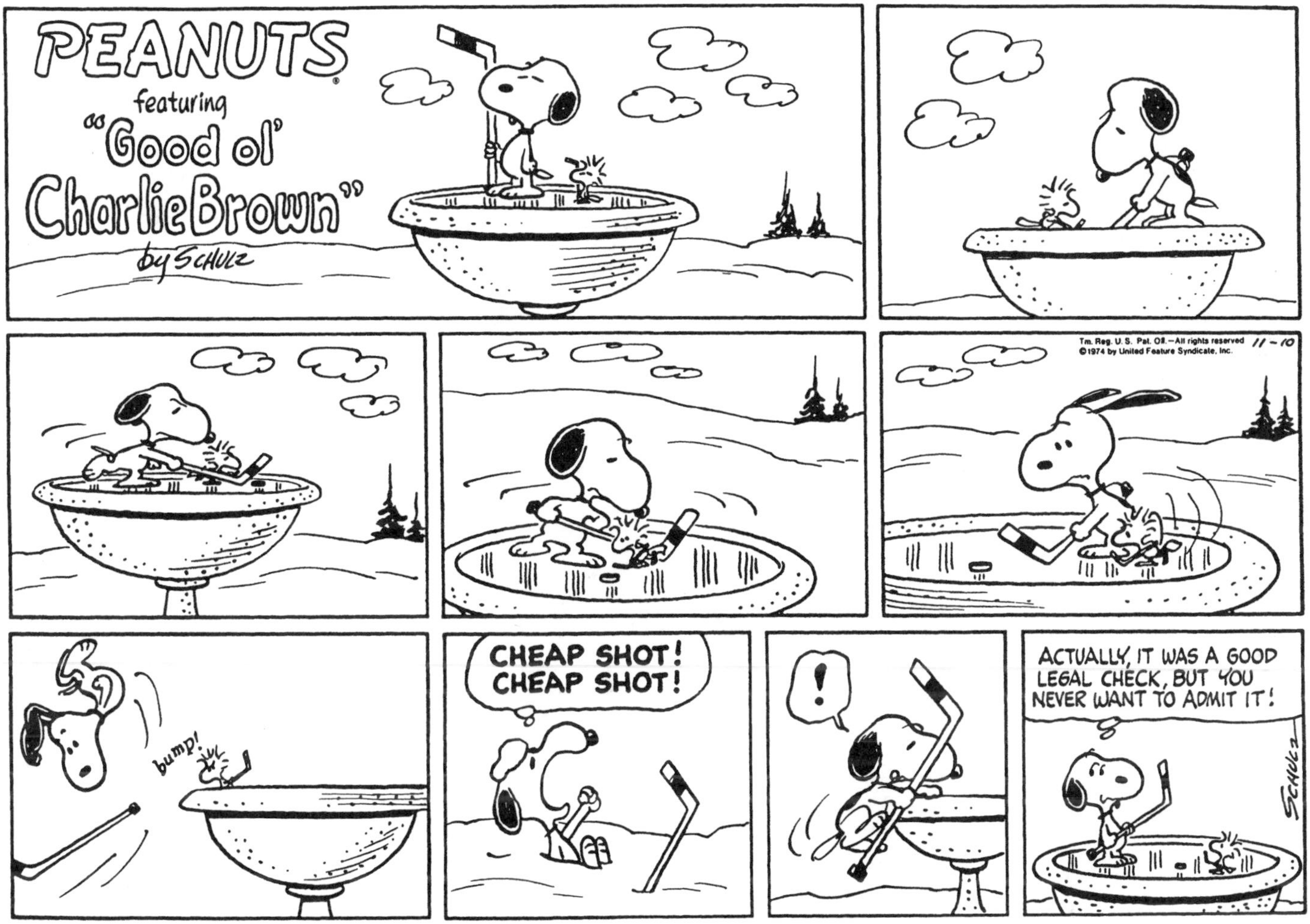

PEANUTS
featuring
"Good ol' Charlie Brown"
by SCHULZ
Tm. Reg. U. S. Pat. Off.—All rights reserved
©1974 by United Feature Syndicate, Inc.
11-10
bump!
CHEAP SHOT! CHEAP SHOT!
!
ACTUALLY, IT WAS A GOOD LEGAL CHECK, BUT YOU NEVER WANT TO ADMIT IT!
SCHULZ

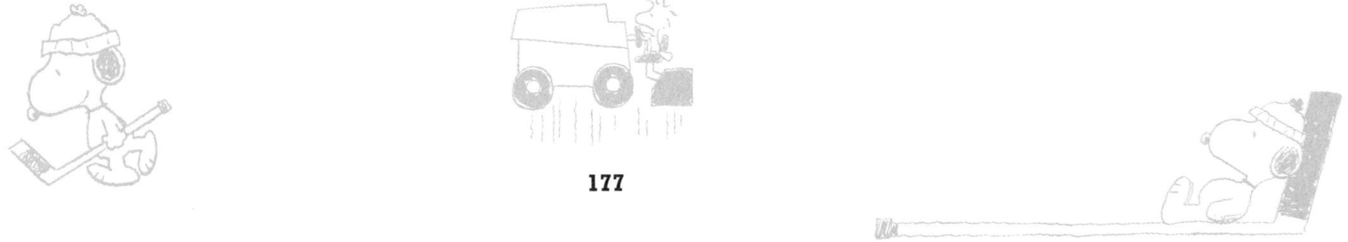

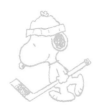

PEANUTS

HERE'S THE WORLD-FAMOUS HOCKEY PLAYER SKATING OUT ONTO THE ICE...

THERE'S A BIG CROWD TONIGHT, AND THEY'RE OUT FOR BLOOD!

HERE'S THE WORLD-FAMOUS HOCKEY PLAYER SKATING OFF THE ICE...

I **NEED** MY BLOOD!

11-27

SCHULZ

179

Panel 1: HOW CAN WE PLAY HOCKEY WITH THAT STUPID GIRL LYING ON THE ICE?

Panel 2: DO YOU GUYS HAVE A PUCK? / SURE! WHAT DO YOU THINK THIS IS?

1-10

Panel 3: GIVE IT TO ME... I WANT TO SHOW YOU A LITTLE TRICK...

Panel 4:

© 1978 United Feature Syndicate, Inc.

Panel 5: I WAS THE HERO! I SCORED THE WINNING GOAL!

11-1

Panel 6: LUCKY SHOT?!

© 1979 United Feature Syndicate, Inc.

Panel 7: I WOULDN'T SAY THAT

Panel 8: JUST BECAUSE IT BOUNCED OFF A WAITRESS IN THE COFFEE SHOP!

YOU DON'T HAVE ANY SHIN PADS?

12-27

YOU CAN'T PLAY HOCKEY WITHOUT SHIN PADS...

I WONDER IF A COUPLE OF MAGAZINES WOULD WORK...

NO, I GUESS NOT

© 1979 United Feature Syndicate, Inc.

THAT STUPID WOODSTOCK!

HE COST US THE HOCKEY GAME...

HE TRIED TO USE MAGAZINES FOR SHIN PADS...SO WHAT HAPPENED?

12-28

THE OTHER TEAM SCORED WHILE HE WAS READING HIS SHIN PADS!

© 1979 United Feature Syndicate, Inc.

Panel 1: SNOOPY? WHERE ARE YOU?

3-2

Panel 2: I THINK HE WENT OFF TO PLAY HOCKEY...

Panel 3: A HOCKEY GAME SHOULDN'T LAST THIS LONG...

© 1981 United Feature Syndicate, Inc.

Panel 4: I HATE THESE ALL-NIGHT PENALTIES!

SCHULZ

Panel 5: HERE WE GO FOR THE FIRST HOCKEY GAME OF THE SEASON...

© 1981 United Feature Syndicate, Inc.

Panel 6: I CAN SEE MYSELF NOW OUT ON THE OL' POND RACING DOWN THE ICE WITH THE PUCK!

Panel 7: 11-2

Panel 8: AFTER IT GETS A LITTLE COLDER

SCHULZ

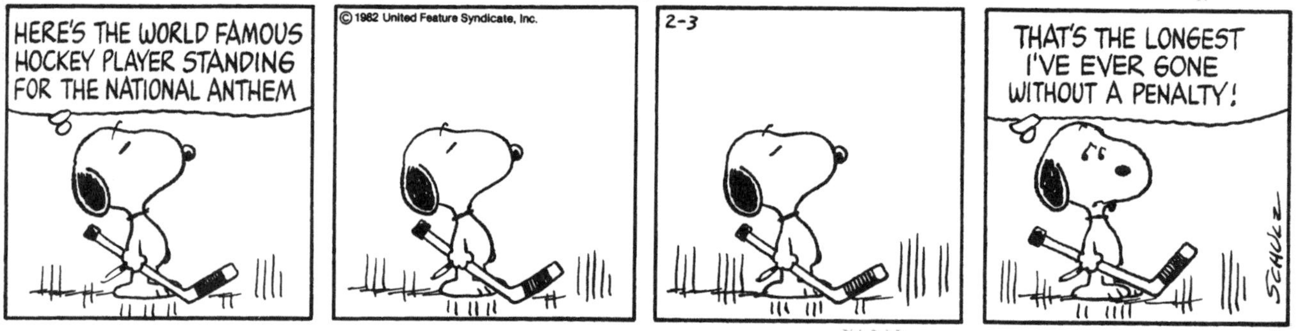
HERE'S THE WORLD FAMOUS HOCKEY PLAYER STANDING FOR THE NATIONAL ANTHEM
© 1982 United Feature Syndicate, Inc.
2-3
THAT'S THE LONGEST I'VE EVER GONE WITHOUT A PENALTY!
SCHULZ

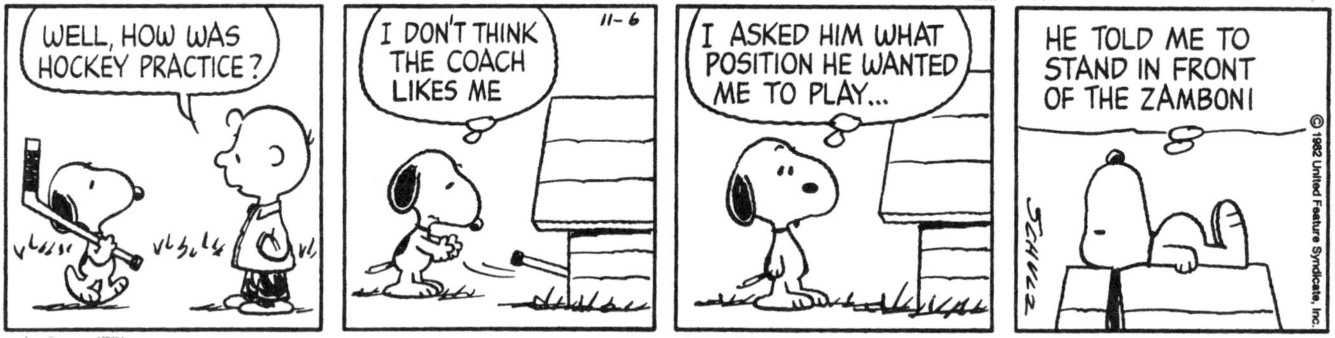
WELL, HOW WAS HOCKEY PRACTICE?
I DON'T THINK THE COACH LIKES ME
11-6
I ASKED HIM WHAT POSITION HE WANTED ME TO PLAY...
HE TOLD ME TO STAND IN FRONT OF THE ZAMBONI
SCHULZ
© 1982 United Feature Syndicate, Inc.

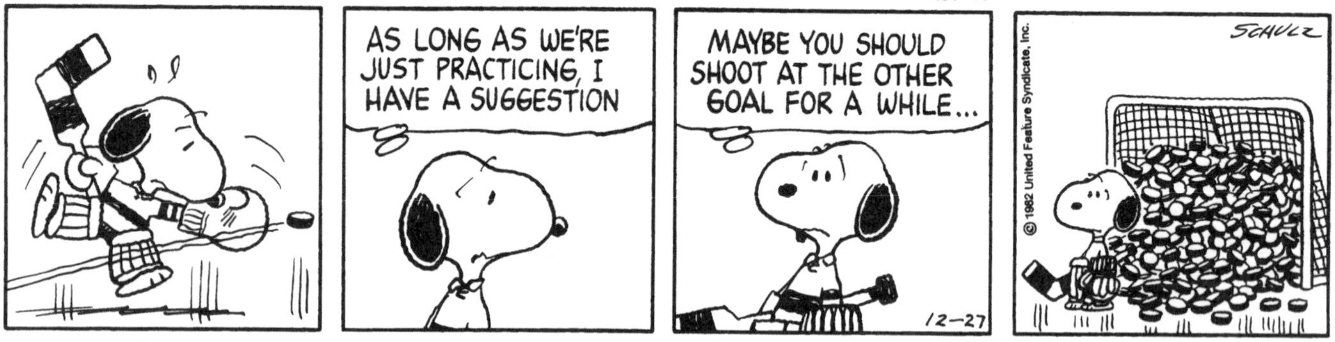
AS LONG AS WE'RE JUST PRACTICING, I HAVE A SUGGESTION
MAYBE YOU SHOULD SHOOT AT THE OTHER GOAL FOR A WHILE...
12-27
SCHULZ
© 1982 United Feature Syndicate, Inc.

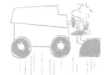

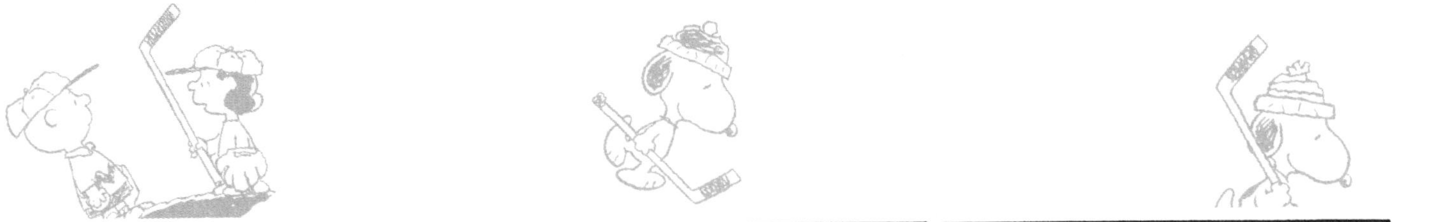

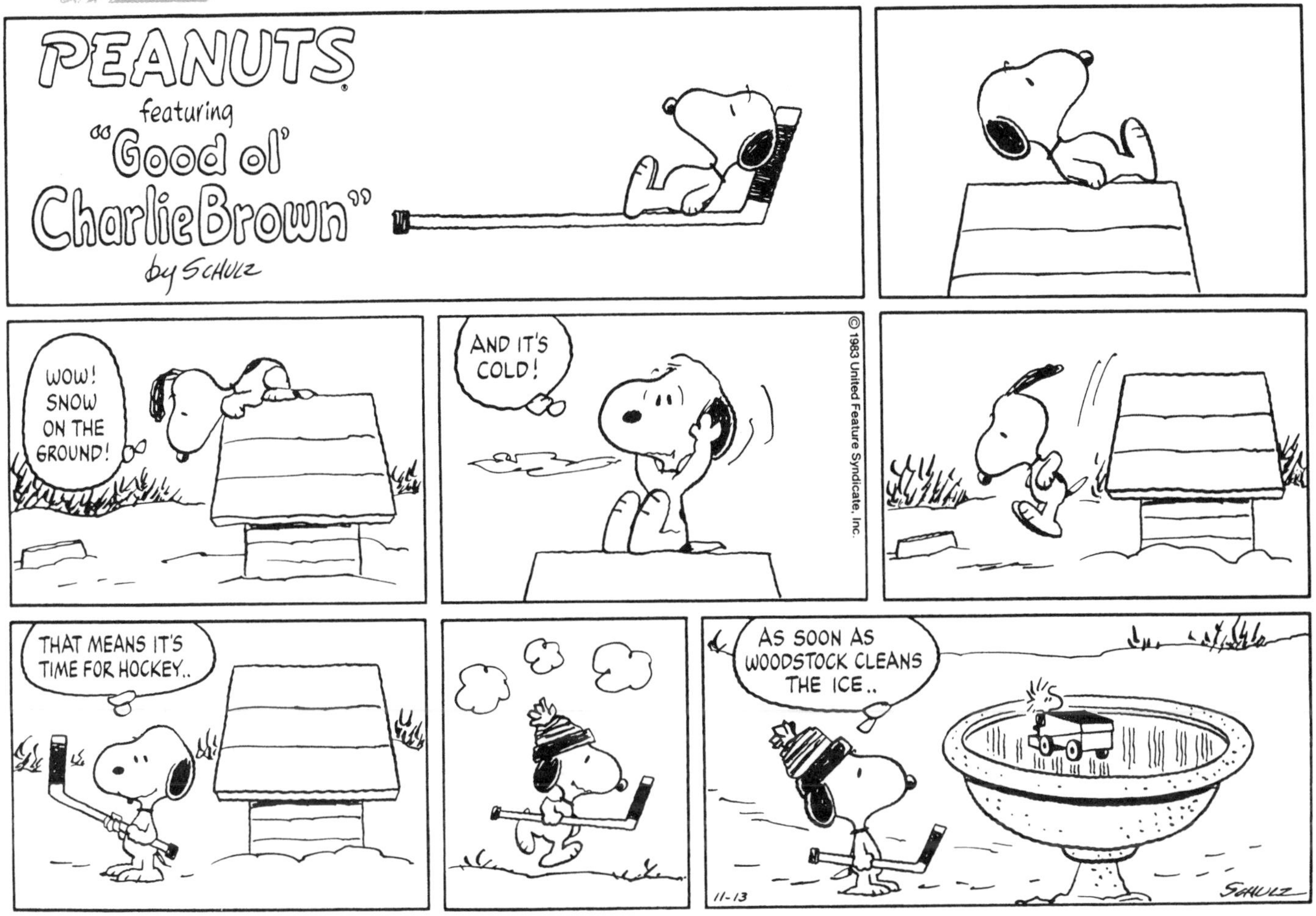
PEANUTS
featuring
"Good ol' Charlie Brown"
by SCHULZ
© 1983 United Feature Syndicate, Inc.
WOW! SNOW ON THE GROUND!
AND IT'S COLD!
THAT MEANS IT'S TIME FOR HOCKEY..
AS SOON AS WOODSTOCK CLEANS THE ICE..
11-13
SCHULZ

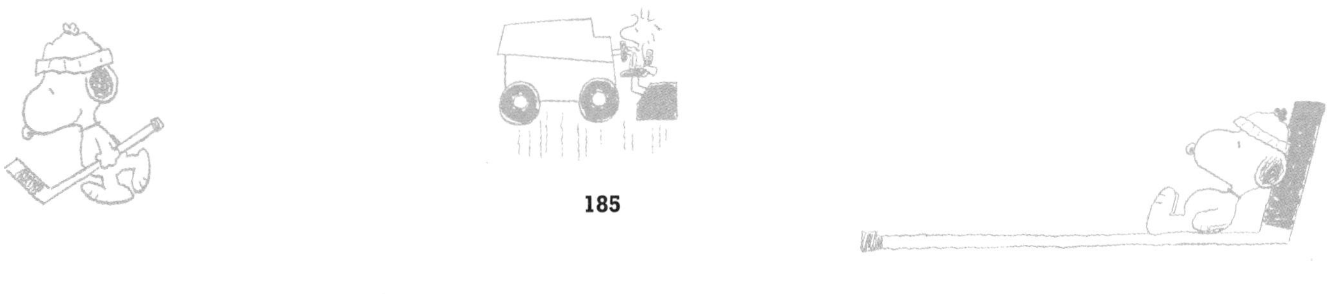

DESERT HOCKEY IS A GREAT GAME..

© 1984 United Feature Syndicate, Inc.

JUST DON'T GET NEAR THE GOALIE

1-19

Panel 1: I HATE PLAYING HOCKEY WITH WOODSTOCK AND HIS FRIENDS...

© 1984 United Feature Syndicate, Inc.

Panel 2: TINY LITTLE PLAYERS WITH TINY LITTLE STICKS...

Panel 3: ..ON A TINY LITTLE RINK..

12-11

Panel 4: ..BUT BIG BODY CHECKS!

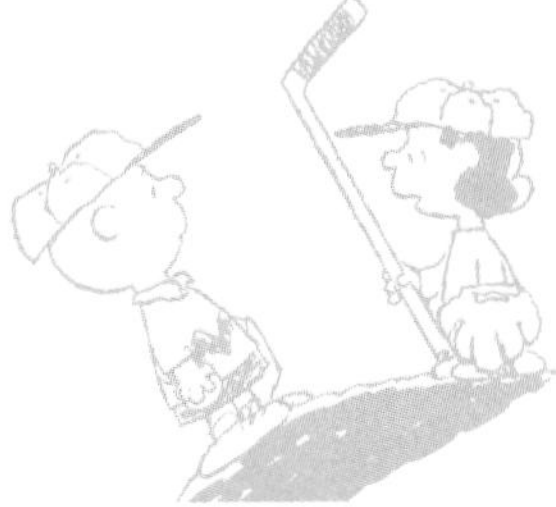

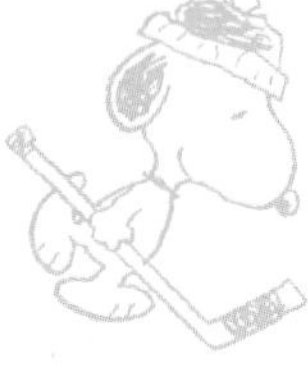

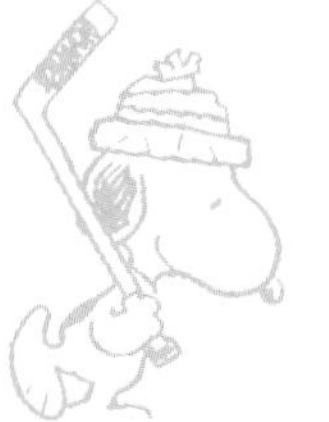

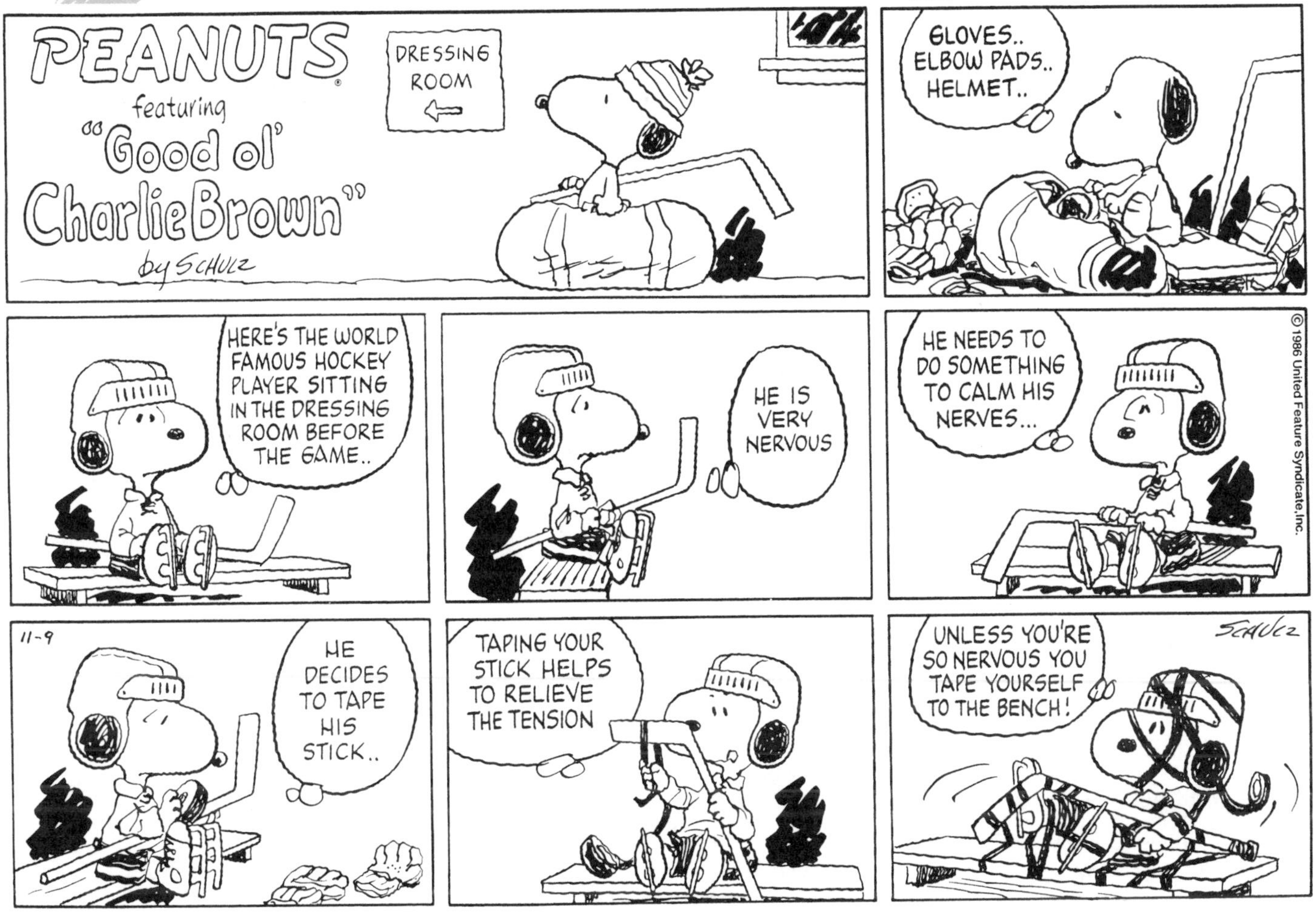
PEANUTS®
featuring "Good ol' Charlie Brown"
by SCHULZ
DRESSING ROOM
GLOVES.. ELBOW PADS.. HELMET..
HERE'S THE WORLD FAMOUS HOCKEY PLAYER SITTING IN THE DRESSING ROOM BEFORE THE GAME..
HE IS VERY NERVOUS
HE NEEDS TO DO SOMETHING TO CALM HIS NERVES...
© 1986 United Feature Syndicate, Inc.
11-9
HE DECIDES TO TAPE HIS STICK..
TAPING YOUR STICK HELPS TO RELIEVE THE TENSION
UNLESS YOU'RE SO NERVOUS YOU TAPE YOURSELF TO THE BENCH!
SCHULZ

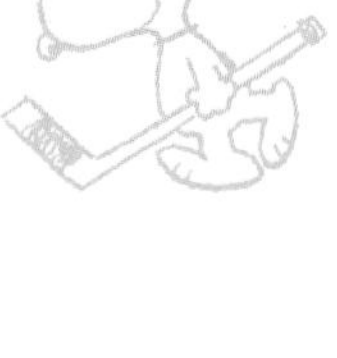

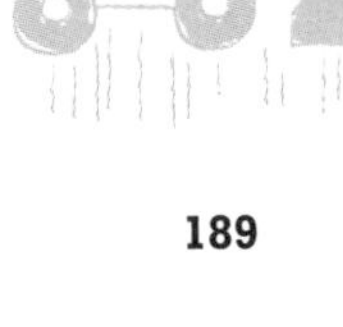

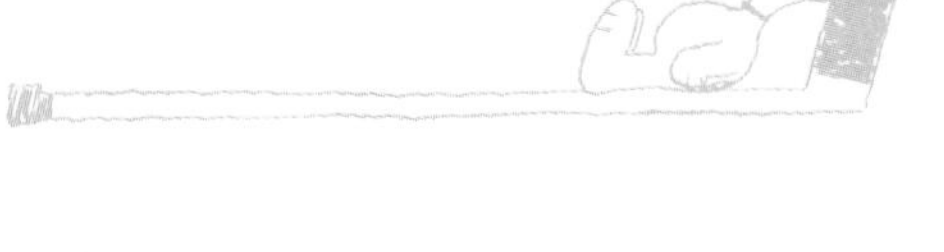

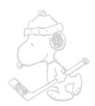

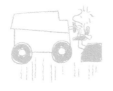

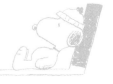

HERE'S THE WORLD FAMOUS HOCKEY PLAYER RACING DOWN THE ICE!

HE FAKES A SLAPSHOT..

11-29

BUT IT DOESN'T FAZE THE GOALIE..

HE KNOWS I DON'T HAVE A SLAPSHOT..

ANOTHER BIG HOCKEY GAME TODAY..

12-17

SOMEHOW, WE ALWAYS END UP PLAYING ON WOODSTOCK'S HOME ICE

IT WOULDN'T BE SO BAD EXCEPT FOR ONE THING..

HE NEVER LETS ME DRIVE THE ZAMBONI !

SOMEONE ON YOUR HOCKEY TEAM SAID YOU AREN'T AS FAST AS YOU USED TO BE..

BUT DON'T WORRY ABOUT IT...

ONE OF THE OTHER PLAYERS STUCK UP FOR YOU..

11-14

HE SAID YOU NEVER WERE VERY FAST !

© 1988 United Feature Syndicate, Inc.
12-27
WHY DO TWELVE BIRDS THINK THEY CAN PLAY HOCKEY ON ONE FROZEN WATER DISH?
SCHULZ

I HATE PLAYING HOCKEY ON WOODSTOCK'S HOME ICE..
1-30
AT OTHER RINKS THEY PLAY THE NATIONAL ANTHEM BEFORE THE GAME...
© 1989 United Feature Syndicate, Inc.
HERE WE HAVE TO DO THE "HOKEYPOKEY"!
SCHULZ

THIS IS A BIG GAME TODAY..
© 1989 United Feature Syndicate, Inc.
12-1
EVERY SEAT IN THE ARENA IS TAKEN..
SCHULZ

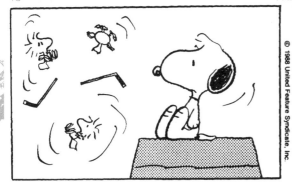

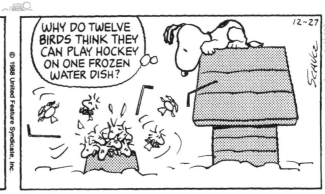

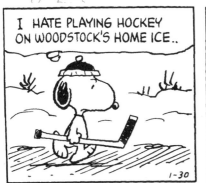

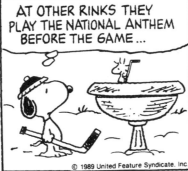

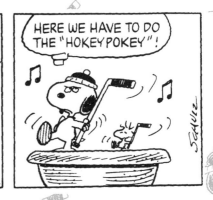

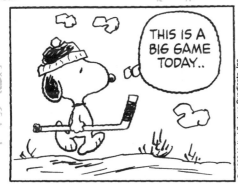

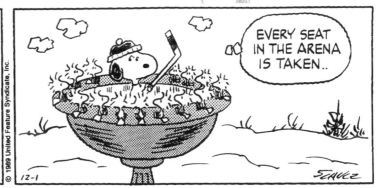

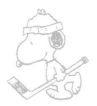

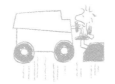

193

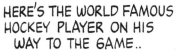

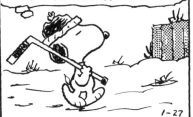

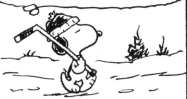

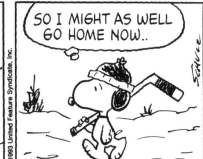

HERE'S THE WORLD FAMOUS HOCKEY PLAYER ON HIS WAY TO THE GAME..
1-27
UNDER THE NEW RULES IF YOU START A FIGHT, YOU ARE AUTOMATICALLY EJECTED FROM THE GAME...
© 1993 United Feature Syndicate, Inc.
SO I MIGHT AS WELL GO HOME NOW..
SCHULZ

MY DAD TOOK ME TO MY FIRST HOCKEY GAME LAST NIGHT..
IT WAS REALLY GREAT..
© 1993 United Feature Syndicate, Inc.
9-21
I LOVED WATCHING THE ZAMBONI GO AROUND..
YOU'RE VERY WEIRD, MARCIE..
SCHULZ

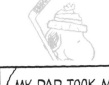

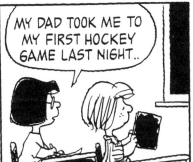

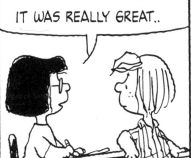

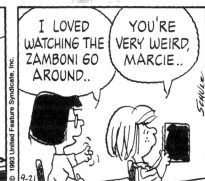

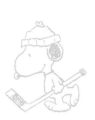

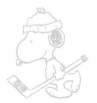

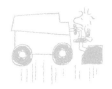

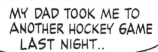

MY DAD TOOK ME TO ANOTHER HOCKEY GAME LAST NIGHT..

I GOT TO MEET THE MAN WHO DRIVES THE ZUCCHINI..

ZAMBONI..

WHATEVER

9-27

MY DAD'S TAKING ME TO ANOTHER HOCKEY GAME TONIGHT..

I THINK WE'RE GOING TO SEE THE "MIGHTY FLAMINGOS"

"DUCKS," MARCIE

SOMETHING LIKE THAT..

DON'T GET RUN OVER BY THE ZUCCHINI..

ZAMBONI, SIR..

YOU'RE GETTING THERE, MARCIE

MY DAD AND I WENT TO ANOTHER HOCKEY GAME LAST NIGHT..

IT'S AMAZING HOW FAST THE PLAYERS SKATE UP AND DOWN THE COURT..

RINK

NEXT WEEK WE'RE GOING TO A BASKETBALL RINK

ALL RIGHT, I'LL ASK HIM..

THAT LITTLE KID WANTS YOU TO COME OUT AND PLAY HOCKEY..

OKAY, WE'LL PLAY THREE TWENTY-MINUTE PERIODS, AND I GET TO DRIVE THE ZAMBONI!

1-13

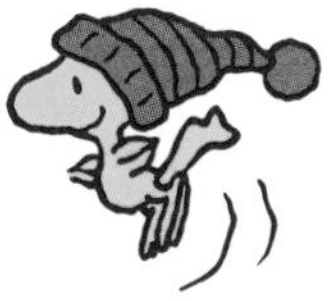

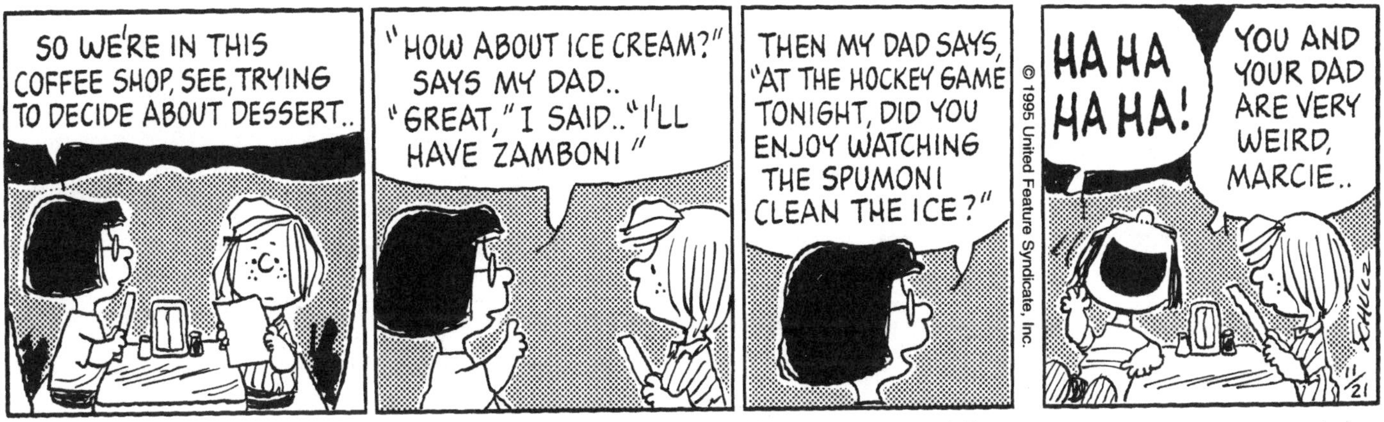
SO WE'RE IN THIS COFFEE SHOP, SEE, TRYING TO DECIDE ABOUT DESSERT..
"HOW ABOUT ICE CREAM?" SAYS MY DAD.. "GREAT," I SAID.."I'LL HAVE ZAMBONI"
THEN MY DAD SAYS, "AT THE HOCKEY GAME TONIGHT, DID YOU ENJOY WATCHING THE SPUMONI CLEAN THE ICE?"
© 1995 United Feature Syndicate, Inc.
HA HA HA HA!
YOU AND YOUR DAD ARE VERY WEIRD, MARCIE..
SCHULZ
11/21

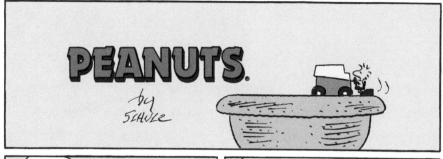

© 1997 United Feature Syndicate, Inc.

1-12

www.unitedmedia.com

PEANUTS
by SCHULZ
© 1997 United Feature Syndicate, Inc.
www.unitedmedia.com
BEST GAME WE'VE EVER HAD!
SCHULZ
2-2

Tennis

205

206

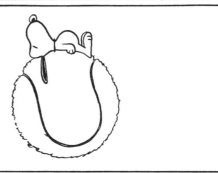

PEANUTS Tm. Reg. U.S. Pat. Off. All rights reserved. © 1973 by United Feature Syndicate, Inc.

BOUNCE
BOUNCE
BOUNCE

BOUNCE BOUNCE BOUNCE
BOUNCE BOUNCE
BOUNCE
BOUNCE
BOUNCE

7-7

IT UNNERVES YOUR OPPONENT IF YOU BOUNCE THE BALL A LOT BEFORE YOU SERVE!

SCHULZ

The comic strip:

| PEANUTS |
HERE'S THE WORLD-FAMOUS TENNIS PLAYER WALKING OUT ONTO THE COURT..
7-18

THIS IS THE MOST IMPORTANT MATCH OF THE SEASON...

THIS IS THE BIG ONE! THIS IS IT!!

FIRST SERVE IN?

PEANUTS

I'VE BEEN ANXIOUS TO HAVE WOODSTOCK SEE MY NEW RACKET...

7-24

HOW DISAPPOINTING...HE HATES MY GUT!

Schulz

PEANUTS

8-7

OVERHEAD SMASH!

Schulz

PEANUTS

I HOPE HE DOUBLE-FAULTS...

PLEASE DOUBLE-FAULT! DOUBLE-FAULT! DOUBLE-FAULT! DOUBLE-FAULT!

THAT WAS TOO BAD!

9-3

PEANUTS

RATS!

4-6

HE WHO LIVES BY THE LOB DIES BY THE LOB!

PEANUTS

4-13

OUT ?!!

BAD CALL !

IT HIT THE EXACT MIDDLE OF THE OUTER PART OF THE EDGE OF THE FRONT PART OF THE BACK PART OF THE LINE !

PEANUTS

6-20

RATS!

I WOULD HAVE WON, BUT I GOT OFF TO A BAD FINISH!

POW!

HE WHO LIVES BY THE POACH DIES BY THE POACH!

WHAM!

RATS!

I SHOULD'VE HAD THAT POINT, AND I SHOULD'VE HAD THAT GAME AND I SHOULD'VE HAD THAT SET...

UNFORTUNATELY, WE'RE NOT PLAYING "SHOULD'VES"!

!!!!

PAW FAULT ?!!

PEANUTS

7-20

OKAY, HERE COMES THE BIGGIE!

I HAVE A SUGGESTION...LET'S NOT PLAY "FIRST SERVE IN"

PEANUTS

THE BIGGIE WAS A SMALLIE!

8-2

216

PEANUTS

AH!

THIS IS GOING TO BE A GOOD DAY...

I GOT THE NEW CAN OF BALLS OPEN WITHOUT CUTTING MYSELF!

9-19

PEANUTS

HA!

I GOT 'IM NOW!

TWO GOOD SERVES AND A COUPLE OF BAD CALLS, AND I'M IN!

10-26

CLANK

THE NEXT TIME YOU SERVE, TAKE THE BALLS OUT OF THE CAN!

SCHULZ

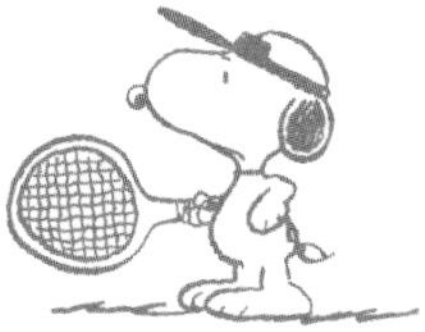
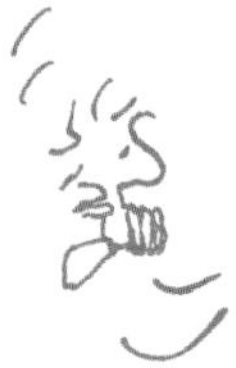
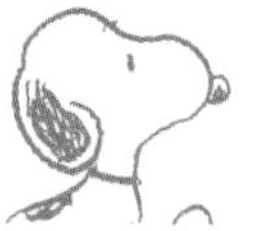
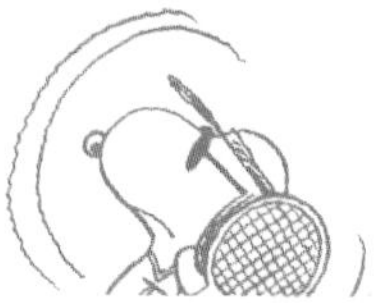

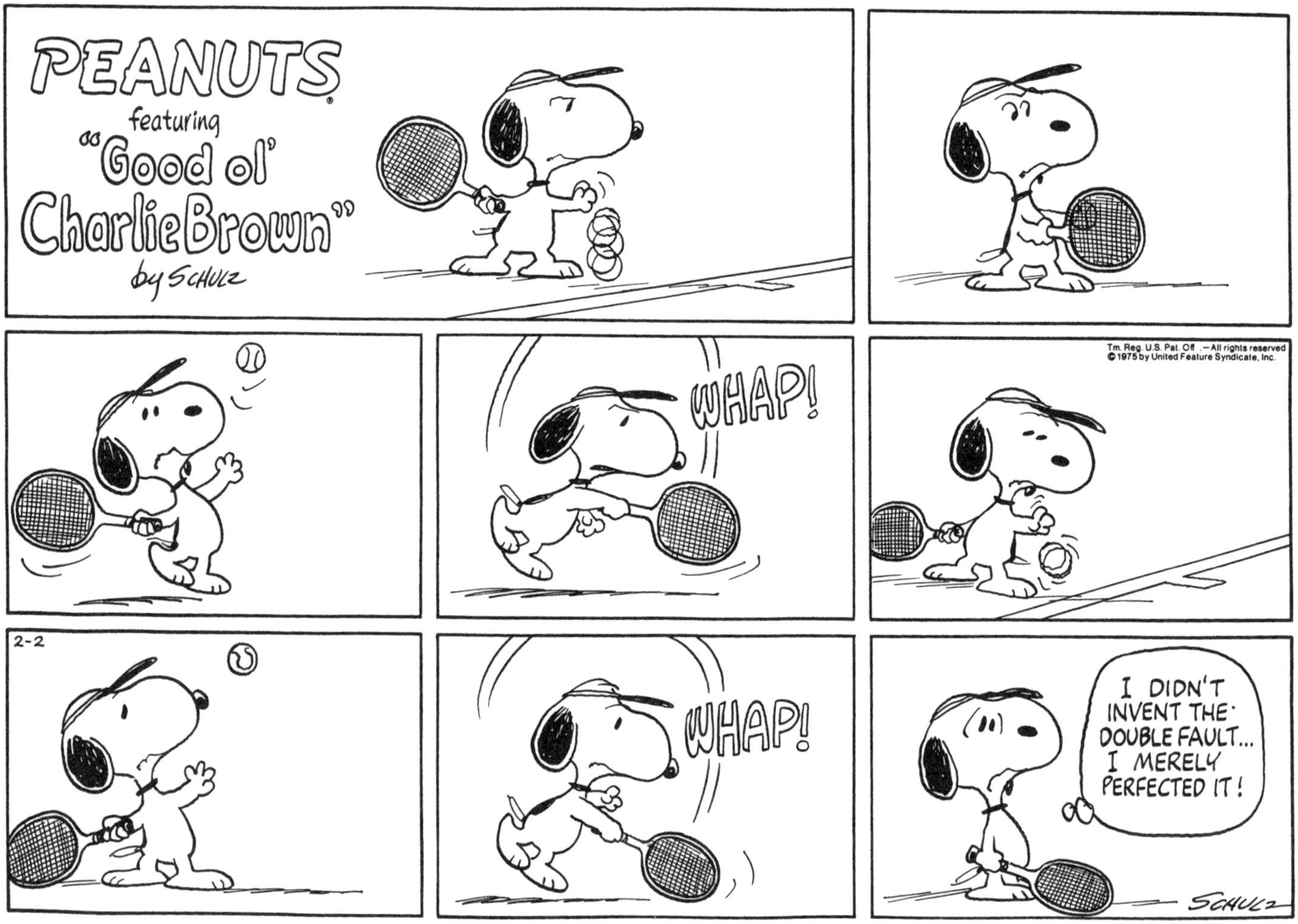
PEANUTS
featuring
"Good ol' Charlie Brown"
by SCHULZ
WHAP!
Tm. Reg. U.S. Pat. Off.—All rights reserved
© 1975 by United Feature Syndicate, Inc.
2-2
WHAP!
I DIDN'T INVENT THE DOUBLE FAULT... I MERELY PERFECTED IT!
SCHULZ

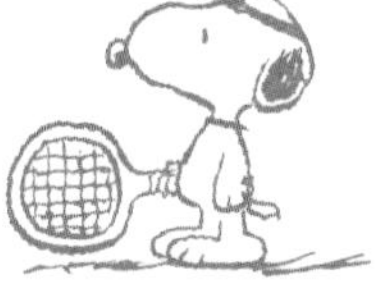
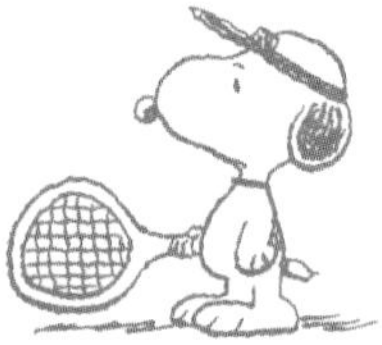
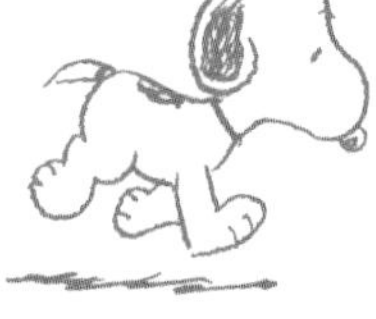
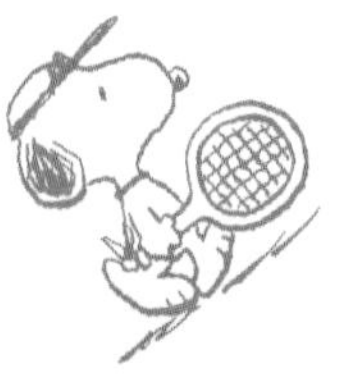

PEANUTS
featuring
"Good ol' CharlieBrown"
by SCHULZ

3-9

I HATE PLAYING ON A WINDY DAY!!

SCHULZ

PEANUTS
6-2
Tm. Reg. U.S. Pat. Off.—All rights reserved © 1975 by United Feature Syndicate, Inc.
POW!
ACED HIM AGAIN!
SCHULZ

PEANUTS
HOLD IT! THERE'S A BUG CROSSING THE COURT!
6-3
HURRY UP, YOU STUPID BUG! DO YOU WANNA GET STEPPED ON? C'MON, YOU'RE HOLDING UP THE GAME!
WHAT?
Tm. Reg. U.S. Pat. Off.—All rights reserved © 1975 by United Feature Syndicate, Inc.
LOVE-THIRTY... WE'RE FOUR-ALL IN THE FIRST SET!
SCHULZ

PEANUTS
HOLD IT! HERE COMES THAT BUG ACROSS THE COURT AGAIN..
6-4
WHAT? NO, THIS ISN'T HIGHWAY TWELVE...THIS IS A TENNIS COURT...
HIGHWAYS ARE BLACK... TENNIS COURTS ARE GREEN..
Tm. Reg. U.S. Pat. Off.—All rights reserved © 1975 by United Feature Syndicate, Inc.
IT WAS THE STRIPE DOWN THE MIDDLE THAT CONFUSED HIM.......SERVICE!!
SCHULZ

PEANUTS
OH, GOOD GRIEF... A LOB!
6-5
I HOPE IT GOES OUT! I HOPE IT GOES OUT!
Tm. Reg. U.S. Pat. Off.—All rights reserved © 1975 by United Feature Syndicate, Inc.
I HOPED IT OUT!
SCHULZ

PEANUTS
AAUGH!! THIS GAME DRIVES ME CRAZY!
6-6
HAVE YOU EVER CONSIDERED SWITCHING TO A METAL RACKET?
Tm. Reg. U.S. Pat. Off.—All rights reserved © 1975 by United Feature Syndicate, Inc.
NEVER!
A METAL RACKET HURTS WHEN YOU BITE IT!
SCHULZ

PEANUTS
WHAP!
AAUGH!
Tm. Reg. U.S. Pat. Off.—All rights reserved © 1975 by United Feature Syndicate, Inc.
6-7
I'M SERIOUSLY THINKING OF NOT TAKING MY TENNIS SO SERIOUS...
SCHULZ

PEANUTS
HOLD IT! THERE'S A BUG CROSSING THE COURT!
C'MON, BUG, HURRY UP BEFORE YOU GET STOMPED ON...
WHAT'S THAT? OH.... ALL RIGHT, THANK YOU...
HE SAID I SHOULD BEND MY KNEES MORE
7-15
SCHULZ

PEANUTS
9-9
Tm. Reg. U.S. Pat. Off.—All rights reserved ©1975 by United Feature Syndicate, Inc.
HE'S BEEN HITTING BALLS AGAINST THAT GARAGE FOR WEEKS...
HE'S PRACTICING FOR A MIXED-DOUBLES TOURNAMENT
OH? WHO'S GOING TO BE HIS PARTNER?
THE GARAGE!
SCHULZ

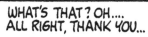

PEANUTS

I HEARD YOU AND THE GARAGE PLAYED IN A MIXED-DOUBLES TOURNAMENT

HOW DID YOU COME OUT? DID YOU PLAY WELL?

I PLAYED GREAT...

BUT THE GARAGE CHOKED!

9-15

PEANUTS

HITTING BALLS AGAINST THE GARAGE AGAIN, I SEE...

I FIND IT INTERESTING THAT YOU SHOULD HAVE THE GARAGE FOR A PARTNER WHEN YOU PLAY MIXED-DOUBLES

I WAS ALSO WONDERING WHAT THE BEST PART OF HIS GAME IS...

HE NEVER FOOT-FAULTS!

9-16

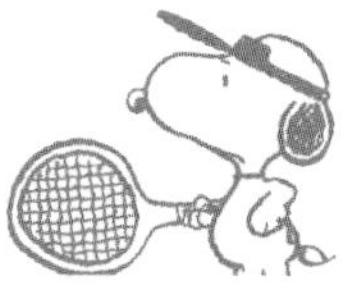
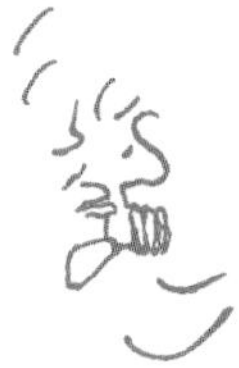
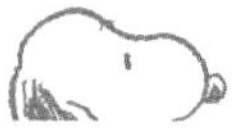
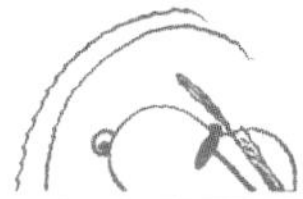

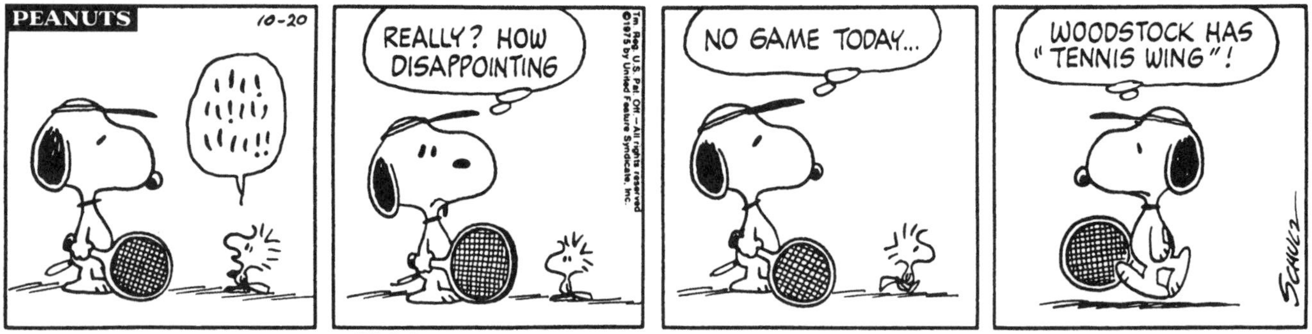
PEANUTS
10-20
Tm. Reg. U.S. Pat. Off.—All rights reserved © 1975 by United Feature Syndicate, Inc.
!!! !!!! !!!!!
REALLY? HOW DISAPPOINTING
NO GAME TODAY...
WOODSTOCK HAS "TENNIS WING"!
SCHULZ

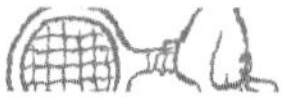
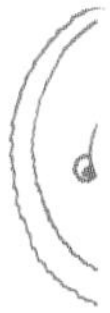

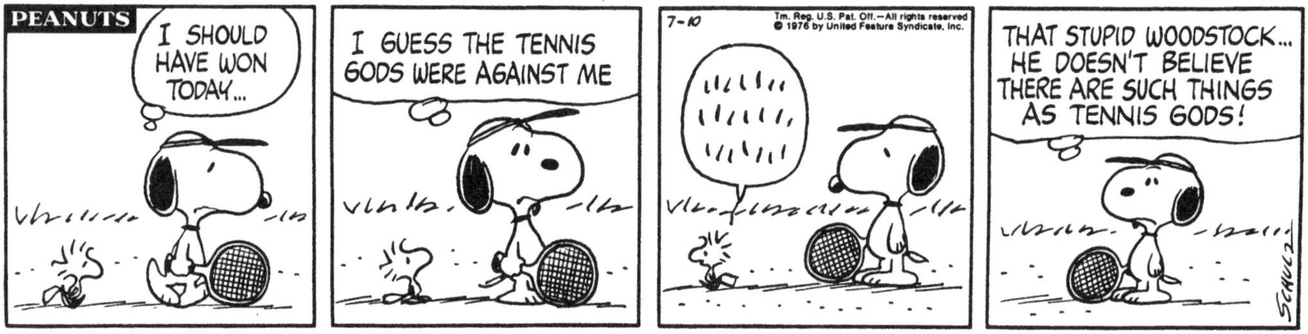
PEANUTS
I SHOULD HAVE WON TODAY...
I GUESS THE TENNIS GODS WERE AGAINST ME
7-10
Tm. Reg. U.S. Pat. Off.—All rights reserved © 1976 by United Feature Syndicate, Inc.
THAT STUPID WOODSTOCK... HE DOESN'T BELIEVE THERE ARE SUCH THINGS AS TENNIS GODS!
SCHULZ

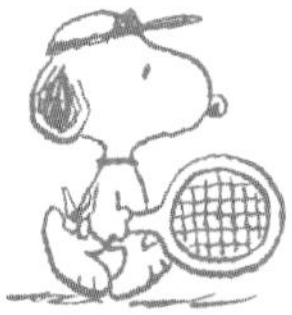
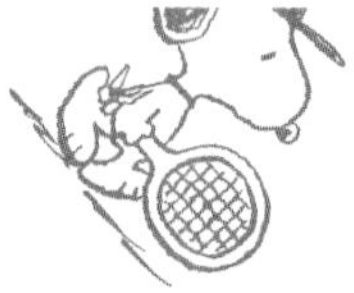
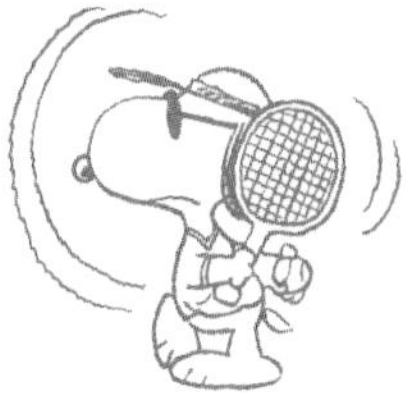
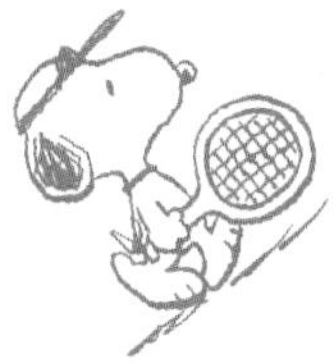
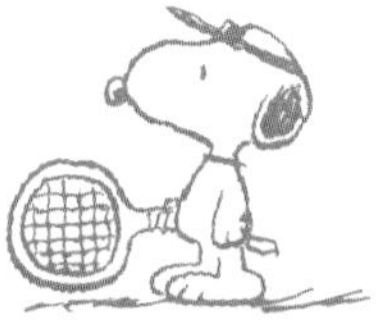
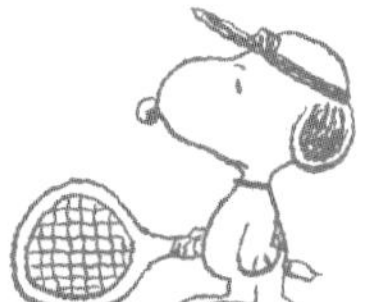
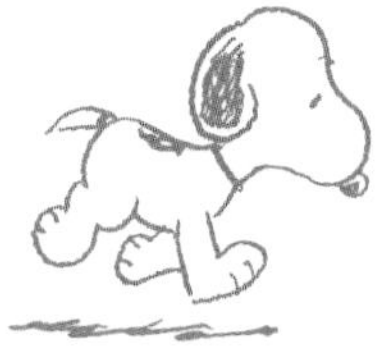
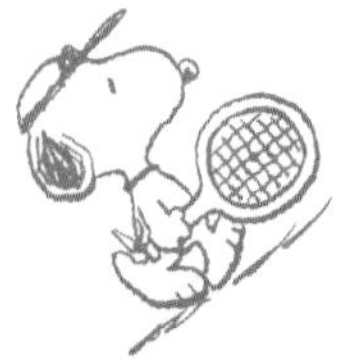

PEANUTS
Tm. Reg. U.S. Pat. Off.—All rights reserved © 1976 by United Feature Syndicate, Inc.
HERE'S A TENNIS TOURNAMENT YOU SHOULD ENTER...
AFTER THE TOURNAMENT IS OVER, THEY'RE HAVING A BIG BANQUET
7-14
I NEVER ATTEND TENNIS BANQUETS
IF I LOSE, I'M ALWAYS TOO MAD TO EAT!
SCHULZ

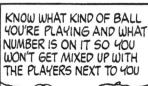

PEANUTS
Tm. Reg. U.S. Pat. Off.—All rights reserved © 1976 by United Feature Syndicate, Inc.
HERE'S SOMETHING YOU SHOULD THINK ABOUT WHEN YOU'RE PLAYING TENNIS
KNOW WHAT KIND OF BALL YOU'RE PLAYING AND WHAT NUMBER IS ON IT SO YOU WON'T GET MIXED UP WITH THE PLAYERS NEXT TO YOU
8-30
MINE HAS A LITTLE SNOWMAN ON IT...
THAT'S A NUMBER EIGHT
ANYONE FINDS A BALL WITH A SNOWMAN ON IT, IT'S MINE!!!
SCHULZ

PEANUTS featuring "Good ol' CharlieBrown" by SCHULZ

Please proceed to your next lesson.

We are very pleased with your progress.

?

A CORRESPONDENCE COURSE?! IN TENNIS?!?

HOW IN THE WORLD CAN YOU STUDY TENNIS BY MAIL?

SIMPLE! WE READ THE TEXTBOOKS CAREFULLY...

LESSON IV

10-10

WE STUDY PHOTOS...

WE TAKE QUIZZES..

AND EVERY AFTERNOON WE GO DOWN TO THE CORNER...

SCHULZ

..AND HIT BALLS AGAINST THE MAILBOX!

US MAIL

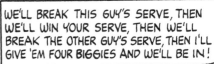

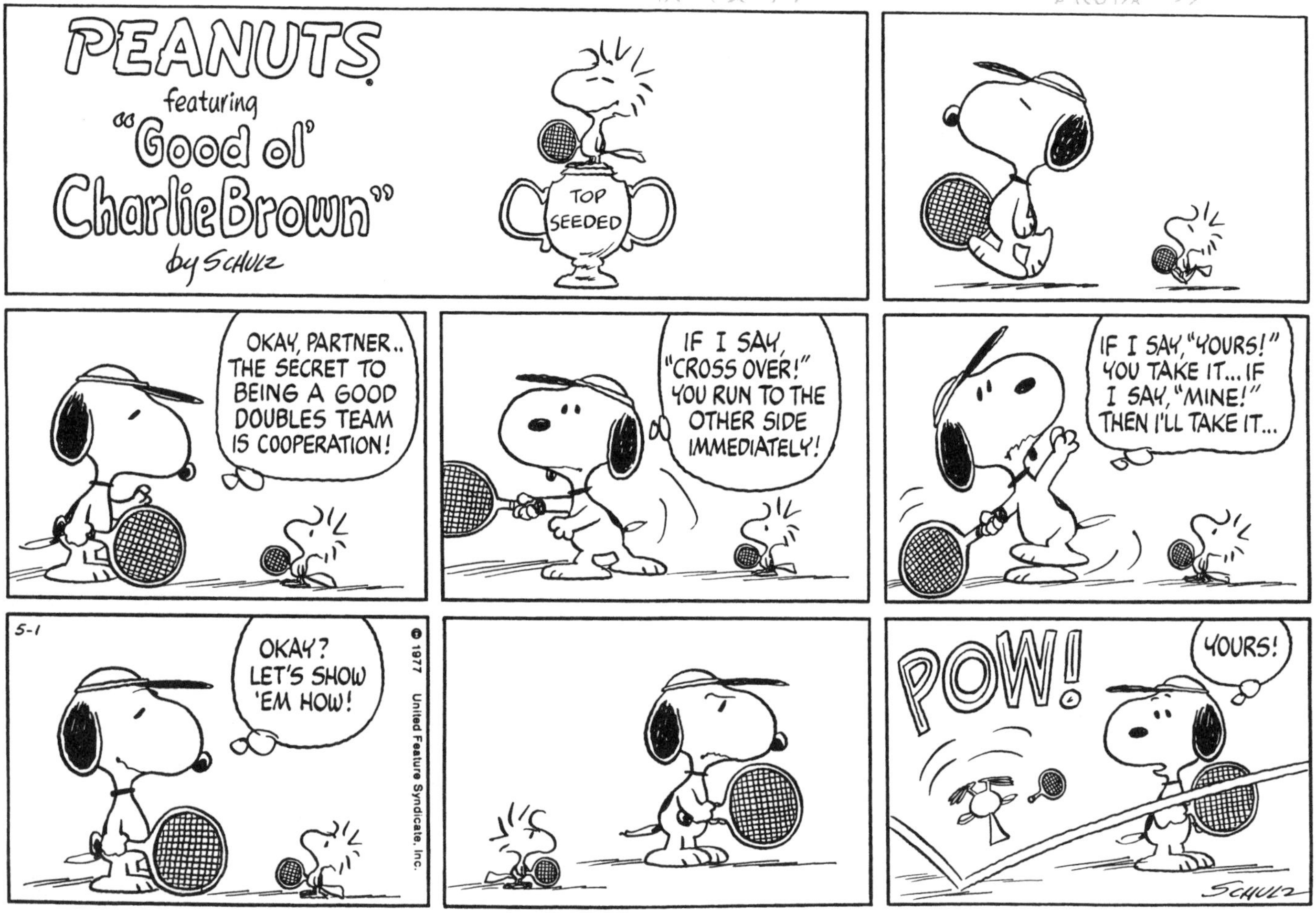
PEANUTS
featuring
"Good ol' CharlieBrown"
by SCHULZ
TOP SEEDED
OKAY, PARTNER.. THE SECRET TO BEING A GOOD DOUBLES TEAM IS COOPERATION!
IF I SAY, "CROSS OVER!" YOU RUN TO THE OTHER SIDE IMMEDIATELY!
IF I SAY, "YOURS!" YOU TAKE IT... IF I SAY, "MINE!" THEN I'LL TAKE IT...
5-1
OKAY? LET'S SHOW 'EM HOW!
© 1977 United Feature Syndicate, Inc.
POW!
YOURS!
SCHULZ

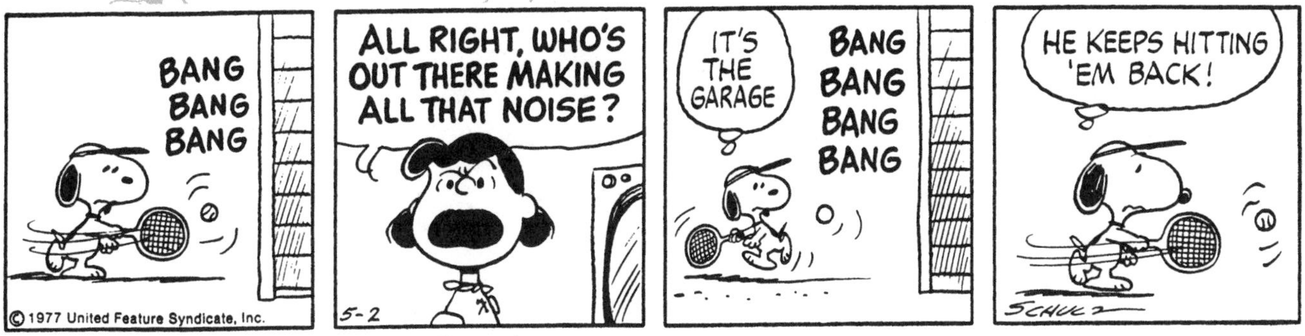
BANG
BANG
BANG
© 1977 United Feature Syndicate, Inc.
ALL RIGHT, WHO'S OUT THERE MAKING ALL THAT NOISE?
5-2
IT'S THE GARAGE
BANG
BANG
BANG
BANG
HE KEEPS HITTING 'EM BACK!
SCHULZ

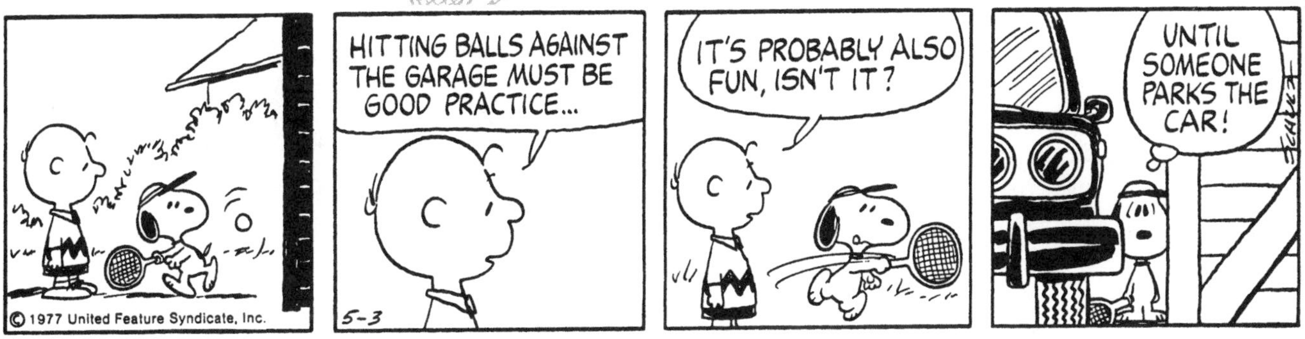
© 1977 United Feature Syndicate, Inc.
HITTING BALLS AGAINST THE GARAGE MUST BE GOOD PRACTICE...
5-3
IT'S PROBABLY ALSO FUN, ISN'T IT?
UNTIL SOMEONE PARKS THE CAR!
SCHULZ

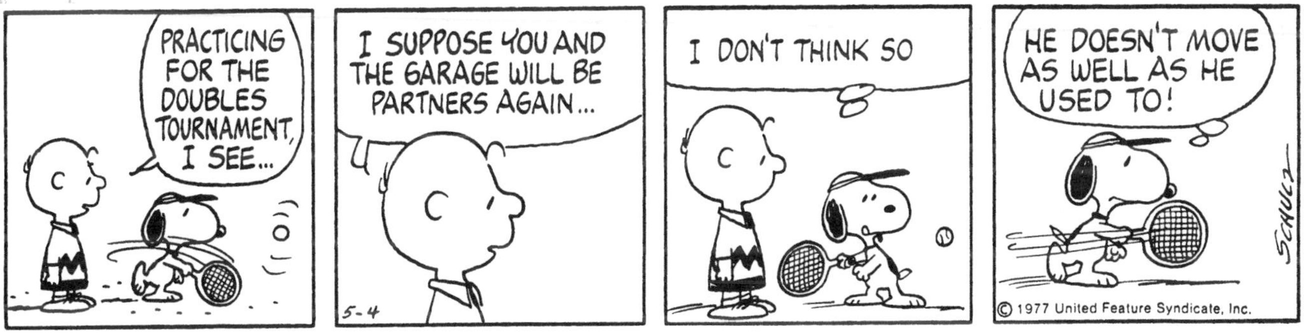
PRACTICING FOR THE DOUBLES TOURNAMENT, I SEE...
I SUPPOSE YOU AND THE GARAGE WILL BE PARTNERS AGAIN...
5-4
I DON'T THINK SO
HE DOESN'T MOVE AS WELL AS HE USED TO!
SCHULZ
© 1977 United Feature Syndicate, Inc.

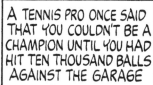

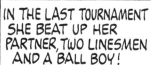

HI, I'M MOLLY VOLLEY!

HI, MY NAME IS CHARLIE BROWN

THIS IS SNOOPY...HE'S GOING TO BE YOUR PARTNER IN THE TOURNAMENT

I'VE HEARD OF MIXED DOUBLES, BUT THIS IS RIDICULOUS!

OKAY, "PARTNER"..

LET'S GET A FEW THINGS STRAIGHT... I HATE TO LOSE!

I'LL MAKE ALL THE LINE CALLS AND TAKE ALL THE OVERHEADS! ALL YOU HAVE TO DO IS GUARD YOUR ALLEY!

AND JUST ONE SMART REMARK ABOUT MY FAT LEGS GETS YOU A KNOCK ON THE NOGGIN!!

HERE'S SOMETHING TO THINK ABOUT, PARTNER..

THE FIRST TIME YOU DOUBLE FAULT, I'M GONNA HIT YOU RIGHT OVER THE HEAD WITH MY RACKET!

OKAY, GO AHEAD AND SERVE! AND DON'T BE NERVOUS...

233

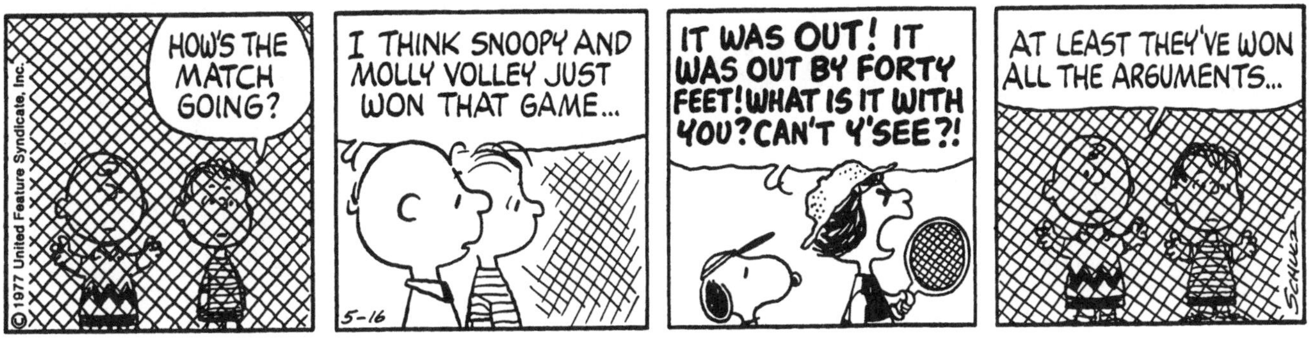
© 1977 United Feature Syndicate, Inc.
HOW'S THE MATCH GOING?
I THINK SNOOPY AND MOLLY VOLLEY JUST WON THAT GAME...
5-16
IT WAS OUT! IT WAS OUT BY FORTY FEET! WHAT IS IT WITH YOU? CAN'T Y'SEE?!
AT LEAST THEY'VE WON ALL THE ARGUMENTS...
SCHULZ

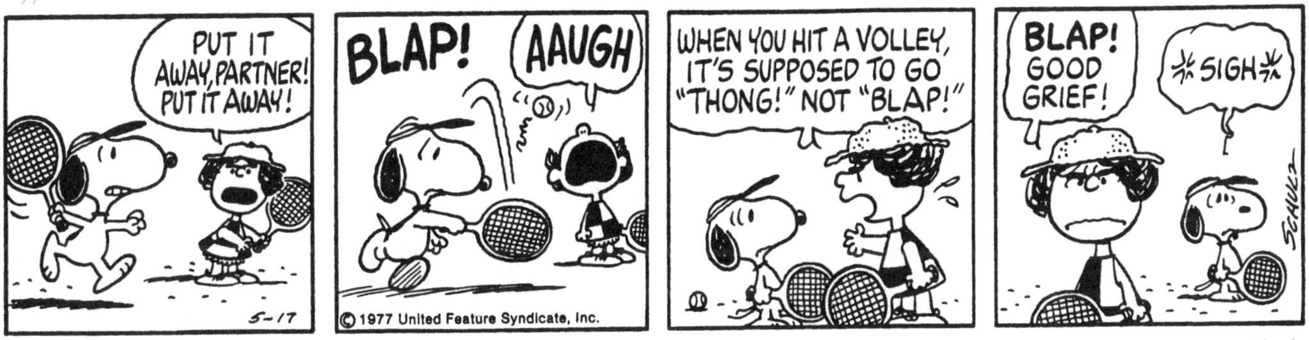
PUT IT AWAY, PARTNER! PUT IT AWAY!
5-17
BLAP!
AAUGH
© 1977 United Feature Syndicate, Inc.
WHEN YOU HIT A VOLLEY, IT'S SUPPOSED TO GO "THONG!" NOT "BLAP!"
BLAP! GOOD GRIEF!
SIGH
SCHULZ

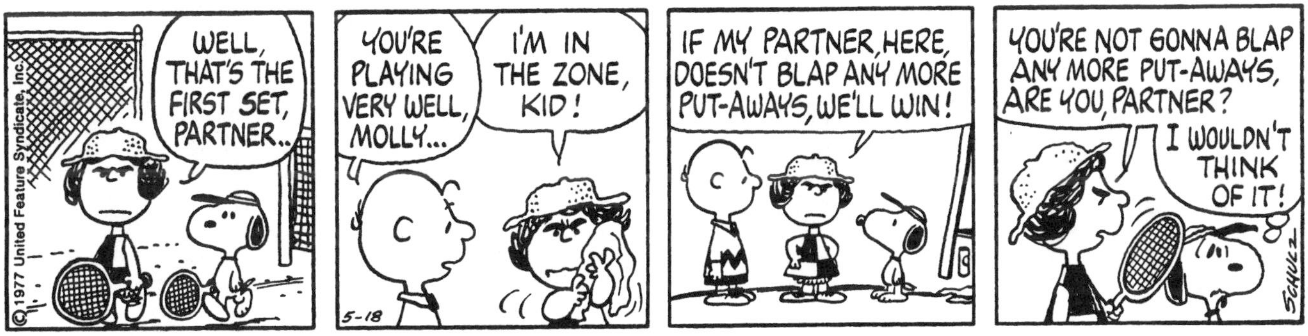
© 1977 United Feature Syndicate, Inc.
WELL, THAT'S THE FIRST SET, PARTNER...
YOU'RE PLAYING VERY WELL, MOLLY...
I'M IN THE ZONE, KID!
5-18
IF MY PARTNER, HERE, DOESN'T BLAP ANY MORE PUT-AWAYS, WE'LL WIN!
YOU'RE NOT GONNA BLAP ANY MORE PUT-AWAYS, ARE YOU, PARTNER?
I WOULDN'T THINK OF IT!
SCHULZ

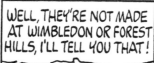

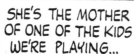

IT'S THREE TO FOUR IN THE TIE-BREAKER..

MINE!

WAP!

FOUR-ALL IN THE TIE-BREAKER!

WHERE'S THE BALL?

I LOST IT IN THE SUN! WHERE DID IT GO? DID YOU SEE IT?

DID IT GO OUT?! WAS IT IN, OR WAS IT OUT? DID WE WIN, OR DID WE LOSE?

DON'T JUST STAND THERE! CALL IT IN, OR CALL IT OUT!!

YOU CALL IT, PARTNER!
WAS IT IN OR OUT? DO WE WIN OR LOSE?
5-26
IN!
© 1977 United Feature Syndicate, Inc.
SORRY, PARTNER!
SMAK!
AAUGH!!
SCHULZ

MOLLY VOLLEY'S ON THE PHONE
NOW WHAT?
SHE WANTS TO KNOW IF YOU'D BE INTERESTED IN ANOTHER MIXED-DOUBLES TOURNAMENT ON SUNDAY...
5-28
I DOUBT IT...
© 1977 United Feature Syndicate, Inc.
I'VE HAD DISTEMPER, AND I'VE PLAYED MIXED-DOUBLES... I'D RATHER HAVE DISTEMPER
SCHULZ

DOUBLE FAULT!
JOE CHOKE
6-11
SCHULZ
© 1977 United Feature Syndicate, Inc.

ARE YOU READY TO PLAY?

OKAY...SPIN FOR SERVE!

© 1977 United Feature Syndicate, Inc.

THAT ISN'T EXACTLY WHAT I MEANT..

11-7

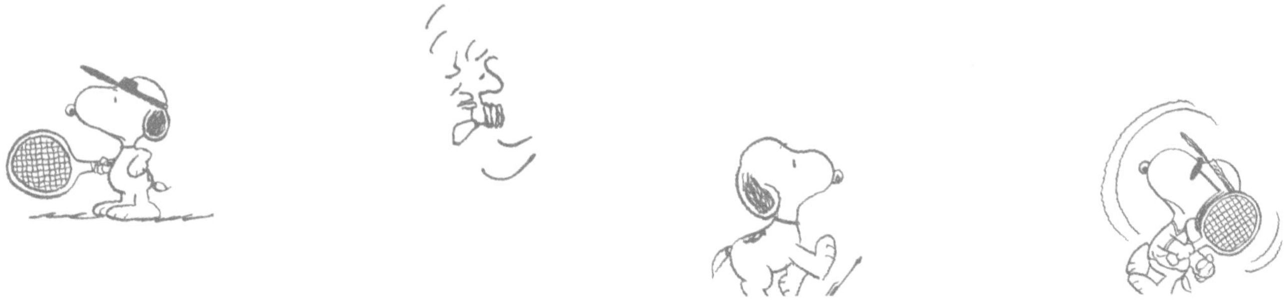

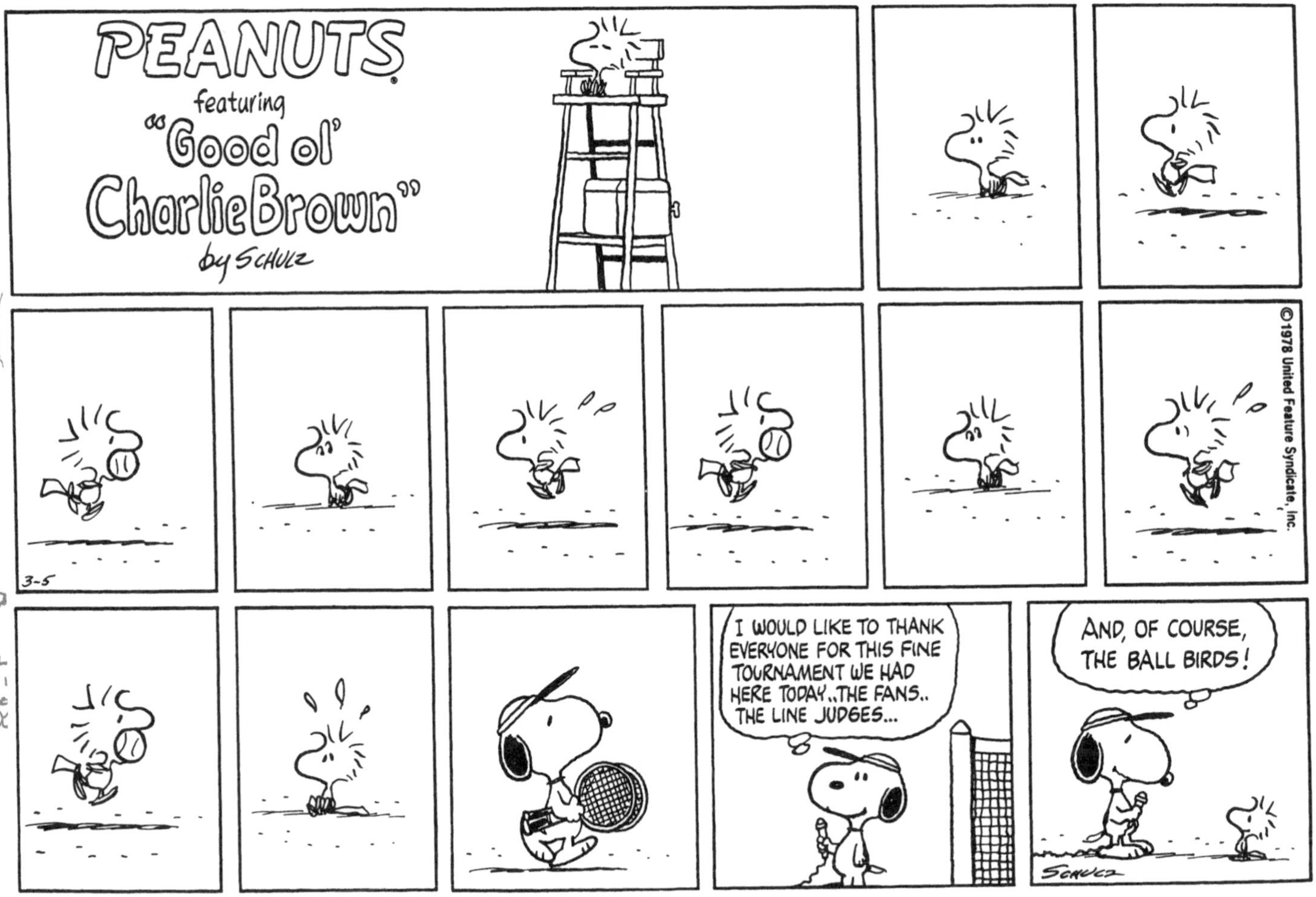
PEANUTS
featuring
"Good ol' CharlieBrown"
by SCHULZ
3-5
© 1978 United Feature Syndicate, Inc.
I WOULD LIKE TO THANK EVERYONE FOR THIS FINE TOURNAMENT WE HAD HERE TODAY..THE FANS.. THE LINE JUDGES...
AND, OF COURSE, THE BALL BIRDS!
SCHULZ

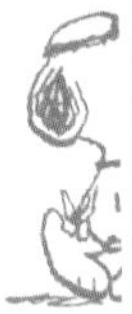

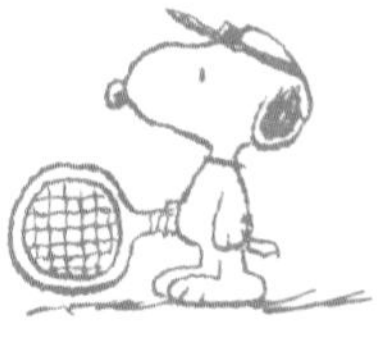

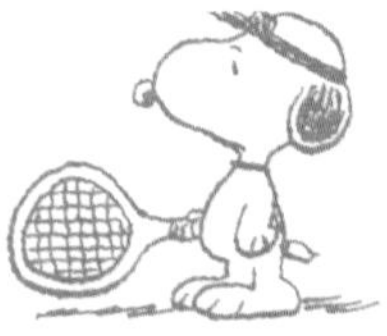

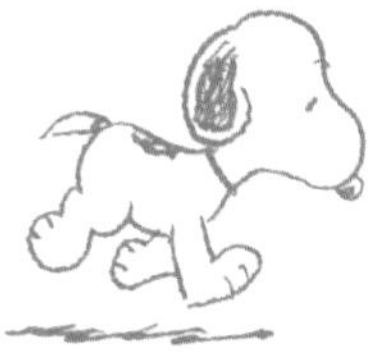

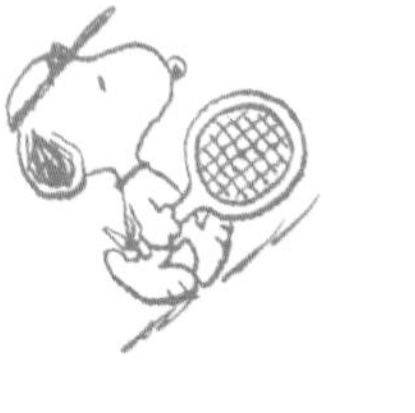

HE HAS TENNIS ELBOW?

I HAVE A STRAP THAT MIGHT HELP

TELL HIM TO WEAR IT THE NEXT TIME HE PLAYS...

© 1978 United Feature Syndicate, Inc.

5-16

I HAVE MY DOUBTS, BUT I'LL TRY ANYTHING

YOUR SERVE AGAIN, PARTNER

THIS COULD BE GAME POINT

5-24

IT ALSO COULD BE SET POINT AND MATCH POINT...

© 1978 United Feature Syndicate, Inc.

HOW ABOUT CHOKE POINT?

Panel 1: MOLLY VOLLEY JUST CALLED

Panel 2: SHE SAID THE MIXED DOUBLES TOURNAMENT STARTS TOMORROW

7-3

Panel 3: YOU GUYS PLAY "CRYBABY" BOOBIE IN THE FIRST ROUND

Panel 4: "CRYBABY" BOOBIE ?!

© 1978 United Feature Syndicate, Inc.

Panel 5: I'VE PLAYED AGAINST "CRYBABY" BOOBIE BEFORE! IT'S AN EXPERIENCE!

© 1978 United Feature Syndicate, Inc.

Panel 6: HER BROTHER, BOBBY BOOBIE, DOESN'T SAY MUCH, BUT SHE COMPLAINS ABOUT EVERYTHING

7-4

Panel 7: JUST DON'T LET HER GET TO YOU...JUST LET IT ALL GO IN ONE EAR AND OUT THE OTHER...

Panel 8: THAT'S THE SPIRIT, PARTNER!

Panel 1: OKAY, WE'LL RECEIVE ON THIS SIDE / THAT'S NOT FAIR!

Panel 2: THAT MEANS WE HAVE THE SUN IN OUR EYES! WHY DO WE ALWAYS SERVE WITH THE SUN IN OUR EYES?! 7-5

Panel 3: SEE? DIDN'T I TELL YOU? "CRYBABY" BOOBIE COMPLAINS ABOUT EVERYTHING! ©1978 United Feature Syndicate, Inc.

Panel 4: I THINK THE NET IS TOO HIGH! THESE BALLS FEEL DEAD! I CAN'T PLAY ON A SLOW COURT! THESE BALLS ARE TOO LIVELY! I THINK THE NET IS TOO LOW! SCHULZ

Panel 5: HEY, "CRYBABY," WHY DON'T YOU SHUT UP AND SERVE?

Panel 6: THESE BALLS FEEL TOO LIGHT! MY SHOULDER HURTS! THE SUN IS KILLING ME! THE NET LOOKS TOO HIGH! 7-6

Panel 7: I SAID, "SHUT UP AND SERVE!" ©1978 United Feature Syndicate, Inc.

Panel 8: NOW YOU'RE TRYING TO PSYCHE ME OUT!! SCHULZ

Panel 1: FAULT!

Panel 2: FAULT?! THAT WAS A BAD CALL! THAT BALL WAS IN! HOW COULD YOU CALL IT OUT? YOU'RE CHEATING ME!

7-7

Panel 3: SHUT UP, "CRYBABY" BOOBIE, AND SERVE!

©1978 United Feature Syndicate, Inc.

Panel 4: THIS IS GOING TO BE A LONG DAY!

Panel 5: HONK! ALL RIGHT, "CRYBABY," TELL YOUR MOTHER TO CUT IT OUT!

Panel 6: SHE SITS THERE IN HER CAR, AND EVERY TIME YOU MAKE A GOOD SHOT, SHE HONKS THE HORN!

7-8

Panel 7: THE NEXT TIME SHE DOES THAT I'M GONNA TEAR OFF A WHEEL!

©1978 United Feature Syndicate, Inc.

Panel 8: I COULD HAVE STAYED HOME AND GOTTEN INTO A NICE GENTLE DOGFIGHT

"ACE!"
AAUGH!
WE WON!!!
HONK! HONK! HONK! HONK! HONK! HONK!
I'M GONNA KILL SOMEBODY!
7-12
©1978 United Feature Syndicate, Inc.
SCHULZ

IT'S MATCH POINT, AND YOU STAND THERE LOOKING AT A LETTER FROM YOUR STUPID BROTHER!
NO WONDER YOU GOT ACED!
NOW WE HAVE TO GO AND CONGRATULATE "CRYBABY" BOOBIE! THIS IS GONNA KILL ME!
NICE MATCH, GUYS! LA DE DA DE DA DE DA
© 1978 United Feature Syndicate, Inc.
7-13
SCHULZ

BEATEN BY "CRYBABY" BOOBIE! WHAT A BLOW!

NOW I HAVE TO CONGRATULATE HER..

7-14

©1978 United Feature Syndicate, Inc.

I DON'T KNOW WHY I PLAY THIS GAME..

CONGRATULATIONS, BOOBIE!

SCHULZ

HE NEEDS A HOME, YOU SAY?

©1978 United Feature Syndicate, Inc.

WELL, I DON'T KNOW...

IS HE VICIOUS?

HE CAN BE IF HE GETS AHEAD IN THE THIRD SET!

SCHULZ

7-27

STILL HITTING BALLS WITH THE GARAGE, I SEE...

IT'S GOOD PRACTICE..HE GETS EVERYTHING BACK

8-7

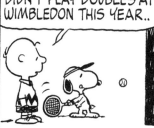
I WAS SURPRISED YOU DIDN'T PLAY DOUBLES AT WIMBLEDON THIS YEAR..

THE GARAGE HATES TO FLY

© 1978 United Feature Syndicate, Inc.

A PRESENT? FOR ME?

I LOVE GETTING PRESENTS

© 1978 United Feature Syndicate, Inc.

WOW! JUST WHAT I NEED...

8-23

A DOZEN FOREHAND VOLLEYS!

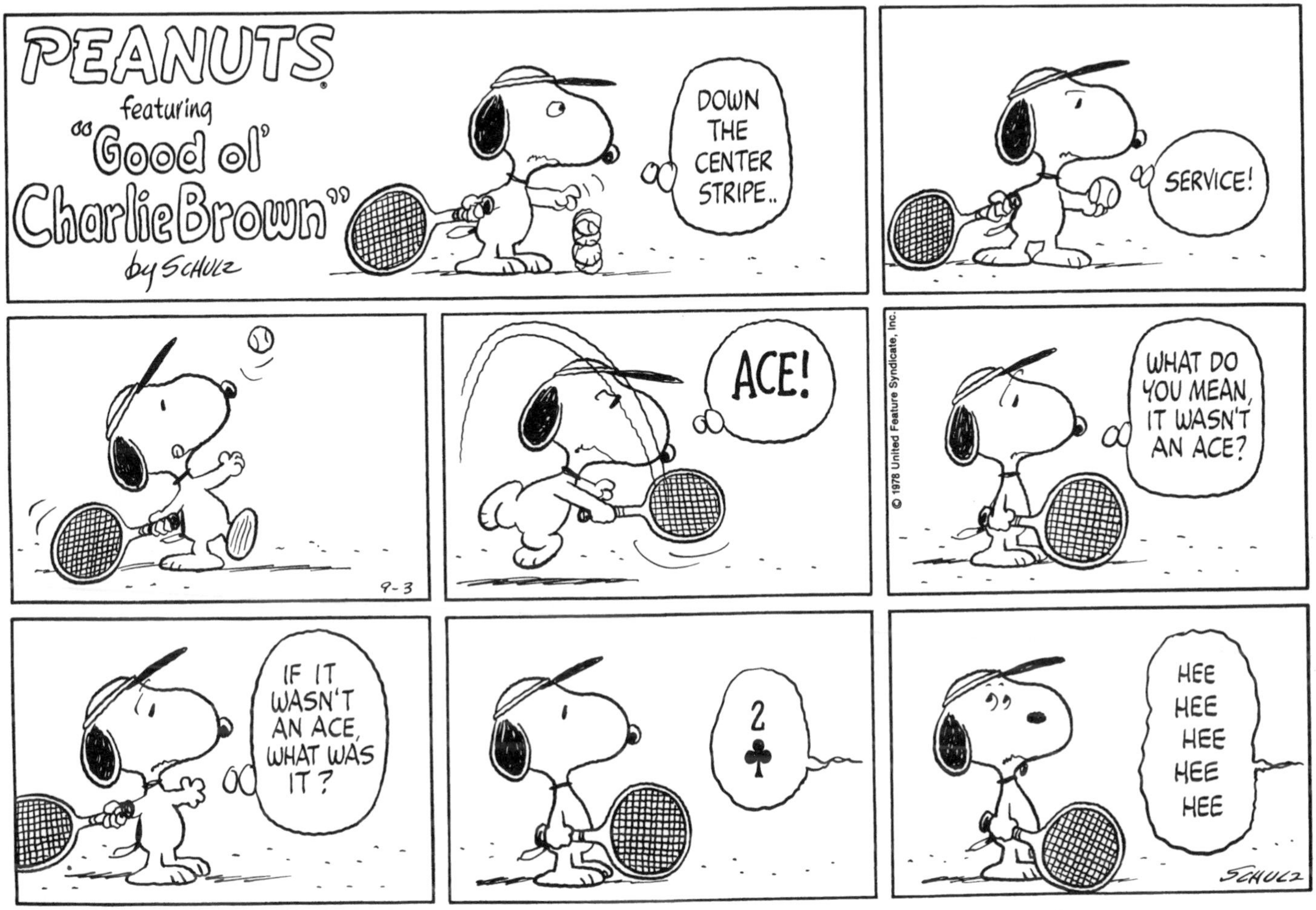
PEANUTS
featuring "Good ol' Charlie Brown"
by SCHULZ
DOWN THE CENTER STRIPE..
SERVICE!
9-3
ACE!
© 1978 United Feature Syndicate, Inc.
WHAT DO YOU MEAN, IT WASN'T AN ACE?
IF IT WASN'T AN ACE, WHAT WAS IT?
2 ♣
HEE HEE HEE HEE HEE
SCHULZ

Panel 1: TOURNAMENT TIME AGAIN, HUH?

Panel 2: I HEAR YOU'RE PLAYING IN THE THIRTY-FIVES...

4-5

Panel 3: YOU'RE NOT THIRTY-FIVE YEARS OLD

Panel 4: YEARS? I THOUGHT THEY MEANT INCHES!

© 1979 United Feature Syndicate, Inc.

Panel 5: I'VE BEEN WATCHING YOU WHEN YOU'RE GETTING READY TO SERVE

Panel 6: ARE YOU SUPERSTITIOUS?

Panel 7: I NOTICE THAT YOU NEVER STEP ON THE BASELINE...

4-14

© 1979 United Feature Syndicate, Inc.

Panel 8: I DON'T WANT TO OFFEND IT

256